Small Business Terms

Financial Education Is Your Best Investment

Published March 06, 2020

Revision 2.2

Financial Terms Dictionary

Copyright And Trademark Notices

Limits of Liability and Disclaimer of Warranties

The materials in this book are provided "as is" and without warranties of any kind either express or implied. The Author disclaims all warranties, express or implied, including, but not limited to, implied warranties of merchantability and fitness for a particular purpose.

The Author does not warrant that defects will be corrected, or that that the site or the server that makes this eBook available are free of viruses or other harmful components. The Author does not warrant or make any representations regarding the use or the results of the use of the materials in this book in terms of their correctness, accuracy, reliability, or otherwise. Applicable law may not allow the exclusion of implied warranties, so the above exclusion may not apply to you.

Under no circumstances, including, but not limited to, negligence, shall the Author be liable for any special or consequential damages that result from the use of, or the inability to use this eBook, even if the Author or his authorized representative has been advised of the possibility of such damages.

Applicable law may not allow the limitation or exclusion of liability or incidental or consequential damages, so the above limitation or exclusion may not apply to you. In no event shall the Author's total liability to you for all damages, losses, and causes of action (whether in contract, tort, including but not limited to, negligence or otherwise) exceed the amount paid by you, if any, for this eBook.

Facts and information are believed to be accurate at the time they were placed in this book. All data provided in this book is to be used for information purposes only. The information contained within is not intended to provide specific legal, financial or tax advice, or any other advice whatsoever, for any individual or company and should not be relied upon in that regard. The services described are only offered in jurisdictions where they may be legally offered. Information provided is not all-inclusive and is limited to information that is made available and such information should not be relied upon as all-inclusive or accurate.

You are advised to do your own due diligence when it comes to making business decisions and should use caution and seek the advice of qualified professionals. You should check with your accountant, lawyer, or professional advisor, before acting on this or any information. You may not consider any examples, documents, or other content in this eBook or otherwise provided by the Author to be the equivalent of professional advice.

The Author assumes no responsibility for any losses or damages resulting from your use of any link, information, or opportunity contained in this book or within any other information disclosed by the author in any form whatsoever.

About the Author

Thomas Herold is a successful entrepreneur, mediator, author, and personal development coach. He published over 35 books with over 200,000 copies distributed worldwide and the founder of seven online businesses.

For over ten years Thomas Herold has studied the monetary system and has experienced some profound insights on how money and wealth are related. After three years of successful investing in silver, he released 'Building Wealth with Silver - How to Profit From The Biggest Wealth Transfer in History' in 2012. One of the first books that illustrate in a remarkable, simple way the monetary system and its consequences.

He is the founder and CEO of the 'Financial Terms Dictionary' book series and website, which explains in detail and comprehensive form over 1000 financial terms. In his financial book series, he informs in detail and with practical examples all aspects of the financial sector. His educational materials are designed to help people get started with financial education.

In his 2018 released book 'The Money Deception', Mr. Herold provides the most sophisticated insight and shocking details about the current monetary system. Never before has the massive manipulation of money caused so much economic inequality in the world. In spite of these frightening facts, 'The Money Deception' also provides remarkable and simple solutions to create abundance for all people, and it's a must-read if you want to survive the global monetary transformation that's underway right now.

In 2019 he released an entirely new financial book series explaining in detail and with practical examples over 1000 financial terms. The 'Herold Financial IQ Series' contains currently of 16 titles covering every category of the financial market.

His latest book "High Credit Score Secrets" offers the most effective strategies to boost the average credit score from as low as 450 points to over 810. It teaches the tactics to build excellent credit, repair credit, monitor credit and how to guard that good score for a lifetime. It reached bestseller status in 2020 in three categories.

For more information please visit the author's websites:

High Credit Score Secrets - The Smart Raise & Repair Guide to Excellent Credit
https://highcreditscoresecrets.com

The Money Deception - What Banks & Government Don't Want You to Know
https://www.moneydeception.com

The Herold Financial IQ Series - Financial Education Is Your Best Investment
https://www.financial-dictionary.com

The Online Financial Dictionary - Over 1000 Terms Explained
https://www.financial-dictionary.info

Please Leave Your Review on Amazon

This book and the Financial IQ Series are self-published and the author does not have a contract with one of the five largest publishers, which are able to support the author's work with advertising. If you like this book, please consider leaving a solid 4 or 5-star review on Amazon.

Herold Financial IQ Series on Amazon

Table Of Contents

Accountant

Accountants are professional financial personnel whose careers are centered on dealing with money and figures. Their responsibilities cover compiling financial records, certifying them, and recording them for businesses, individuals, government organizations, and not for profit organizations. As such, they track a company or individual's money through the development of reports.

Managers of companies and organizations and other individuals read these accounting reports. The managers learn the state and progress of their company from them. Governments utilize these reports to determine the taxes that companies are required to pay. Investors and other businesses look at them to determine if they wish to work with a company. Banks and others investigate these reports in their decisions of lending money to a company.

The majority of accountants are specialized. Four main types of accountants practice their trade. Management accountants follow the money that is both earned and spent by their employing companies.

Public accountants work at public accounting firms. Here, they perform auditing, accounting, consulting, and tax preparation work. These types of accountants perform numerous tasks for individuals who are clients of the accounting firm. Some public accountants have their own small business.

Government auditors and accountants ensure that the accounting records of government agencies are correct. Besides this, they double check the record of those individuals who transact business with the government. This helps to keep governments responsible.

Internal auditors are accountants who ensure that the accounting records of their company are correct. In this role, they are investigating to make certain that no person within the firm is stealing. Besides this, they investigate to make certain that no individual in the company is wasting the firm's capital.

Accountants perform their tasks in offices. Those accountants who work for public companies and government groups often travel to perform audits of their own company's other branches or outside companies. Regarding their hours, accountants typically work for a normal forty hours per week. Some accountants ply their trade for more than fifty hours each week. Especially in tax season that runs from January through April, tax accountants commonly work incredibly long hours.

The outlook for accountants is exceptionally strong. Their field of work is anticipated to grow substantially faster than the average occupation through at least 2018. The reasons for this have much to do with the complex nature of both income tax laws and mandatory financial reporting. Because of the nature of these laws and rules, the demand for accountants will always exist. Working as an accountant entails a wide variety of requirements and prerequisites. Some very important positions mandate advanced degrees. Other accountant positions only need an ability and compliance to learn the trade, along with the necessary patience to see the training through.

Adjusted Gross Income (AGI)

Adjusted Gross Income (AGI) refers to a means of calculating income off of an individual's actual gross income. People use this figure in order to determine the amount of their income which the Internal Revenue Service will subject to tax assessment. It is ultimately the United States tax code which creates this AGI figure. This number should never be confused with the actual gross income. Gross income is merely the total amount of all money individuals realize and earn over a year long period.

The Adjusted Gross Income considers a range of deductions which it subtracts from the individuals in question's actual gross incomes. The result is the basis off of which the person's individual income taxes become calculated at the end of the tax year. Where tax activities and the Internal Revenue Service are concerned, this figure generally proves to be more useful than gross income alone.

All relevant deductions that apply to gross income and turn it into Adjusted Gross Income come from above the line deductions. This simply signifies that they must be reflected on the tax calculations ahead of dependents, military service, and other exemptions. There are a number of such deductions which count in the compiling of this AGI. Among the best known and most common are the following: contributions to retirement plans, business expenses which are not reimbursed, medical expenses, losses from property sales, and alimony or child support.

To calculate up individuals' Adjusted Gross Income, it is first necessary to figure up all reported income in the year being considered. Additional taxable income sources also have to be added in to the total. This includes any compensation for unemployment, property sales' profits, Social Security payments, pensions, and other sources of income that did not become reported on the tax return. Once this complete earnings' total has been figured up, it is necessary to subtract out all relevant deductions to come up with the appropriate AGI.

The Internal Revenue Service makes it easier to come up with all of the potential deductions pertaining to gross income by going to their IRS website. Here they provide a rules list for all potential deductions' requirements. Some of these prove to be extremely specific. This is why people have to carefully study the tax code in order to be certain of their eligibility for any and all deductions that they take.

Once individuals have figured out their AGI, they are able to then add in the government's normal federal tax deductions to finish calculating their taxable income. For some tax payers, this will mean itemizing out their various expenses to come up with the itemized deductions alternatively. Sometimes this works out better for taxpayers. One thing that a tax payer must be careful to never do is to not confuse their Adjusted Gross Income with their MAGI modified adjusted gross income.

In fact the modified adjusted gross income is supposed to be totally separate from the AGI. It is utilized to figure out the deductible dollar amount from the person's IRA individual retirement account. It will also be employed to decide if the private parties are eligible for specific tax deductions. In order to figure up this MAGI, tax payers have to add back in some items like foreign housing deductions, foreign earned income, IRA contribution deductions, higher education cost deductions, and student loan deductions.

In many cases, the MAGI is often much the same as the AGI for a given individual. Yet it is important to be aware that even tiny differences can significantly impact the overall tax return for an individual. In particular, such variances will impact a person's eligibility to receive particular benefits allowed under the ACA Affordable Care Act.

Amortization

The word amortization is one that is commonly utilized by financial officers of corporations and accountants. They utilize it when they are working with time concepts and how they relate to financial statements of accounts. You typically hear this word employed when you are figuring up loan calculations, or when you are determining interest payments.

The concept of amortization possesses a lengthy history and it is currently employed in numerous different segments of finance. The word itself descends from Middle English. Here amortisen meant to "alienate" or "kill" something. This derivation itself comes from the Latin admortire that signified "plus death." It is loosely related to the derivation of the word mortgage, as well.

This accounting principle is much like depreciation that diminishes a liability or asset's value over a given period of time through payments. It covers the practical life span of a tangible asset. With liabilities, it includes a pre-set amount of time over which money is paid back. Like this, a certain amount of money is set aside for the loan repayment over its lifetime.

Even though depreciation is similar to amortization, they are not the same concepts. The main difference between them lies in what they cover. While depreciation is most commonly employed to describe physical assets like property, vehicles, or buildings, amortization instead covers intangibles such as product development, copyrights, or patents. Where liabilities are concerned, it relates to income in the future that will be paid out over a given amount of time. Depreciation is instead a lost income over a time period.

Several different kinds of amortization are presently in use. This varies with the accounting method that is practiced. Business amortization deals with borrowed funds and loans and the paying of particular amounts in different time frames. When used as amortization analysis, this is the means of cost execution analysis for a given group of operations. Where tax law is concerned, amortization pertains to the interest amount that is paid over a given span of time relevant to payments and tax rates.

Amortization can also be employed with regards to zoning rules and regulations, since it conveys a property owner's time for relocating as a result of zoning guidelines and pre-existing use. Another variation is used as negative amortization. This pertains specifically to increasing loan amounts that result from total interest due not being paid up at the appropriate time.

Amortization can also be employed over a widely ranging time frame. It could cover only a year or extend to as many as forty years. This depends on the kind of loan or asset utilized. Some examples include building loans that span over as many as forty years and car loans that commonly span over merely four to five years. Asset examples would be patent right expenses that commonly are spread out over seventeen years.

Annual Percentage Rate (APR)

The annual percentage rate, or APR, is the actual interest rate that a loan charges each year. This single percentage number is truthfully used to represent the literal annual expense of using money over the life span of a given loan. Annual percentage rate not only covers interest charged, but can also be comprised of extra costs or fees that are attached to a given loan transaction.

Credit cards and loans commonly offer differing explanations for transaction fees, the structure of their interest rates, and any late fees that are assessed. The annual percentage rate provides an easy to understand formula for expressing to borrowers the real and actual percentage number of fees and interest so that they can measure these up against the rates that other possible lenders will charge them.

Annual percentage rate can include many different elements besides interest. With a nominal APR, it simply involves the rate of a given payment period multiplied out to the exact numbers of payment periods existing in a year. The effective APR is often referred to as the mathematically true rate of interest for a given year. Effective APR's are commonly the fees charged plus the rate of compound interest.

On a home mortgage, effective annual percentage rates could factor in Private Mortgage Insurance, discount points, and even processing costs. Some hidden fees do not make their ways into an effective APR number. Because of this, you should always read the fine print surrounding an APR and the costs associated with a mortgage or loan. As an example of how an effective APR can be deceptive with mortgages, the one time fees that are charged in the front of a mortgage are commonly assumed to be divided over a loan's long repayment period. If you only utilize the loan for a short time frame, then the APR number will be thrown off by this. An effective APR on a mortgage might look lower than it actually is when the loan will be paid off significantly earlier than the term of the loan.

The government created the concept of annual percentage rate to stop loan companies and credit cards issuers from deceiving consumers with fancy expressions of interest charges and fees. The law requires that all loan issuers and credit card companies have to demonstrate this annual percentage rate to all customers. This is so the consumers will obtain a fair comprehension of the true rates that are associated with their particular transactions. While credit card companies are in fact permitted to promote their monthly basis of interest rates, they still have to clearly show the actual annual percentage rate to their customers in advance of a contract or agreement being signed by the consumer.

Annual percentage rate is sometimes confused with annual percentage yield. This can be vastly different from the APR. Annual percentage yield includes calculations of compounded interest in its numbers.

Annual Percentage Yield (APY)

APY describes the amount of compound interest which individuals or businesses will earn in a given year (or longer time period). Investments in money market accounts, savings accounts, and CD Certificates of Deposit all pay out such interest. It is the annual percentage yield that demonstrates precisely the amount in interest individuals will receive. This is helpful for people or businesses trying to ascertain which investments and banks offer superior returns by comparing and contrasting their real yields. In general, higher Annual Percentage Yields are better to have (unless one is comparing interest on credit card debts).

This APY is practical to understand and measure simply because it considers compound interest and the miracle of compounding within any account. Simple interest rates do not do this. Compounding is simply earning interest on interest that has already accrued and been paid. It signifies that individuals are gaining a greater amount in interest than the corresponding interest rate literally indicates.

It is always a good idea to consider a real world example for clarification purposes. If Fred deposits $10,000 into a particular savings account that provides a two percent yearly interest rate, then at the end of that first year Fred will have $10,200. This assumes that the interest is paid one time per year. If the bank were to figure up and pay out the interest on a daily basis, it would increase the amount to $10,202. The extra $2 may seem small, but given a longer time frame of from 10 to 30 years, this amount can add up, particularly if larger deposits are involved.

APY should never be confused with APR. They have some similarities, but APR does not consider compounding. It is once again a simpler means of computing interest. Credit card loans are an area where it is important to understand the differences between annual percentage rate and annual percentage yield. When people carry a balance, they will be paying higher APY's then the APR the firm actually quotes. This is because interest is assessed monthly, which means that interest on the interest will be computed on each following month.

The key to obtaining a better APY on investments and savings accounts lies in getting as frequent a compounding period as possible. Quarterly compounding is better than annually, yet daily is the most superior form of compounding possible. This means that as individuals are looking to increase their APY's personally, it is important to have the money compounding as frequently as they can practically achieve.

When two CD Certificates of Deposit pay out the same rate, it is best to select that one which actually pays out both more frequently and also boasts the greater APY. With CD's, the interest payments become automatically reinvested. More frequent reinvestment is always better. This will help any individual or business to earn a greater amount of interest on the interest payments already earned and paid out.

Calculating the annual percentage yield is not an easy task. Business calculators as well as computer algorithms mostly do it for people nowadays. The simplest way to find the APY for a given account is to plug in the information including the initial deposit, compounding frequency period, interest rate, and amount of overall time for the period considered. These smart calculators will then tell you both the effective annual percentage yield as well as the ending balance on the hypothetical account at the end of the given time period.

Assets

Assets are any thing that can be owned by a company or an individual person. These are able to be sold for cash. Commonly, assets produce income or give value to the owner.

In the world of financial accounting, assets prove to be economic resources. They can be physical objects or intangible concepts that can be utilized and owned to create value. Assets are deemed to have real and positive value for their owners. Assets must also be convertible into cash, which itself is furthermore considered to be an asset.

There are several different types of assets as measured by accountants and accounting processes. These might be current assets, longer term assets, intangible assets, or deferred assets. Current assets include cash and other items that are readily and easily able to be sold to raise cash. Longer term assets are those that are held and useful for great periods of time, including such physical items as factory plants, real estate, and equipment. Intangible assets are non physical rights or concepts, like patents, trademarks, goodwill, and copyrights. Finally, deferred assets are those that involve monies spent now for the costs in the future of things like rent, insurance, or interest.

Though tangible, physical assets are not hard to conceptualize, intangible assets are often confusing for people to understand. Even though these are not physical items that may be touched, they still have value that can be controlled and sold to raise cash. Intangible assets include rights and resources which provide a company with a form of marketplace advantage. These can cover many different elements beyond those listed above, such as computer programs, stocks, bonds, and even accounts receivable.

On balance sheets, tangible assets are commonly divided into further categories. These include fixed assets and current assets. Fixed assets are objects that are immobile or not easily transported, such as buildings, office locations, and equipment. Current assets are comprised of inventory that a business holds. Balance sheets of companies keep track of a firm's assets and their value as expressed in monetary terms. These assets are both the cash and other items that the business or person owns.

Assets should never be confused with liabilities. Assets create positive cash flow that represents value or money coming into a business, organization, or individual's accounts. Liabilities are obligations that have to be paid and that create negative cash flow, or take money out of a business, individual, or organization's accounts. As an example of the difference between the two, assets would be houses that are rented out that bring in more rent every month than the expenses, interest, and upkeep of the houses. Liabilities would be homes that have payments that must be paid every month and do not provide any income stream to effectively offset this.

Audit

An audit refers to a third party evaluation and review of a business or individual's financial statements. The goal is to ensure that the financial records are both accurate and reflective of the transactions for the entity they represent. Such a review can be carried out by an external auditing firm or by accounting employees within an organization itself.

There is also the possibility for the Internal Revenue Service itself to conduct audits in order to confirm the veracity of a business or individual's tax payer returns and transactions. As the IRS engages in such audits, this usually creates a dark cloud over the victim organization or individual. This is because such IRS audits come with a negative connotation. It is as if the government suspects the taxpayers in question have engaged in illegal activities with their taxes or income declarations.

For those audits which an external company performs on behalf of corporations, these are often very useful in taking away the tendency towards personal bias. It means that the final picture of the corporation should be more complete, unbiased, and accurate. Such audits are often seeking any inadvertent material error in the corporations' statements or activities. They reassure shareholders of the company that the financial statements are accurate. As third parties undertake audits, the bias of the internal accountant who would otherwise be engaging in the auditing tasks is eliminated.

This could be regarding a company subsidiary or division, the entire corporation or one system within it, or the financial books of the business. There is also no pressure that a member of management will think negatively of the employee for producing less than stellar outcomes from the audit when the corporation engages and retains an external accounting firm.

The majority of publicly traded firms become audited one time each year. Enormous corporations can be audited even every month. There are companies in industries where their oversight organization requires legally that the firm receive routine audits so as to eliminate any temptation to deliberately misrepresent financial information. Such misrepresentation is literally called fraud. Still other large corporations look at audits and auditors as a valuable tool to ascertain how effective their financial reports and associated internal controls of them actually are.

Two different types of auditors exist in the realm of external audits. These are statutory auditors and external cost auditors. The statutory varieties independently labor to consider the quality of the financial statements and reports. The external cost auditors consider and review the cost sheets and statements to make certain they do not contain any errors, misrepresentations, or fraudulent facts or figures. Each of the two different kinds of auditing personnel work with a range of varying standards that are different than those which the corporation hiring them would engage in otherwise.

Such internal auditors will be hired by the firm or other organization on whose behalf they are engaging in the audit in the first place. They do their fiduciary best to deliver reliable and accurate information and certification to the management of the company, the board of directors, and shareholders regarding the books and all internal operating systems and procedures of the company in question.

Other auditors will be consultants. They will still utilize the standards of the corporation which they are auditing instead of an independent set of standards, even though they are not internal employees of the organization. Such consultants are brought in when the corporation or other organization lacks the necessary resources to perform their own internal operational audits.

Auditors must meet certain specified standards which their jurisdictional governments lay out when they conduct these audits. The American Institute of Certified Public Accountants has its respected external audit standards which they call the GAAS Generally Accepted Auditing Standards. Internationally, the International Auditing and Assurance Board maintain their International Standards on Auditing. The U.S. also has a regulatory body dating back to 2002 called the PCAOB, or Public Company Accounting Oversight Board.

Bankruptcy

Bankruptcy is a term that refers to the elimination or restructuring of a person or company's debt. Three principal different types of bankruptcy filing are available. These are the personal bankruptcy options of Chapter 7 and Chapter 13 filings, and the business bankruptcy restructuring option of Chapter 11.

Individuals avail themselves of Chapter 7 or Chapter 13 bankruptcy filings when their financial situations warrant significant help. With a Chapter 7 filing, all of an individual's debt is erased through discharge. This provides a new start for the debtor. Due to changes in laws made back in October 2005, not every person is able to obtain this type of total debt relief any longer. As a result of this new bankruptcy law, a means test came into being that prospective bankruptcy filers must successfully pass if they are to prove eligibility for this kind of bankruptcy relief.

The net effect of this new test is that consumers find it much more difficult to qualify for total debt elimination under Chapter 7. Besides the means test, the cost of bankruptcy attorneys has now risen dramatically by upwards of a hundred percent as a result of the new laws. Before these laws went into effect, Chapter 7 filings represented around seventy percent of all personal filings for bankruptcy. Chapter 7 offered the individual the advantage of simply walking away from debts that they might be capable of paying back with sufficient time and some interest rate help.

Chapter 13 Bankruptcy filings prove to be much like debt restructuring procedures. In these proceedings, a person's creditors are made to agree to the repayment of principal and zero interest on debts over a longer span of time. The individual gets to keep all of her or his assets in this form of filing. The most common motivation for Chapter 13 proves to be a desire to stop a foreclosure on a home. Individuals are able to achieve this by halting foreclosure proceedings and catch up on back mortgage payments. Once a court examines the debtor's budget, it will sign off on the plan for repayment proposed by the person. Depending on the level of an individual's income, he or she may have no choice but to file a Chapter 13 filling, as a result to the 2005 law changes.

Companies and corporations that are in financial distress may avail themselves of bankruptcy protection as well. Chapter 11 allows for such businesses to have protection from their creditors while they restructure their debt. Some individuals who have a higher income level will take advantage of this form of filing as well, since it does not place income restrictions on the entity filing. It has been instrumental in saving many large and well known companies over the years, including K-Mart, that actually emerged strong enough from the Chapter 11 bankruptcy to buy out higher end rival Sears afterward.

Business Cycle

Business Cycle refers to changes in economic activity which economies around the globe undergo in a certain time-frame. Such cycles are generally framed under the concepts of recession or expansion. When an economy is expanding, it is growing in true terms, which means faster than inflation. This is demonstrated with economic indicators such as industrial production, personal income levels, employment levels, and consumer goods sales.

Conversely in times of economic recession, the economy is shrinking. Economists measure this with the same economic indicators as with expansion. In expansions, analysts measure the period from the bottom called the trough of the prior business cycle to the height (or peak) of the present cycle. With recessions, they instead measure them from the peak up to the trough.

There are organizations which decide what the official technical dates for any such business cycles actually are. Within the U.S., the group that makes these calls is the NBER National Bureau of Economic Research. The American NBER has decided for official purposes that fully 11 business cycles have occurred between the years of 1945 and 2009. They have also broken down the average times of such cycles.

The average business cycle length has run approximately 69 months. This means that they typically last for slightly under six years. Meanwhile, the average expansion in that time frame has run for 58.4 months long. In the same time period, the average length of contraction has amounted to a mere 11.1 months. This is good news as recessions or contractions are often painful and sometimes deep, bringing unemployment and financial hardship on millions of individuals.

The business cycle is also useful for investment positioning. Personal investors can effectively utilize it to allocate and position their various investments and funds. Looking at an example helps to clarify this idea. When an expansion is underway in the early months and years, the best cyclical stocks in different industries like technology and commodities usually outperform the other sectors. Within the recessionary periods, it is more effective to position in defensive sectors. These include consumer staples, health care, and utilities. Such segments commonly outperform their peers as they possess high and dependable dividend yields and reliable cash flows.

The NBER declared (per January of 2014) that the prior expansion began at the end of the Global Financial Crisis and Great Recession which ended officially in June of 2009. This represents the point when the Great Recession that held from years 2007 to 2009 attained its trough.

Economists consider that expansion is the normal mode of the American and Western based economies. Recessions are commonly far shorter and less frequent as well. Many people have wondered why recessions must happen. There is no general consensus among economists. Usually though, a definitive and destructive pattern of speculation that becomes carried away reveals itself in the end stages of the prior expansion. This is the case with many different business cycles.

As an example, the recession from 2001 had a mania which former Federal Reserve Chairman Alan Greenspan referred to as "Irrational Exuberance" that came before it. In this time, the various technology and especially "dot-com" stocks went from boom to bust in a short matter of months. Similarly the recession of 2007 to 2009 came after a time when real estate activity, primarily in housing, had experienced its greatest speculation in American history.

Since the 1990s began, the average time span for expansions has grown substantially. With the last three business cycles that ran from July of 1990 through June of 2009, the average expansion ran for 95 months, nearly eight years. At the same time, the typical recession lasted around 11 months. Some overly optimistic economists believed that this somehow meant the business cycles were finished.

This euphemistic hope became dashed when the world financial markets, banks, and economies melted down in spectacular free fall from 2007 to 2009. During this terrible time in the global economy, the majority of stock markets throughout the world suffered eye-watering declines exceeding even 50 percent in only 18 months. This amounted to the most severe contraction worldwide since the Great Depression of the 1930s.

C Corporation

C Corporations refers to the primary subchapter under which American businesses decide to incorporate themselves in order to restrict the total financial and legal liabilities of the owners. Such C Corporations prove to be the principle alternatives to S Corporations, whose profits are able to pass directly through to the owners and so only become taxable on the individual level. Limited liability companies are the other main choice to the C corporations. They deliver all of the legal safeties of corporations yet become tax treated as if they were sole proprietorships.

Unfortunately for C Corporations, they do suffer the effects of double taxation. Yet they do also permit the businesses to reinvest their profits back into the firm with a lower corporate tax rate penalty. The majority of incorporated companies within the United States turn out to be C Corporations.

Organizing a corporation starts with the new owners selecting the new entity's name (and in many states registering or reserving it with the secretary of state) of the new business enterprise. The owners must draft up the articles of incorporation and file them with the appropriate state business department. The first shareholders will then be issued their stock certificates once the business is established. Every C Corporation has to first file the Form SS-4 in order to get their EIN employer identification number. Every jurisdiction has its own varying requirements for these obligations, yet the corporations generally must file income, state, payroll, disability, and unemployment taxes for their employees.

Such C Corporations must hold minimally one meeting per year for the benefit of both the directors and the shareholders. These must have meeting minutes kept in order to transparently display the ways and means in which the business functions. There will have to be voting records maintained of the company directors as well as a full list of all owners' names and their ownership percentages in the firm. The company bylaws are required to be kept on the business headquarter premises at all times. Such enterprises also have to file all necessary financial disclosure reports, annual reports, and relevant financial statements with the SEC.

There are many benefits to such C Corporations. Most importantly for owners, they first limit the liability of all shareholders, directors, officers, and employees. It is not possible for the legal and debt obligations from the company to transfer over to one or more individuals under this type of corporate structuring. Even if each of the company owners become changed out, the corporation continues its existence. There is no limit to the numbers of shareholders and owners with this kind of corporation either as there would be with an S Corporation. Yet these must be registered properly with the SEC Securities and Exchange Commission once they reach a certain number of shareholders.

The primary downside to the C corporations centers on the idea of double taxation. As the firm generates its income, it will have to file a corporate tax return with the IRS Internal Revenue Service. Once the appropriate business expenses (including salaries) have been deducted from the gross income, the rest becomes subjected to corporate income taxes. Much of the remaining net income will then be distributed out to shareholders in what is called dividends. The income to the shareholders must be reported on the recipients' tax returns. This means that the C Corporation profits are being twice taxed, once at the corporate tax rate level and a second on the individuals' tax rate level. That income which is retained earnings will avoid double taxation only. It helps to explain why mega corporations like Apple hold on to billions of dollars in retained earnings routinely.

Capital Inflow

Capital Inflow refers to money (in the form of investments) moving into a certain benefitting nation. The country which is the recipient of the inflow is best known as the host country. The source countries are the ones sending or investing the initial funds. Host nations often have a range of causes for attracting such capital inflows.

Direct foreign investment occurs when multinational corporations purchase literal tangible assets in the host country. This could come in the form of purchasing a local company outright or building a manufacturing plant locally. There could also be portfolio investment in the host nation's financial securities. This might include bonds and stocks which may be bought by international banks, foreign residents, insurance companies, pension funds, hedge funds, or other cross-border groups.

A third way that this occurs is when host governments are forced to borrow money off of international governments or foreign banks in order to pay their deficit on the balance of payments. It also occurs when domestic corporations or citizens elect to borrow from foreign banks. Finally inter-company transfers can finance investment and consumption in this category of capital inflow.

A last form of capital inflow happens when the host country has higher interest rates than the source nations' own corresponding rates. In this scenario, shorter term deposits will often flock to the banks' and money market instruments of the host nation. This could be straight up investment or speculation that the host national exchange rate will increase and so lead to a capital gain. This is the opposite of capital outflows. Outflows occur as funds move out of the host nation into other competing countries for the same reasons detailed above.

There are many beneficial effects to a country which receives capital inflows. As money comes into the host country via a business or stock purchase on the nation's stock market exchange, the recipient firm will deploy the funds either for startup purposes or to expand their existing business products and lines. This is really good for the companies which receive the funds. Such expansion of the companies in question then leads both job creation and employment growth in the host nation. Businesses will finally realize profits utilizing the original capital investment and the projects they subsequently fund with it. With these profits, the company is able to pay for additional expansion or investment in other projects and/or financial investments.

In the last few decades, foreigners have invested literally hundreds of billions worth of foreign capital into the United States economy. This has massively advantaged the American economy and workers (besides just creating countless jobs) as it boosted the international value of the dollar, lowered interest rates for American individuals and businesses, and grew the capital supply for loans which banks could make to residents and companies alike. With the onset of the catastrophic Global Financial Crisis from 2007-2009, the capital inflows to the United States dropped considerably. The subsequent Sovereign Debt Crisis in Europe dramatically decreased the capital inflow to Europe as well.

Years later by 2012, China finally surpassed the U.S. to capture the spot as the globe's greatest host of direct foreign investment . At the conclusion of 2012, the United States managed to recapture this coveted top spot. China had several reasons to steal the American thunder this way. The Chinese economy grew quicker than the United States as well as the other developed nations. Besides this, China has finally matured into a country that does not appear to be a high risk investment any longer. This has helped to draw in direct foreign investment by the hundreds of billions over the decades.

Capital Loss

Capital Loss refers to a type of loss that companies or individuals experience as one of their capital assets decreases by value. This includes a real estate or investment asset. The loss only becomes realized when the asset itself sells for less than the price for which it was originally purchased. Another way of looking at these capital losses is that they represent the difference from the asset's purchase price and the asset's selling price. In other words, for it to be a loss the selling price must be less than the original price. As an example, when investors purchase a home for $300,000 and then sell the same home six years later for only $260,000, they have taken a capital loss amounting to $40,000.

Where income taxes are concerned, capital losses often offset capital gains. Capital losses in fact reduce the personal or business income in a like dollar for dollar amount. When net losses are higher than $3,000, then the overage amount can not be applied. Instead, this amount higher than net $3,000 simply carries over against any other gains or taxable income to the following year when they will similarly offset capital gains and income. When losses are multiple thousands, they continue to carry forward as many years as it takes for them to be fully exhausted.

Both capital losses and capital gains will be reported using a Form 8949. This form helps taxpayers to determine if the sale dates allow for the transactions to be counted as long term or short term losses or gains. When such transactions are deemed to be short term gains, they become taxable by the individual's ordinary income tax rates. These ranged from only 10 percent to 39.6 percent as of 2015. This is why the shorter term losses when paired off against shorter term gains give significant tax advantages to higher income earning individuals. It benefits them when they have earned profits by selling off any asset or assets in under a year from original purchase point.

With longer term capital gains, investors become taxed by rates of zero percent, 15 percent, or 20 percent. This occurs when they take a gain which results from a position they possessed for over a year. Such capital gains also can only be offset by capital losses which they realize after holding the investments for over a year. It is also on form 8949 that these assets become reportable. Here investors list out both the gross proceeds from the sales and assets' cost basis. The two figures are compared to determine if the total sales equate to a loss, gain, or wash. Such losses become reported on Schedule D. Here the taxpayer is able to ascertain the amount that may be utilized to lower overall taxable income.

These wash sale rules can be confusing to individuals without an example. Consider an investor who dumps his IBM stock on the last day of November in order to realize a loss. The taxing authority of the Internal Revenue Service will disallow such a capital loss if the exact stock was bought again on the day of December 30th or before this. This is because investors have to wait at least 31 days before such a security can be repurchased then sold off once more in order to realize another loss.

Yet the regulation does not affect sales and re-buys of different mutual funds that possess similar positions and holdings. As an example, $10,000 worth of Vanguard Energy Fund shares may be entirely reinvested in the Fidelity Select Energy Portfolio at any point. This would not forfeit the investors' ability to recognize another loss even as they continue to own an equity portfolio (through the mutual fund) that is similar to their earlier mutual fund holdings.

Capital Outflow

Capital Outflow is a phenomenon where financial assets and money move away from a given nation. All countries of the world consider this to be a negative action. It typically occurs as a result of economic and/or political instability or at least the perception of it. Such asset flight results from domestically and especially foreign-based investors choosing to sell their stakes within a certain nation. They do this as they see potential weakness in the economy or political establishment of a country. They begin to feel that greater and safer opportunities for investment lie overseas.

When such Capital Outflows become too fast and great, it is a serious indicator that economic and political turmoil is present and a primary cause of the asset and capital flight. Many governments will begin to set limitations for capital choosing to exit. The connotation of such actions tends to warn still other investors who have not left that the condition of the host nation and economy is rapidly deteriorating.

Abnormal capital outflow creates increasingly severe pressure on the macroeconomics of a country and its economy. It tends to dissuade domestic and foreign investors alike from investing in the state and its companies. There are a range of valid explanations for why such capital flight actually occurs. Among them are unnaturally low national interest rates and growing political unrest.

It often helps to look at a real world example to better understand a difficult concept. Japan chose to decrease its interest rates to actual negative levels back in 2016. This applied to all government bonds and securities. They simultaneously began unprecedented aggressive stimulatory measures to boost the growth of the GDP Gross Domestic Product at the same time. The economic problems in Japan started after massive capital outflows from the island nation throughout the decade of the 1990s kicked off two long decades of sub-par stagnated growth in the country which formerly boasted the position of second greatest economy in the world.

Often times, governments impose severe restrictions on capital flight in a valiant effort to stop the fleeing money and financial assets. This is in an endeavor to shore up the capital markets and especially domestic banking institutions and system which can fail if all the money is simultaneously withdrawn. Too few bank deposits often cause banks to crater into insolvency when a great number of assets depart all at once. Subsequently, many banks find it difficult if not outright impossible to call back in existing issued loans in order to make good on customer withdrawal demands.

Consider the sad case study of Greece. Back in 2015, the government of the world's first democracy had no other choice than to instate a week long bank holiday. Wire transfers became restricted only to those recipients with Greek bank accounts. When such events occur in developing (or sometimes third world) countries, the weakness it institutes can create a vicious downward spiral that leads to domestic public panic and foreign investment fear and resistance.

There are also dramatic effects on exchange rates. The supply of a given country's currency rises dramatically as investors cash out of the state. Investors in China have periodically sold off the Yuan in order to obtain American dollars. This drives down the value of the Chinese Yuan, which has the additional side benefit of reducing the costs of Chinese exports while simultaneously boosting the costs to import foreign goods. It unfortunately also leads to inflation since import demand will fall while exported goods demand increases. During the second half of the year 2015, Chinese assets to the tune of $550 billion departed China looking for a higher ROI return on investment. This caused not only Chinese government fears but ensuing worldwide government worries.

Similarly Argentina suffered from sudden, unexpected, and runaway capital outflows back in the decade of the 1990s following a dramatic currency realignment. Their new fixed exchange rate created a resulting recession. The nation has now become the popular example and poster country for fledgling economies and the difficulties they all too often encounter in boosting their economic development.

Cash Flow

Cash Flow is either an incoming revenue or outgoing expense stream that affects the value of any cash account over time. Inflows of cash, or positive cash flows, typically result from one of three possible activities, including operations, investing, or financing for businesses or individuals. Individuals are also able to realize positive cash flows from gifts or donations.

Negative cash flow is also called cash outflows. Outflows of cash happen because of either expenses or investments made. This is the case for both individuals' finances, as well as for those of businesses.

Where both individual finances and business corporate finances are concerned, positive cash flows are required to maintain solvency. Cash flows could be demonstrated because of a past transaction like selling a business product or a personal item or investment. They might also be projected into a future time for some consideration that a company or individual anticipates receiving and then possibly spending. No person or corporation can survive for long without cash flow.

Positive cash flow is essential for a variety of needs. Sufficient cash flow allows for money for you to pay your personal bills and creditors. It also allows a business to cover the costs of employee payroll, suppliers' bills, and creditors' payments in a timely fashion. When individuals and businesses lack sufficient cash on hand to maintain their budget or operations, then they are named insolvent. Lasting insolvency generally leads to personal or corporate bankruptcy.

For businesses, statements of cash flows are created by accountants. These demonstrate the quantity of cash that is created and utilized by a corporation in a certain time frame. Cash flows in this definition are calculated by totaling net income following taxes with non cash charges like depreciation. Cash flow is able to be assigned to either a business' entire operations or to one particular segment or project of the company. Cash flow is often considered to be an effective measurement of a business' ongoing financial strength.

Cash flows are also used by business and individuals to ascertain the value or return of a project or investment. The numbers of cash flows in to and out of such projects and investments are often utilized as inputs for indicators of performance like net present value and internal rate of return. A problem with a business' liquidity can also be determined by measuring the entire entity's cash flow.

Many individuals prefer investments that yield periodic positive cash flow over ones that pay only one time capital gains. High yielding dividend stocks, energy trusts, and real estate investment trusts are all examples of positive cash flow investments. Real estate properties can also be positive cash flow yielding investments when they provide greater amounts of rental income than their combined monthly mortgage payments, maintenance expenses, and property management upkeep costs and outflows total.

Cash Flow Quadrant

The cash flow quadrant is a diagram that shows four types of individuals involved in a business. These four people make up the entire business world. The four quadrants are E, S, B, and I.

The E quadrant stands for employees. Employees have the same core values in general. This is security. When any employee sits down with a manager or a president, they will always tell them the same thing. This is that they are looking for a secure and safe job that includes benefits.

The S in the cash flow quadrant represents a small business owner or a self employed person. They are generally solo actors or one person outfits. These types would rather operate on their own, as their motto is always to have something done right, you should do it yourself.

On the right side of the cash flow quadrant are the B's. B stands for Big Business people. Big businesses have five hundred or greater numbers of employees. They are completely different from the others in the quadrants, as they are constantly looking for the most intelligent and capable people, networks, and systems to aid them in running their large business. They do not want to micro manage the company themselves, rather they want good people to do it on their behalf.

The last quarter of the cash flow quadrants is the I, which stands for Investor. Investors are those individuals who make money work effectively and efficiently for themselves. The main difference between them and the B quadrants it that the investors have their money working hard while the Big Business people have other people working hard for them. Both groups of B's and I's represent the wealthy. The employees and the self employed are the people who work hard for the business people and investors on the right, or wealthy side of the quadrant.

The cash flow quadrant explains the differences between the rich and the working poor. It is useful to describe four types of income that a person can generate as well. The smartest people in the cash flow quadrant are the ones who manage to make the other people and their money work hard for their benefit. That is why they are the wealthy, while the hard working members of society on the left side are the ones who do all of the working on the wealthy people's behalf. Learning to become wealthy means effectively changing which square of the cash flow quadrant a person occupies.

Cash Management

Cash management refers to the corporate functions of gathering, handling, and short term investing cash. This represents a critical part of making certain a firm is financially viable and stays solvent. In many cases, the business managers of a company or corporate treasurers of a large corporation will handle the aggregate cash management responsibilities. This means they will be responsible for ensuring the firm continues to be financially viable and solvent on a week to week basis.

There is more to successfully handled cash management than simply sidestepping financial problems or even bankruptcy. This job also involves bringing in invoice payments and account receivables, boosting the rates and speed of collection, improving the level of available cash at hand, and picking out relevant short term investment instruments which will all contribute to better profits and a stronger cash position for the firm in question.

Those small business managers and developers must learn to manage cash flow well since they do not enjoy low cost access to easy credit. They also encounter many ongoing running costs that they have to stay on top of while they are waiting for their customers to pay their receivables. By properly and prudently managing their cash flow, firms are able to cover unanticipated costs and to effectively cover their routine financial events like payroll on a bi-weekly or semi-monthly basis. The point of cash management is to effectively balance out two main corporate counteracting forces. These are the receivables for incoming cash and the outflows of payables.

Part of the dilemma for many companies struggling to effectively run their cash management operations is that invoices and receivables are positive cash flow on the books, yet in practice they are not always received immediately. Some invoice terms allow for the customer to wait from 30 to 60 to even 90 days to settle their invoices. This is how businesses can actually find themselves in the uncomfortable position of their sales growing even rapidly and still have cash flow problems because their receivables come in slowly or even unfortunately late.

Businesses have a variety of tools and means to speed up their receivables so that their payment float becomes reduced. Some of these are to deploy an auto billing service that immediately invoices the customers electronically, to make clear the billing and payment terms to the clients, to keep on top of all collections with an aging receivables spreadsheet, to offer incentives for same as cash 10 day invoice payments, and to collect payments via electronic payment processing at a bank.

Businesses which are successful in controlling their payables will be better capable of maintaining positive cash flows. Through streamlining the efficiency of the payables operations, firms are able to lower their costs all the while holding on to more cash which they can put to work in the company operations. There are a wide variety of effective payable management solutions available today. Some of these include direct payroll deposits, payment processing which is handled electronically, and closely and carefully controlled cash disbursements. Each of these processes will help to both automate and make efficient all of the payout operations.

Thanks to the variety of digital age offerings, the vast majority of payable management and receivable operations may be simply automated through current day solutions in business banking. Smaller companies are now able to operate with the same big scale technologies for cash management as the mega corporations. This is in no small part due to the rapid march of technological advances across business solutions and banking. Such cost savings created by these cutting-edged cash management techniques effectively more than offset the costs of utilizing them. The best part of the process nowadays is that a firm's management is capable of allocating critical resources to expanding the core business better than ever before possible.

Cash Reserves

Cash reserves refer to money which an individual person, a company, or a corporation saves in order to be ready to cover any emergency funding or short term requirements. They can also be utilized to refer to a kind of extremely liquid, short term investment which usually garners a poor rate of return (under three percent in a year).

An example of this would be Fidelity Cash Reserves, one of the Fidelity mutual families of funds particular investments. Sometimes individuals will hold money they need rapid access to in such a fund which can be instantly liquidated on the same day they issue the order. Possessing a major amount in a cash reserve fund provides corporations, companies, individuals, families, or communities with the necessary capability to engage in a significant purchase right away.

There are various reasons why firms wish to maintain some cash reserves. They need to have sufficient money on hand in order to cover all of their costs which may be anticipated or even unanticipated over the short term time-frame. Besides this, they often prefer to have enough cash readily available for such interesting possible investments which could arise with little to no warning.

Though cash is always considered to be the most liquid type of wealth and assets, there are also short term kinds of assets like three month U.S. Treasury bills which investors also deem to be a type of a cash reserve because of the ease and frequency with which they can exchange them and their close proximity to maturity date. Major corporations like Alphabet (Google), General Electric, IBM, and Apple keep enormous cash reserves available. These typically range from fifty billion dollars to one hundred and fifty billion dollars.

At the beginning of 2016, Apple boasted such cash reserve ranging from fifty billion to one hundred fifty billion dollars. At the same time, Alphabet (Google) counted $75.3 billion in their immediate cash on hand reserves. This permitted Google to buy out major corporate purchases like their acquisition of Nest, which they bought for a hefty $3 billion price tag back in 2014.

With banks, governmental oversight agencies require that they maintain a minimum quantity of cash reserves on hand. This is because their operations are critical for the functioning of any economy. In the United States, it is the American Federal Reserve that determines these cash reserve amounts for the banks. In other countries, it is often the national central bank or some other governmental oversight regulator who makes the call.

Banking cash reserves will typically be set as a certain percentage of the banks' liabilities or net transaction accounts. With those banks which contain in excess of $110.2 million in their net transaction accounts, this amount within the U.S. proves to be 10 percent of such liabilities. This amount became effective on January 1st of 2016. Such bank reserves have to be kept in either deposits at a Federal Reserve Bank or in their own vaults as cash on hand. With euro currency liabilities or time deposits of a non-personal nature, these liabilities are not subjected to such a cash reserve requirement.

Economists and personal finance gurus generally state that individuals are wise to keep minimally sufficient cash on hand to cover from three to six months of expenses in the event they suffer a family emergency. Such an emergency fund is a form of a cash reserve. These reserves would be kept in either their local bank accounts or otherwise in a stable and short term time frame investment which will maintain its value regardless of what happens in the markets. In this way, individuals are able to draw on their own emergency funds or alternatively to sell such investments at a moment's notice without taking a financial loss. This needs to be the case no matter how the financial investment markets are performing.

Other forms of personal cash reserves could be held in a savings account, checking account, money market account, money market fund, or even CDs and Treasury Bills. For those businesses or individuals who do not plan ahead with enough cash reserves, they may have to instead to fall back on credit, loans, or in some drastic cases, declaring bankruptcy.

Certified Public Accountant (CPA)

CPA's, or certified public accountants, are accountants who have taken and successfully completed a series of demanding exams that are given by the American Institute of Certified Public Accountants. Many states also have their own state level exams that have to be passed along with the national one.

CPA'a are accountants in every sense of the word, but not every accountant is qualified as a CPA. Because of the difficulties in becoming a CPA, there are many accountants who either never attempt or never succeed in successfully passing the Certified Public Accountant exam. This does not mean such an accountant is not qualified to practice accounting tasks, only that he or she will not be allowed to do tasks that require specific CPA credentials.

Such Certified Public Accountants do a number of varying tasks and jobs. Many will provide advice and simple income tax preparing for various clients who might be comprised of corporations, small companies, or individuals. Besides this, Certified Public Accountants practice many other tasks that include auditing, keeping the records of businesses, and consulting for business entities.

Keeping a CPA license is not accomplished through automatic renewal. Certified Public Accountants are required to engage in a full one hundred and twenty hours of courses on continuing education in every three year period. This is so that they will be on top of any and all changes going on in the field of their chosen profession.

The opportunities for Certified Public Accountants are many and varied. The FBI seeks to hire them routinely, preferring applicant candidates with either such a CPA background or alternatively an attorney background. Numerous state and Federal government agencies offer CPA's opportunities by providing CPA positions. Businesses ranging from small companies to large corporations also seek them out. With these firms, CPA's can occupy positions ranging from controllers, to CFO or Chief Financial Officers, to CEO's or Chief Executive Officers.

Among the most significant parts that CPA's can play proves to be one of a consultant. As a consultant, Certified Public Accountants can be looking into possible means of saving small businesses or even enormous corporations money on expenses or putting together specific financial plans that permit a corporation or business to appear more appealing to investors or possible buyers. Certified Public Accountants are sworn to a particular code of ethical conduct. They are required to provide their clients with honest and reliable advice that is also ethical.

Certified Public Accountants who do not stay within the bounds of their ethical code can lead to the total financial failure of a firm. This turned out to be the case in recent years at Enron, the energy trading and producing giant. Not only were Enron corporate executives charged for illegal accounting activities, but also a number of CPA's from nationally renowned accounting firm Arthur Anderson were charged with unethical practices of accounting.

Chapter 11 Bankruptcy

Chapter 11 Bankruptcy proves to be a specific type of bankruptcy. This kind has to do with the business assets, debts, and affairs being reorganized. The business reorganization filing was named for the Section 11 of the United States' Bankruptcy Code. Corporations commonly file it that need some time to rearrange the terms of their debts and their business operations. It gives them a fresh start on repaying their debt obligations. Naturally the indebted company will have to stick to the terms of the reorganization plan. This proves to be the most highly complex type of bankruptcy filing possible. Companies have been advised to only entertain it once they have contemplated their other options and analyzed the repercussions of such a filing.

This Chapter 11 bankruptcy rarely makes the news unless it is a nationally known or famous corporation which is filing. Among the major corporations that have filed such a Chapter 11 bankruptcy are United Airlines, General Motors, K-Mart, and Lehman Brothers. The first three successfully emerged from it and became as great or stronger than they were before falling into hard times financially. In reality, the vast majority of these cases are unknown to the general public. As an example, in the year 2010, nearly 14,000 separate corporations filed for Chapter 11.

The point of this Chapter 11 Bankruptcy is to assist a corporation in restructuring both obligations and debts. The goal is not to close down the business. In fact it rarely leads to the corporation closing. Instead, corporations like K-mart, General Motors, and tens of thousands of others were able to survive and once again thrive thanks to the useful process of protection from creditors and reorganization of business debts.

It is typically LLCs Limited Liability Companies, partnerships, and corporations that make application for Chapter 11 Bankruptcy. There are cases where individuals who are positively saddled with debt and who are not able to be approved for a Chapter 13 or Chapter 7 filing can be qualified for Chapter 11 instead. The time table for successfully completing Chapter 11 bankruptcy ranges from several months to as long as two years.

Businesses that are in the middle of their Chapter 11 cases are encouraged to keep operating. The debtor in possession will typically run the business normally. Where there are cases that have gross incompetence, dishonest dealings, or even fraud involved, typically trustees come in to take over the business and its daily operations while the bankruptcy proceedings are ongoing.

Corporations in the midst of these filings will not be permitted to engage in specific decisions without first having to consult with the courts to proceed. They may not terminate or sign rental agreements, sell any assets beyond regular inventory, or expand existing business operations or alternatively cease them. The bankruptcy court retains full control regarding any hiring and paying of lawyers as well as signing contracts with either unions or vendors. Lastly, such indebted organizations and entities may not sign for a loan that will pay once the bankruptcy process finishes.

After the business or person files their chapter 11 bankruptcy, it gains the right to offer a first reorganization plan. Such plans often include renegotiating owed debts and reducing the company size in order to slash expenses. There are some scenarios where the plan will require every asset to be liquidated in order to pay off the creditors, as with Lehman Brothers.

When plans are fair and workable, courts will approve them. This moves the reorganization process ahead. For plans to be accepted, they also have to maintain the creditors' best interests for the future repayment of debts owed to them. When the debtor can not or will not put forward a plan of their own for reorganization, then the creditors are invited to offer one in the indebted company or person's place.

Chapter 7 Bankruptcy

Chapter 7 bankruptcy is a form of protection from creditors. Unlike Chapter 13 bankruptcy, it does not have any repayment plan. In the Chapter 7 a bankruptcy trustee determines what eligible assets the debtor individual or company has. The trustee then collects these available assets, sells them, and distributes proceeds to the creditors against their debts. This is all done under the rules of the Bankruptcy Code.

Debtors are permitted to keep specific property that is exempt, such as their house. Other property that the debtor holds will be mortgaged or have liens put against it to pledge it to the various creditors until it is liquidated. Debtors who file chapter 7 will likely forfeit property in partial payment of debts.

Chapter 7 bankruptcy is available to corporations, partnerships, and individuals who pass a means test. The relief can be granted whether or not the debtor is ruled to be insolvent.

Chapter 7 bankruptcy cases start when debtors file their petitions with their particular area's bankruptcy court. For businesses, they use the address where the main office is located. Debtors are required to give the court information that includes schedules of current expenditures and income and liabilities and assets.

They are also required to furnish a financial affairs statement and a schedule of contracts and leases which are not expired. The debtors will also have to deliver the trustee tax return copies from the most current tax year along with any tax returns which they file while the case is ongoing.

Debtors who are individuals also have to furnish their court with other documents. They are required to file a credit counseling certificate and any repayment plan created there. They must also file proof of income from employers 60 days before their original filing, a monthly income statement along with expected increases in either, and notice of interest they have in tuition or state education accounts. Husbands and wives are allowed to file individually or jointly. They must abide by the requirements for individual debtors either way.

The courts are required to charge debtors who file $335 in filing, administrative, and trustee fees. Debtors typically pay these when they file to the clerk of court. The court can give permission for individuals to pay by installments instead. When the income of debtor's proves to be less than 150% of the amount of the poverty level, the court can choose to drop the fee requirements.

Debtors will have to provide a great amount of information in order to complete their Chapter 7 filing and receive a discharge of debts. They have to list out each of their creditors along with the amounts they owe then and the type of claim. Debtors have to furnish a list of all property the own. They must also give the information on the amount, source, and frequency of income they have to the court.

Finally, they will be required to provide an in depth list of all monthly living expenses that includes housing, utilities, food, transportation, clothing, medicine, and taxes. This helps the court to determine if the debtor is able to set up a repayment plan instead of discharging the debts.

From 21 to 40 days after the debtor files the petition with the courts, the trustee hosts a creditors' meeting. The debtor will have to cooperate with the trustee on any requests for additional financial documents or records. At this meeting, the trustee will ask questions to make sure the debtor is fully aware of the consequences of debt discharge by the bankruptcy court. Sometimes trustees will deliver this in written form to the debtor before or at the meeting. Assuming the trustee makes the recommendation for discharge, the Federal bankruptcy court judge will discharge the debts when the process is completed.

Closeout Sale

A closeout sale represents the last sale for a given item from a retailer. It could also refer to the last offers from a retailer in its inventory it provides to the public or another company. Sometimes certain items simply are not selling effectively. Other time it may be that a retailer is forced to sell off its inventory thanks to a fire, moving to another location, or too much inventory. In many cases, the company has simply gone bankrupt and has to liquidate everything. In these last cases, this type of sale is also referred to as a "going out of business sale."

Car dealerships also offer these types of inventory-moving events following hail storms. These are called "hail sales" in this case because the car dealership inventory has suffered extensive damage from the inclement weather. In any of these last chance scenarios, stores or outlets make an effort to get the word out to their customers and the general buying public.

A closeout sale should never be confused with a closeout store. These outlets are stores that concentrate their efforts on purchasing wholesale closeout items off of retailers. They then sell them to their own customer base for a price discount. In the United States, there are several nationally known examples of this type of operation. Closeout store chains include Big Lots, Marshalls, Ross Dress for Less, TJ Maxx, and Value City. They mostly specialize in goods that are house ware or clothes related.

It is a well-known fact that many times, items purchased in closeout sale offers cannot be returned according to the company policy of many stores. The goal is to move these items, not exchange them for other closeout sale items. In the cases of store closing and liquidation efforts, this is usually the policy. In other jurisdictions outside of the United States, like the United Kingdom, the buying customers maintain their typical rights of return in any sale. This means that they are allowed to return defective goods under the country's Distance Selling Regulations.

Holiday-themed merchandise is often the subject of closeout sales in the U.S. and other Western nation economies. This is because it is expensive and space-intensive to store Christmas merchandise for the better part of a year. Most American stores therefore engage in after-Christmas clearance sales. Some of them even commence ahead of the holidays. The discounts at such events can typically be 25 percent or more, though they actually range from five percent to as high as 50 percent. Sometimes stores will later boost this discount from 75 percent to even 90 percent rather than store the final merchandise, allowing it to age. In Canada, these post-Christmas sales are called "Boxing Day sales." They attract enormous shopping crowds looking for their closeout deals following Christmas.

Merchandise which is specific to a given season is often seen at clearance sales. This is especially true for winter wear or summer time patio furniture. This allows the store to bring out more current styles and fashions in their limited showroom or shelf space.

Thrift stores that are normally better priced than traditional big box department stores also practice what they call "rolling" closeouts. In these stores, they simply take all of the merchandise which they offer in a particular week and tag it with a special color or sometimes letter to make it clear which items are part of the closeout sale. In these cases, they rotate out the clearance goods once per month.

In the more traditional department stores, they also utilize closeout sales in their physical locations. They will take merchandise they wish to discontinue and place it on their clearance racks. The price will continue to drop until the point that a shopper finally takes the item to buy it. Stores have taken this concept and reproduced it on online in recent years. The first Internet-based operation to imitate the retail store clearance idea was the now-failed Drop.com. They permitted sellers on the site to auto reduce the price of their items for the online customers.

Collateral

Collateral refers to an asset or piece of Real Estate which borrowers provide as security to lenders in exchange for a loan. This property actually secures the mortgage or other form of loan. In the event that the borrowers do not continue to make the agreed upon payments on the loan according to the laid out schedule, the financial institution has the right to seize this property in order to recover the principal losses.

Because such collateral provides at least nominal security to the lending institution in the scenarios where the borrower refuses to or is unable repay the loan, these forms of loans are commonly provided with lower interest rates as compared to those loans which are unsecured entirely. When such a lender has interest in the underlying property provided by the borrower then this is referred to as a lien.

In the end there are several arrangements with such collateral. The type of loan often determines which form will be required within the contract. With car loans or mortgages, the loans are secured by the property upon which the financial institution issues the loan. Other forms of loans have more flexible security, as with collateralized personal loans. In order for any loan to be called secured, the backing security has to be at least equal to or greater than the balance that remains on the loan in question.

Such secured loans entail far less risk for lenders because the underlying property serves as an incentive for the borrower to keep paying back the loan. Borrowers know all too well that if they do not complete the required payments then the financial institution which holds the loan may legally possess (or repossess) this collateral in order to recoup the money it is owed on the rest of the loan.

With mortgages, the collateral in question will always be the home that the borrower buys using the loan in the first place. If and when they fail to pay the debts, then the lender may seize possession of the property by utilizing a procedure called foreclosure. After the lender completes the necessary court process and has the property back in its possession, it is allowed to sell off the home to someone else. This will permit the bank to cover the principal which remains on the original loan along with their costs for the foreclosure.

Houses also can also be utilized for second mortgage collateral, or against HELOC's (Home Equity Lines of Credit). In such scenarios, the credit delivered by the financial institution may not be greater than the equity which exists within the home itself. As a tangible example, a home could have a market value of $300,000. At the same time, it might be that $175,000 of the original mortgage balance remains to pay. This would mean that the majority of HELOC's or even second mortgages would not exceed the available equity of $125,000.

Collateral is also utilized in margin accounts' trading of stocks, commodities, and futures. In this case, it is the securities themselves that become the property which secures the brokerage loan. In the event that a margin call has to be issued and the account holder will not or can not pay it on demand, then the securities' value ultimately makes certain that the brokerage will get back its loaned money.

Sometimes financial institutions will require additional collateral be put up for a given existing loan, if the contract allows such a scenario. This will reduce increasing risks for the lending institution. A creditor could give notice that without such additional security, they will be forced to raise the interest rate on the loan. Additionally accepted security could be certificates of deposit, cash, equipment, letters of credit, or even shares of stock.

Compound Interest

Compound interest represents interest which calculates on both the original principal amount as well as the interest that was accumulated previously during the loan or investment. Economists have called this miraculous phenomenon an interest on interest. It causes loans or invested deposits to increase at a significantly faster pace than only simple interest, the opposite of compound interest. Simple interest proves to be interest that calculates on just the principal amount of money.

Compound interest accrues at an interest rate which determines how often the compounding occurs. The higher the compound interest rate turns out to be, the faster the principal will compound and the more compounding periods will occur. Consider an example of how effective compounding truly is. $100 that is compounded at a rate of 10% per year will turn out to be less than $100 which is compounded at only 5% but semi annually during the same length of time.

Compound interest is important to individuals as it is able to take a few dollars worth of savings now and transform them into significant money throughout lifetimes. Investors do not need an MBA or a Wall Street background in order to benefit from this principle. Practically all investments earn compounding interest if the owners leave these earnings in the investment account over the long term.

This form of interest cuts both ways on the receiving and paying sides. When individuals are saving and investing money, it helps them grow the amount faster. When they are borrowing and paying the same interest on the debt, it grows against them faster. Individuals who are saving wish their money to compound as often as they can. Individuals who are borrowing wish it to compound as infrequently as possible. Savers are better off if they are able to compound quarterly instead of annually while just the opposite is true for borrowers.

For people who are compounding their investments, time works on their side. Money that grows at a rate of 6% each year doubles every 12 years. This means that it increases to four times as much as the original amount in only 24 years. For individuals paying compound interest, time is similarly working against them. Credit card companies utilize this principle to keep their card owners in debt forever by encouraging them to only make minimum monthly payments on the bills.

Thanks to compounding, a smaller amount of money that a person adds to an account upfront is more valuable than a larger sum of money he or she adds decades later. This cuts both ways. By paying down principal on a credit card with an extra $5 per month, the amount of compound interest individuals pay on a 14% interest rate credit card decreases by $1,315 over ten years. This is true even though they have paid only $600 in extra payments over this amount of time.

Anyone can make the miracle of compounding work for them. The idea works the same whether individuals are investing $100 or $100 million instead. Millionaires have greater ranges of investment choices. Even relatively poor people can compound their interest to increase their original amount and double their money as often as possible.

Compounding interest means that participants have to give up using some dollars today in order to obtain a greater benefit from them in the future. The little money may be missed now, but the rewards for the more significant amounts in the future will more than make up for the little sacrifice the individual makes now. Financial planners have claimed that the difference between poverty and financial comfort in the future amounts to even a few dollars in savings each week invested now rather than later.

Consumer Debt

Consumer debt refers to debts which individuals owe because of goods they have purchased. These goods must be consumable forms which do not appreciate in value to qualify for the designation. Having huge amounts of consumer debts is generally considered to be negative for individuals since it raises the burden on their resources to keep up with the debt servicing. It also makes it harder to remit the installment payments which are often laden with interest. When these types of debts are not well managed, they can cause a consumer to be forced into bankruptcy.

There are cases where some analysts and economists feel that a little consumer debt can benefit the individual. These scenarios mostly center on instances where the debt is run up in purchasing an asset that will increase the earning power of the individual. Several examples of this are useful to consider. One of them surrounds buying a car with financing in order to reach a job which pays more. Another might be incurring student debt to obtain a higher degree that will make it possible to secure a promotion or better job.

There are differences between this consumer debt and those that governments or businesses owe. Consumer debt is also referred to as consumer credit. This type of debt can be obtained from credit unions, commercial banks, and sometimes the United States federal government. Among the two categories of consumer debt are revolving debt and non-revolving debt.

Revolving debt is represented by credit cards. These debts are called revolving as they were originally intended to be repaid every month when the bill comes due. In practice this does not often happen, as consumers carry balances forward much of the time. Non-revolving debts are fixed installment payment loans. They are not paid off fully in a typical given month. They are more commonly held against the underlying asset's useful life. Mortgages on homes are not considered to be consumer debt. Rather they are counted as personal forms of investment in real estate under the category of personal residential.

As of January 2017, the total debt of American consumers increased to

$3.77 trillion. This represented a 2.8 percent increase over the prior month. Around $2.78 trillion of this consumer debt was comprised of non-revolving loans. It had grown by 5.5 percent. Debts on credit cards represented $995 billion at this point. This had dropped by 4.6 percent in January versus December of 2016.

There are three reasons why Americans find themselves so deeply in debt today. These are school loans, car loans, and credit cards. School loans commonly last for ten years. They can also be pushed to an over 25 year repayment schedule by extension. The federal government guarantees most of these loans since there are no assets with which to back a college degree. The rates are low to encourage higher education. During the Great Recession, these loan defaults skyrocketed as the loans increased massively with many people who were unemployed "going back to school" to improve their prospects. The Affordable Care Act gave the Federal government authority to take over this national student loan program from Sallie Mae, the private company which previously administered it.

Car loans typically run from three to five years, which is considered to be the safe collateral life of the new vehicle. After this point, the value of these cars depreciates so highly that they are no longer considered to be valuable collateral. Banks simply repossess the vehicle if the borrowers default on the payment schedule. There are more of these loans now thanks to the low interest rates which encourage borrowing to buy vehicles.

Finally, credit card debt soared because of the Bankruptcy Protection Act of 2005. People could no longer easily declare bankruptcy, so they were forced to run up their credit cards in an effort to pay bills, especially healthcare. In July of 2008, the credit card debt peaked at its historic high of $1.028 trillion. This amounted to a per household average of $8,640.

Consumer Price Index (CPI)

The Consumer Price Index, also known by its acronym of CPI, actually measures changes that take place over time in the level of the pricing of various consumer goods and services that American households buy. The Bureau of Labor Statistics in the U.S. says that the Consumer Price Index is a measurement of the over time change in the prices that urban consumers actually pay for a certain grouping of consumer goods and services.

This consumer price index is not literal in the sense of what inflation really turns out to be. Instead, it is a statistical estimate that is built utilizing the costs of a basket of sample items that are supposed to be representative for the entire economy. These goods and services' prices are ascertained from time to time. In actual practice, both sub indices such as clothing, and even sub-sub indices, such as men's dress shirts, are calculated for varying sub-categories of services and goods. These are then taken and added together to create the total index. The different goods are assigned varying weights as shares of the total amount of the expenditures of consumers that the index covers.

Two essential pieces of information are necessary to build the consumer price index. These are the weighting data and the pricing data. Weighting data comes from estimates of differing kinds of expenditure shares as a percentage of the entire expenditure that the index covers. Sample household expenditure surveys are sourced to figure what the weightings should be. Otherwise, the National Income and Product Accounts estimates of expenditures on consumption are utilized. Pricing data is gathered from a sampling of goods and services taken from a sample range of sales outlets in varying locations and at a sampling of times.

The consumer price index is figured up monthly in the United States. Some other countries determine their CPI's on a quarterly basis. The different components of the consumer price index include food, clothing, and housing, all of which are weighted averages of the sub-sub indices. The CPI index literally compares the prices of one month with the prices in the reference month.

Consumer Price Index is only one of a few different pricing indices that the majority of national statistical agencies calculate. Inflation is figured up using the yearly percentage changes in the underlying consume price index. Uses of this CPI can include adjusting real values of pensions, salaries, and wages for inflation's effects, as well as for monitoring costs, and showing alterations in actual values through deflating the monetary magnitudes. The CPI and US National Income and Product Accounts prove to be among the most carefully followed of economic indicators.

Cost of living index is another measurement that is generated based on the consumer price index. It demonstrates how much consumer expenditures need to adjust to compensate for changes in prices. This details how much consumers need to keep up a constant standard of living.

Core CPI

Core CPI refers to the Consumer Price Index. This term revolves around the idea of core inflation. It reveals the longer term price trend in a given item or economy. Core CPI is a means of measuring inflation which leaves out some specific items, particularly those that experience volatility in their pricing. There is a reason for excluding these items. To learn what long term inflation actually is, volatility in prices over the short term and temporary price changes have to be eliminated.

Core inflation is most typically figured up by using the core CPI. This takes out some products like food and energy items, especially oil and gas. Both of these categories may experience short term price changes. Such short term shocks often differ from the bigger picture trend in inflation and provide a false reading of it.

There is another way of calculating core CPI. This is called the outlier method. This way of figuring core inflation takes away products that show the biggest price movements. Many of these items' prices fluctuate rapidly in commodity markets when speculators trade them for profit. Since their prices do not reflect actual alterations of supply and demand, it can make sense to exclude them.

The government is very concerned about which method of measuring inflation it uses. The Federal Reserve decided to switch from CPI to the PCE Index back in January of 2012. They prefer PCE because it offers trends in inflation which are less dramatically impacted by changes in short term prices. Different agencies find other ways to get to what they believe are more accurate means of measuring inflation.

The BEA Bureau of Economic Administration is concerned with eliminating those short term price changes that speculators and traders cause. To get around this, the BEA works with the gross domestic product numbers that already exist and calculates price changes from it. It then takes the monthly release of Retail Survey numbers and measures them against the CPI data-provided consumer prices. The BEA eliminates irregular fluctuations in the inflation data this way and gains more accurate long term trend information.

Determining core CPI inflation is important. It reveals the correlations between goods and services with their prices and the purchasing value of the general income of consumers. Should the costs of goods and services go up in a given time frame while the consumers' parallel income levels do not rise, the buying power of consumers is weakening. This is because their money's actual value is declining when measured against the costs of critical goods and services.

The process could be virtuous as well. Sometimes inflation occurs only on the income of consumers while the costs of goods and services remain constant. In this case, consumers gain greater purchasing power. This means that they will be able to buy an additional amount of the identical services and goods. Asset inflation can also benefit consumers. If the price of their house or the value of their investment portfolio goes up, the consumer has additional buying power also.

Core Inflation

Core Inflation refers to the change in the cost of goods and services without calculating the important categories of food and energy. The U.S. federal government believes this to be the most accurate means of figuring up true inflationary trends. They claim that both energy products and food components are priced too volatilely to be a part of the core inflation calculation and figure. This is because they constantly change so rapidly that they interfere with inflation readings.

The reason for this is that they are subject to the whims of the traders on the various commodity market exchanges. The majority of core food products like beef, pork, wheat, orange juice, and more and energy products such as oil, natural gas, and gasoline trade each and every week day all throughout the day.

As an example, traders of commodities will likely bid up the prices of oil and its derivative products when they believe its supplies will diminish or if they feel that demand will outpace supplies. It could be that a strike will interrupt production and oil supplies from Nigeria, Venezuela, or Angola. Because of this fear, traders will purchase oil at the prices today and hope to sell it for a higher amount at the anticipated greater prices tomorrow or next week.

That is all that it really takes to radically increase the price of oil. Should the strike wrap up quickly, then the oil prices will plunge when traders suddenly all sell out of their positions. This is why both energy and food prices depend on rapidly changing human emotions rather than real changes to underlying forces of supply and demand. Between this and the inelastic demand of food and energy which people simply have to possess in order to live, these commodities rise and fall crazily sometimes.

Consider how gasoline prices will change when their primary input oil does. Yet as people require gas to travel to school and work, they cannot delay their purchases and wait for prices to decline. Food prices also vary according to gasoline and oil prices as they are shipped by truck throughout the United States. In truth, most foods on your dinner plate have more frequent flyer miles than you ever dreamed of acquiring.

The Fed has a few tools to deal with higher than desired core inflation. The problem comes with their tools needing time to take effect on the broader economy. This might mean as much as from six to 18 months before changes to the Fed Funds rate will show a meaningful impact on the inflation rate in the U.S. As the Fed Funds rate goes higher, so will the bank loans and mortgage rates. Credit will tighten and slow economic growth. Corporations find themselves lowering their core prices in order to keep selling merchandise. This lowers inflation as it finally all feeds through to the economy.

The Federal Reserve targets inflation with their policies. They promise to not take action when the core inflation rate remains at two percent or lower. Consider a real world example. Inflation has a tendency to creep higher throughout the summer as people go on vacations. The Fed does not wish to raise rates each summer though, which would force them to proportionally lower them again in the fall.

Rather, they wait and see if such summer increases boost the prices of the goods and services ex food and energy permanently. Yet ultimately higher food and gas prices force up the prices of all other goods and services if they remain elevated for long. This is why the Federal Reserve will also consider the headline inflation rate, which is the opposite of the core inflation rate. This broader measure of inflation considers food and energy prices alongside all other goods and services.

The core inflation rate can be measured via the Core Price Index, or core CPI, as well as the core Personal Consumption Expenditures price index, or core PCE price index.

Corporation

A corporation refers to a business entity where it is distinctive and separated from the owners. Such corporations may take on many responsibilities similar to individuals. They can borrow and loan out money, make and execute contracts, hire and terminate employees, sue or become sued, pay taxes, and own cash and assets. This is why corporations are many times referred to by the phrase of legal person.

A corporation is a legal construct that controls and runs businesses of all types all over the globe. There may be differing legal arrangements from one government jurisdiction to the next, but they all have the attribute of a limited liability. With this protection, shareholders enjoy important rights like benefitting from dividends as a result of profits and price appreciation from successful business endeavors. While enjoying these advantages, limited liability means that they do not carry any of the personal responsibility for payment of the company's debts.

Practically every famous business and brand in the world is a part of a corporation. This includes such internationally recognized entities as Coca-Cola, McDonalds, Microsoft, and Toyota Motors. Corporations can also do business under a different name. A classic example of this is Alphabet Inc. that runs Google.

Corporations are established as a group of stock holders choose to incorporate. They pursue this follow up after a common goal in their ownership of the business. Such corporations may be charitable as well as for profit. The overwhelming majority of such companies are founded with the ambition of earning positive returns for the stock holders. These shareholders own some percentage of the corporation in exchange for paying for their shares. If they obtain them directly from the company, then their payments remit to the treasury of the company itself.

Corporations sometimes possess thousands of shareholders, especially when they are publicly traded companies. These entities could also have only a few or even one shareholder. The most common corporations within the United States are called "C Corporations."

Shareholders use their one vote per share to vote for the company board of directors every year. This group is responsible for naming the management which they oversee. The managers run the daily activities of the company. It is the corporation's board of directors which must carry out the business plan of the entity. They also do not bear responsibility for the company's debts, but have a fiduciary responsibility to care for the corporation. If they do not fulfill the duty faithfully, they may become personally liable for mistakes. There are tax statutes that allow for board of directors members to be personally liable.

As these corporations fulfill their goals, they can be wound down through a process also known as liquidation. In this process, they appoint a liquidator to sell off the company assets, pay the creditors, and share out all cash assets which remain among the stockholders. This can be done as a result of an involuntary or a voluntary procedure. Creditors can force liquidation when a company can no longer pay its debts. This often leads to corporate bankruptcy.

Corporation Tax

Corporation Tax refers to a United Kingdom jurisdiction method of taxing companies and associations domiciled in Great Britain. For any business that is a limited company, or is a foreign firm that boasts a United Kingdom office or branch, or operates as a cooperative, club, or other type of unincorporated association, they must pay such taxes on any and all profits which they accrue from engaging in business (called trading in Britain) in the U.K. This last qualifier means that even sports clubs and community-based groups will have to pay the tax on all profits in excess of one hundred British pounds sterling (if they have any).

The United Kingdom is similar in its corporate tax collecting efforts to other jurisdictions like the United States. Their taxing authorities do not send out bills. They follow a self-reporting taxation system. Businesses must first register for the corporation tax as they begin conducting business. Those associations which are not incorporated are required to write to HMRC Her Majesty's Revenue and Customs. These companies must maintain official accounting records to prepare a company tax return. They will then figure out how much of the corporation tax they will be required to pay. Finally they pay the tax itself. If they have nothing they are required to pay to HMRC, then they must report this.

Companies in the United Kingdom receive typically nine months and a day from the conclusion of their accounting period as a deadline to pay their taxes. The returns themselves the firms must file with HMRC by the deadline that falls 12 months following the conclusion of the accounting period. Though there are exceptions, accounting periods in Great Britain are commonly the identical 12 months to the financial year which their annual accounts cover.

Not all profits will be corporation tax assessed in the U.K. Profits which companies or associations earn from investments, trading profits (i.e. doing business), or for selling assets for higher than their cost basis (called chargeable gains in the U.K.) will be tax assessed. For those firms which are headquartered within the United Kingdom, they will be required to pay the tax on corporations for their profits which they generate not only within the U.K., but also from overseas. Those firms which merely maintain a branch office in Great Britain will only pay taxes on profits earned on British soil.

Companies which fall into a dormant status will not be required to pay the corporation tax. The definition of dormant simply means that there is no income from the firm (as with investments), nor is the firm engaging in business. Those companies that are new limited companies that have not yet begun trading are also deemed dormant. Associations which are unincorporated or clubs that owe below one hundred British pounds in such tax are also considered to be dormant. Flat management companies similarly fall under the dormant definition. The definition of trading (or doing business) includes any activities that involve selling, renting, or purchasing property, employing any individuals, advertising, or obtaining interest.

Firms that have been dormant can become active again. In scenarios where this occurs, British law requires that the owners alert HM Revenue and Customs once their dormant limited or non-trading company begins trading again. The law of the land also requires that these companies in this restarting status will have to begin amassing statutory accounts so they can once again create and file Company Tax Returns at the end of year for the company. Alerting HMRC that the business has begun to trade once more simply means that the firm should re-register for the corporation tax once again.

Credit Bureaus

Credit bureaus are agencies that collect financial information. They go by different names in various countries around the world. In the United Kingdom they are known as credit reference agencies. In Australia, the bureaus are called credit reporting bodies. India knows their credit agencies as credit information companies.

Within the United States, these organizations are called consumer reporting agencies. Whatever name they go by, they all serve the same function. The bureaus gather information from banks and other financial sources to deliver consumer credit information about individual consumers.

The U.S. consumer reporting agencies are governed by the Fair Credit Reporting Act. Other laws that regulate the activities of the bureaus are the Fair and Accurate Credit Transactions Act, the Fair Credit Billing Act, the Fair Credit Reporting Act, and Regulation B. These acts attempt to safeguard consumers against unfair practices and mistakes made by the data providers and the credit reporting agencies themselves.

The U.S. has two separate government organizations who oversee the credit bureaus and their data suppliers. These are the FTC and the OCC. Primary oversight of the credit reporting agencies as they deal with consumers belongs to the Federal Trade Commission. The banks are monitored for all of the information that they provide the reporting agencies by the Office of the Controller of the Currency. This government agency supervises, regulates, and charters all of the national banks and any information they turn over to the consumer credit reporting agencies.

Three main credit reporting bureaus dominate nearly all credit reporting in the U.S. These are Experian, Equifax, and TransUnion. None of these three agencies are owned by government entities. All of them exist as companies seeking to make a profit and are traded publically. They are carefully monitored for fairness by the government provided oversight organizations.

The consumer reporting agencies operate through a vast network with the credit card issuing companies, banks, and other financial entities with which individuals have accounts. All of these ties ensure that credit account information and histories show up on the credit reports of one, two, or even all of the bureaus.

The credit bureaus compile all of this information into a consumer credit report. They each then utilize proprietary trade secret formulas to determine every individual's FICO credit score. Each of the three bureaus formulates its own score that is different from that of its competitors. They also come up with educational credit score numbers which are often vastly different from the official scores.

Consumers do not have to settle for educational credit scores. They have the rights to see what is on their credit reports. Each and every year, individuals are able to obtain an official credit report from each of the three credit bureaus. This can be done by going to the government mandated website AnnualCreditReport.com.

Besides this, consumers are allowed to go to the websites of the three main consumer reporting agencies and order credit reports and scores from them directly. The only way to get the official credit score is to pay for and order it from the credit bureaus themselves. These are not provided in the annual free reports. Experian and Equifax offer all three credit reports in a single convenient to view document.

Sometimes the credit bureaus will make mistakes with individuals' credit reports. When this happens, it is important to get in touch with the credit bureau itself in order to dispute any information that is inaccurate. These organizations also should be contacted directly if there is concern about fraud so that they can place a security alert or fraud alert on the person's credit report.

Credit Report

A credit report is an individual or business' credit history. This includes their record of borrowing and repaying money in the past. It similarly covers data pertaining to any late payments made or bankruptcies that have been declared. In some countries, credit reports are also referred to as credit reputations.

When an American like you completes a credit application for a bank, a credit card company, or a retail store, this information is directly sent on to one of the three main credit bureaus. These are Experian, Trans Union, and Equifax. These credit bureaus then match up your name, identification, address, and phone number on the application for such credit with the data that they keep in their bureau's files. Because of this match up process, it is essential that lenders, creditors, and other parties always provide exactly correct information to the credit bureaus.

Such information in these files at the three major credit bureaus is then utilized by lenders like credit card companies in order to decide if you are deserving of having credit issued to you by the creditor. Another way of putting this is that they decide how likely that you will be to pay back these debts. Such willingness to pay back a debt is usually indicated by the timeliness of prior payments to other lenders. Such lenders will prefer to see the debt obligations of individual consumers, such as yourself, paid on time every month.

The second element considered in a lender offering loans or credit to individuals like you is based on your actual income. Higher incomes generally lead to greater amounts of credit being accessible. Still, lenders look at both willingness, as shown in the credit report and prior payment history, along with ability, as shown by income, in deciding whether or not to extend you credit.

Credit reports have become even more significant in light of risk based pricing. Practically all lenders of the financial services industry rely on credit reports to determine what the annual percentage rate and grace period of repayment of a loan or offer of credit will be. Other obligations of the contract are similarly based on this credit report.

In the past, a great deal of discussion has gone on considering the information contained in the credit reports. Scientific studies done on the issue have determined that for the most part, this credit report information is extremely accurate. Such credit bureaus also have their own authorized studies of fifty-two million credit reports that show that the information contained therein is right a vast majority of the time.

Congress has heard testimony from the Consumer Data Industry Association that in fewer than two percent of credit report issue cases have there been data which had to be erased because it was wrong. In the few cases where these did exist, more than seventy percent of such disputes are handled in fourteen days or less. More than ninety-five percent of consumers with disputes report being satisfied with the resolution.

Credit Score

Credit Score refers to a number generated by the credit bureaus to represent the creditworthiness of an individual. The credit bureaus possess literally from hundreds to thousands of distinct lines worth of information on each person with a credit profile. This makes it extremely difficult for lending institutions to go through it all. Since they lack the man hours to carefully peruse each applicant's credit reports personally, the majority of financial institutions which lend money employ these credit scores rather than tediously read through credit reports on applicants.

These Credit Scores are actually numbers that a computer program generates after crawling through an individual's credit report. Such programs seek out certain fundamentals, patterns, and so-called warning flags in any credit report and history. They then generate a credit score based on what they find. Lenders love these scores since they can be basically interpreted by a consistent set of comparative rules.

Consider the following examples. Lending institutions might automatically approve any application that comes with an associated 720 credit score or higher. Those profiles with 650 to 720 would likely be approved but with a greater interest rate. Applications with credit scores below 650 might simply be rejected. The computer is consistent and fair using these standards, so no one is treated in a discriminatory way relative to any other applicant.

Federal laws require that each individual be granted a free credit report annually from every one of the big three credit bureaus Experian, Trans Union, and Equifax. This does not mean that anyone is required to hand out free credit scores. In fact there is no such thing as a truly free credit score offer. There are scores provided in exchange for signing up for trial membership services in things like credit monitoring services. In general though, individuals pay for their credit scores from each of the major credit bureaus.

The particulars of a Credit Score are interesting. It is always a three digit formatted number that ranges from 300 to 850. These become created using one of a variety of mathematical algorithms that work off of both the individuals' credit profiles and their credit report's particular information.

This score is crafted with the intention of predicting risk to the lenders, not to benefit the person it covers. It is particularly concerned with the chances of an individual going delinquent on any credit obligations within the next 24 months after the score has been issued.

It is a common misnomer among many individuals that there is only one credit scoring model in the country. There are countless models that exist. It is only the FICO credit score that matters in nearly all cases though. This is because fully 90 percent of financial institutions within the United States rely on FICO credit scores in making their decisions on to whom they will extend credit and at what interest rate.

The higher the FICO score these algorithms generate, the lower the risk is to the various lenders. What makes matters more confusing is that there is not only one FICO credit score in existence for every adult American. Each of the three major bureaus generates its own particular score. Since 2009, consumers are only able to view two of their credit scores, those from both Trans Union and Equifax. This is because Experian chose to terminate its myFICO.com arrangements in 2009. Experian does not share their proprietary credit scores with consumers any longer.

Five different significant categories make up the FICO Credit Score. These are payment history (35 percent of the total component), Amounts owed (30 percent), length of credit history (15 percent), types of credit used (10 percent), and new credit inquiries and accounts opened (10 percent).

Customer Base

A customer base refers to a company's prospective customers who the business might be serving. There are many individuals who believe this only pertains to the customers whom a business already counts. Still analysts tend to include in those customers who share common buying habits in the category. This is the case even when the customer has not come into the relevant store location or bought one of the company products yet.

In this group of all potential customers is a narrower set of the customers who are loyal followers of the company products. Business analysts call this group of consumers repeat customers. Business strategies focus on the critical need to turn every one-time customer into a repeat customer. Every company is interested in this, even when not all companies are focused on growing their entire customer base.

Theories on how to build up reliable and impressive customer bases abound. They run the gamut from offering periodic promotions to advertising the company products, brand, and services effectively to offering the highest possible customer service to clients. Any way a business manages to bring people into the store these are possible customers and could become a part of the reliable customer base. The hardest challenge is to bring them back to the store repeatedly.

It is well known that repeat customers are always the most crucial component of any businesses customer base and ultimately company success. These are the ones who will repeatedly and consistently spend money buying the business' products or services. They are also the best possible word of mouth advertising regarding the finest qualities of the company.

It is interesting to realize that some customer bases do not preexist at all. This is because some businesses provide a unique service that establishes a new customer pool which was not around before they began offering the service to the community. It happens when a company comes up with an idea to provide a service to people that they did not even realize they needed.

The trick for many businesses is to find a way to balance the differences between a company's end goals and the needs of the customer which will change periodically. Businesses have to be capable of adapting their strategies to the shifting requirements of a consumer base. At the same time, the business can not be spread in all directions simply chasing consumer fads.

The trick is to build up a loyal customer base which counts numerous repeat customers. When a business develops these types of customers, analysts call them an installed customer base. This refers to those clients of a company who are already utilizing the various products which the company produces.

It is helpful to look at a tangible example to better understand this idea. A company might sell laptop computers, printers, and software. The installed customer base would be only the customers who count at least one of the business' products working in their house. If they were interested in buying a laptop, they would be merely a member of the potential customer base for the business.

It is always more costly to add new customers than it is to keep those which are already existing customers of a business. This is why so many companies today focus their primary efforts on customer service, retention, and relations with their current customers. It does not take much in the way of advertising to keep an existing customer base. The good news is they already know the products.

This is why some promotions and occasional special pricing offers to loyal customers is enough to keep them coming back for more of the core business products. Companies often do this by maintaining as complete an existing customer mailing or emailing list as they possibly can. It is easy to send them promotions in the mail and even easier via emails.

Debit Card

Debit cards are plastic cards that function like a check and are easily utilized like a credit card. Debit cards are commonly one of two types, either branded Visa or Master Card. When you use such a debit card to pay for a purchase, then this amount is deducted immediately from your checking account. Both convenience and security features are included in the use of a debit card.

Debit cards provide tremendous convenience in their ease of use. No longer do you have to make sure that you are carrying enough money on you, or to take the time to write out a physical check while the long line waits impatiently behind you. Besides this ease of use, debit cards are accepted at literally millions of places around the country and the world.

Nowadays, they can be used for almost any purchase, such as lunches or dinners at restaurants, monthly bill payments, merchandise in retail stores, groceries, prescriptions, gas, online purchases, over the phone orders, and even fast food.

Debit cards' spending is easy to keep track of as well. The majority of such transactions are both deducted and posted to a checking account in twenty-four hours or less. This allows for you to conveniently monitor your constantly updated transaction record and balance either over the phone or the bank or card issuer's website. Besides this, debit cards also offer statements, much like credit cards, that outline all purchases made, with details on the name of the merchant, date, location, and amount of transaction.

Debit cards offer another benefit in their security provisions. These cards include free fraud monitoring that helps to find and stop activity that is suspicious with your debit card. They also come with policies of zero liability that protect you from charges that you did not make or authorize. Fraudulently taken out funds are guaranteed to be returned to your account. The vast majority of debit cards also come with the security feature of three digit security codes that allow you to confirm your identity for both phone and Internet orders and purchases.

Debit cards allow two ways for completing in person transactions. One of these is through swiping the card and then signing the receipt issued by the merchant representative. The other is via using a pad with your PIN, or personal identification code, after the card is swiped.

A final benefit that you gain from a debit card is that most of them provide rewards that are earned simply by utilizing them. These are earned in one of two ways. With Visa Debit cards, you are able to receive discounts from some merchants who provide these special price breaks for the holders of Visa cards.

Other debit cards provide extras rewards programs. These rewards programs pay you back with some type of reward for every purchase that you make. These can be cash rebates or more commonly awards that are earned through the collection of such points.

Debt Ratio

Debt Ratio refers to a highly favored financial ratio. This one measures the consumer or company's debt leverage. This ratio is best explained as the ratio for all of the longer-term and shorter-term debt divided by all assets of the individual or enterprise. It is then expressed out in percentage or decimal format. Another way of stating it is the proportion of a firm's assets financed by outright debt. The debt ratio is sometimes called the debt to assets ratio as well.

All else being equal, as this debt ratio is higher it means that the firm has a higher degree of leverage. This generally implies a higher amount of financial risk. Yet simultaneously it is true that such leverage is a critical tool which many corporations employ to expand. Countless firms have discovered many sustainable uses of such debt.

Naturally, acceptable and average debt ratios will range drastically from one industry to the next. Utilities and pipelines are capital-intensive firms. They will necessarily possess far greater debt ratios than do companies in such industries as technology. Consider a clear example to help understand this term better. When corporations have assets of $200 million and aggregate debts of $50 million, then the debt ratio would amount to 25 percent or .25 alternatively. This company would therefore be in a stronger financial position than a comparable one with a 35 percent debt to asset ratio, but not always.

This is because 25 percent debt to asset ratios can be excessive in an industry that boasts unstable cash flows. These businesses simply cannot assume too much debt. Such a firm that possessed an overly high debt ratio as measured up against its rivals would discover how costly additional borrowing would become. This means that it might fall into a cash crunch in shifting circumstances. The fracking industry starting in summer 2014 found itself in dire straits thanks to its huge debt levels and plunging energy prices.

At the same time, debt levels that amount to 35 percent could be easy to manage for those firms which are in an industry like utilities. The cash flows in these businesses are far stronger and more stable. Higher debt to assets ratios are not only acceptable in this business, they are expected. For those firms that find themselves with an over 100 percent debt ratio, you know that its debt levels actually exceed its amount of assets. Conversely, when firms possess a ratio under 100 percent, the firm possesses more assets than debt. Alongside other metrics for determining financial soundness, this ratio will allow investors to ascertain how high the risk level is for a given business.

Debt ratios do not take into account all money that a firm owes necessarily. While they will always count longer- and shorter-term debts, they will leave out liabilities. Some of these liabilities that do not figure into the calculations are negative goodwill, accounts payable, and "other" items.

Consider a real-world example of how this works out in practice. Starbucks possesses a debt ratio of around 22.5 percent. Morningstar considers that the typical ratio for the industry is more like 40 percent on average. This means that the Starbucks Corporation can easily borrow money on the markets. Creditors understand that its finances are solid as a rock. They anticipate receiving full repayment on time. The non-callable and fixed rate Starbucks' bonds that mature in 2045 possess coupon rates of only 4.3 percent.

Contrast this with a basic materials firm like Arch Coal Incorporated. The industry of coal mining is regarded as highly capital intensive. This is why the industry forgives utilizing leverage to operate effectively. The average debt to assets ratio proves to be 47 percent. Yet Arch Coal Inc. has a 64 percent ratio. This makes it costly for them to borrow money. In fact their non-callable, fixed rate bonds that mature in 2023 come with a painful interest coupon rate amounting to 12 percent.

Debt Restructuring

Debt restructuring refers to a means which corporations or countries with overwhelming debt loads utilize to change the terms of their outstanding debt arrangements so they can gain advantage in repayment. Corporations will often utilize a form of debt restructuring so that they can sidestep defaulting on their already existing debt levels. They might also wish to gain the benefits of lower interest rates that may be available to them on the markets.

One way that companies accomplish this is by issuing a series of callable bonds. These permit them to easily and rapidly restructure their new debts at a given point in the future. In this case, the firms' existing debts will be called. They will then replace them with a newer issued debt for the lower, more advantageous interest rate. Another way that corporations are able to restructure their debt lies in changing the provisions and terms of the current debt issue.

With corporate debt restructuring, a company will typically reorganize its actual obligations by lowering the debt burdens on their firm. They can do this by reducing the payable rates on the debt or by extending the amount of time they have until they repay the debt obligations. By doing either of these, the company ensures it is able to service its relevant debt burdens. There are other cases where the creditors will opt to forgive a part of the debt in exchange for obtaining an equity stake in the firm.

A need for this type of corporate debt restructuring most often occurs when corporations or companies are experiencing financial difficulties. These make it most difficult to keep up with their full range of financial obligations. Sometimes such troubles can be sufficient to create a significant risk of the company declaring bankruptcy. In these cases, they have the ability to engage in a structured negotiation with the creditors to lower the burdens so that they can avoid entering bankruptcy-led defaults.

Within the United States, there is a provision of the corporate bankruptcy code known as Chapter 11. These protocols permit corporations to obtain effective protection from their creditors so that they are able to try to rearrange the debt terms to continue on as a reorganized, ongoing, viable concern. Thanks to federal bankruptcy courts becoming involved in this process, even when the creditors refuse to accept such a settlement and reorganization, the courts can mandate that the creditors accept the plan if they deem it to be reasonable and fair.

It is not only corporations and companies which can avail themselves of such debt restructuring. Governments also have needs for help with their debts when they finally become unsustainable. This is not a new phenomenon. It stretches back to the first historically recorded sovereign debt default of the fourth century B.C. At this time, ten different Greek city-states defaulted on loans they had taken from the sacred temple of Delos. Despite the fact that this has occurred for at least 2,300 years, today no clear and mutually understood rules exist to structure the process for what will occur if a sovereign state can not pay their debts.

The most recent classic example of this dates back to the huge default by Argentina. Their enormous debt default in 2001 was among the largest in modern history. The rules are unclear as to who has jurisdiction and who can set restructuring terms. For years Argentina refused to negotiate terms with the eight percent of its bondholders who would not agree to the terms the country set in 2001. Then a court ruling from the U.S. Supreme Court confused the issue by ordering Argentina to settle with the remaining holdouts at full value plus interest before they could pay the agreed-upon settled amount to the other 92 percent of debt holders.

Argentina then came back to the table for the eight percent of mostly opportunistic hedge funds which had bought their defaulted debt for pennies on the dollar. Grudgingly under duress they paid the hedge fund eight percent claimants. This was an unusual case study that only worked out because the debt had been issued under American debt law. In other cases and scenarios, it is only the IMF International Monetary Fund that is attempting to create some sort of rules on situations like these.

Yet in the end, no one can force a country to pay its debts back to creditors short of going to war with them to seize their physical assets or by freezing assets of the offending country in the banks or vaults of the debt holders' countries.

Debt to Equity

Debt to Equity refers to a ratio that is extremely important and often scrutinized in the world of business. It is the amount of longer term debt on the balance sheet of a corporation as related to and divided by the company equity. Long term debt for a company means money that it will not be expected to pay back in the coming 12 months. Both are critical factors in effective balance sheet analysis.

This ratio tells an analyst or investor a great deal about a company and the amount of debt it is carrying compared to its true net worth. This is accomplished by gathering together all of the company liabilities and then dividing this amount up by the shareholder equity. The end result which comes back in dividing the total debt by the equity proves to be the percentage of the firm which is leveraged (or more accurately stated--- indebted).

Over time, the acceptable and average amount of debt to equity has varied significantly in the corporate world. Today it heavily depends on both the state of the economy, the industry in which the company operates, and the all-around feelings of society concerning credit and debt. If all else is equal, any firm with a debt to equity ratio in excess of 40 percent to 50 percent should be more careful about the risk hidden within its balance sheet and books. These could lead to a liquidity crisis at some point in the future.

When analysts consider the working capital of the company and find that both it and the current ratios of the firm are dramatically low, then this is a glaring sign of significant financial weakness in a corporation. This is why an analyst or investor truly needs to adjust any current profitability numbers to the economic cycle at hand. Many investors have lost fortunes over the years because the plugged in peak earnings at the height of an economic boom as their base case scenario metric for a firm's ability to pay back its various debt obligations.

There is no good reason to fall for this age old trap after all. All that is required to avoid it is to predict that the economy may fall off a proverbial cliff at any point and time. Then consider if the cash flow would be sufficient to cover the liabilities without the corporation being hurt and hampered by a lack of money for critical daily, monthly, and yearly expenses on items such as plant, property, and equipment.

The truth is that debt and elevated debt to equity ratios is not necessarily a bad thing. Many businesses are quite adept at earning a greater return on their capital than the cost of the interest which they incur in borrowing the money. This would make it extremely profitable to borrow money in such cases. It allows such firms to boost their earnings and profitability for one thing. The real key element is that the company management clearly understands the level of debt which will represent a danger level for smart and forward thinking stewardship of their company. Leverage cuts both ways. It dramatically boosts returns when it is working well for a firm, and it similarly can even totally wipe out a company if things turn on the firm in an economic recession or even economic depression.

Investors especially need to be careful in buying corporate bonds in such environments. Bonds issued in the lower interest rate environments of today will suffer drastically when the interest rates invariably rise higher, especially if this is quick and unexpected. This will lead to less profitability for the firm when the bonds have to be financed again. If the management did not wisely prepare for such an issue well in advance, then the company will truly have been mismanaged during the golden boom days and will suffer needlessly during the inevitable bust economic times.

Delinquency

Delinquency refers to primarily an individual (but also conceivably an entity or business) failing to make good on what was expected of them according to their duty or the law. It often pertains to failing to affect the minimum due payment or carry out a fiduciary responsibility. An individual who practices Delinquency is called a delinquent. These persons have contractually undertaken obligations to turn in payments on loan accounts according to a pre-arranged routine deadline.

This might include minimum monthly amounts of money owed on a car payment, a credit card payment, or a mortgage payment. As the individuals do not make these payments on time, they become delinquent. When mortgage holders become delinquent, the financial institutions holding the loans are able to start working through foreclosure processes. They will do this when the mortgage account stays unpaid for a specific length of time.

There are many different types of accounts on which people fall into Delinquency. This could be retail account payments, income taxes, mortgages, lines of credit, and more. Individuals who become delinquent suffer the consequences for these financial actions. Such impacts vary with the kind of Delinquency, cause, and length of time it has continued in this unfortunate state. As individuals become late on credit card bills, they can be charged late fees. Those who do not make their required tax payments can have their wages garnered or even their bank account levied by the Internal Revenue Service.

Besides these financial Delinquencies, there are responsibilities which when they are not carried out can be labeled delinquent. By not carrying out one's fiduciary duties, professional responsibilities, or other contractual obligations as set forth by custom or the law, individuals can be called delinquents as well. Police officers who do not professionally carry out their responsibilities to protect ordinary citizens in the line of duty can be found to be delinquent.

It is important not to confuse Delinquency with default. Individuals are officially delinquent at the point when they miss making a required payment of some sort in a timely fashion. By contrast, loan defaults happen as borrowers do not pay back a loan according to the terms on which they agreed to in their original contract. Loans can stay in the delinquent stage without being treated as in default for an unspecified amount of time. The amount of time this remains delinquent rather than in default varies considerably from one creditor and financial institution to another. For example, with student loans, the United States' Federal Government permits these to be fully delinquent for as long as 270 consecutive days before they become considered to be in default.

The U.S. keeps track of its various national Delinquency rates. Per the year 2016 in the fourth quarter, such Delinquencies amounted to 4.15 percent for real estate loans on residential loans, 2.15 percent on loans for consumer credit cards, and .85 percent for real estate loans on commercial loans. The government also maintains official statistics for these rates by year of loan issued. For 2016, this amounted to 2.04 percent, which was near the historically typical average.

The devastating global financial crisis and U.S. mortgage crisis which erupted in 2007 caused the rates to spike to a high in the Great Recession years which reached fully 7.4 percent in the year 2010 in its first quarter. For residential real estate, the rate topped out at 11.26 percent for these specific types of loans. Up to the year 2008 in its second quarter these Delinquencies had not been higher than three percent all the way back to the year 1994 in its first quarter.

Depreciation

Depreciation is the means of spreading out the price of a usable physical asset during the period of its practical life. Businesses engage in this process of depreciating assets for accounting and taxing purposes. Depreciation can also be the reduction of the value of an asset that poor market conditions create.

Where accounting and taxing purposes are concerned, the process of depreciation demonstrates the portion of the value of the asset in question that has been utilized. Where taxes are concerned, the rules are stricter. The IRS sets out the regulations for taking depreciation of tangible assets.

Businesses are permitted to deduct the expenses of the asset they buy as a business expense. They simply must abide by the IRS' rules as far as when and how much of the deduction they are permitted to log. This all comes down to which category the asset falls in and the amount of time for which it is expected to last.

In accounting, businesses attempt to correlate the cost of a particular asset with the amount of income that it practically earns the company. With regards to an item of equipment that costs them $1 million, it may have a practical life expectancy of 10 years. They would depreciate this asset over the course of ten years. The company would then expense out $100,000 of the asset value each accounting year. They would match up the income that the equipment generated the company every year as well.

Accountants can use depreciation tricks to impact the company's financial bottom line. This is because with enough depreciation, the income statement, cash flow statement, balance sheet, and statement of the owners' equity will all be impacted significantly. It is true that certain depreciation assumptions can have significant impacts on both the long term asset values and the results of short term earnings.

Other assets can see their value depreciated by unfortunate circumstances or poor conditions in the market. Two standout examples of this type include real estate and currencies. In the housing crisis of 2008, many home owners living in the most severely impacted markets like Las Vegas watched helplessly as their home values depreciated by even 50% of the value. The post Brexit vote results day saw the British pound plunge by over 10% in a single day.

Generally accepted accounting principles affect depreciation figures. This is because a company might pay for a long life asset in cash, as with a tractor trailer that delivers its goods to customers. According to GAAP principles though, this expense would not be shown as a cost against income then and there. Rather than this, the expense is listed as an asset on the company balance sheet. The value of the asset is consistently and continuously reduced out during the in-service life of the asset in question. As the expense is reduced, this is a form of depreciating the asset.

This is done because GAAP principles insist that all expenses must be recorded along with the accounting time-frame as are the revenues which they generate. In the example of the tractor trailer that costs $100,000 and lasts for approximately ten years, GAAP would look to see what the salvage value would be at the end of that time. Assuming it expected the trailer to be worth $10,000 at the end of the depreciating period, than the expense would be depreciated at a rate of $9,000 for each of the ten years (using the formula of cost – salvage value/number of years depreciating).

With long term assets, the depreciating typically involves two lines. There would commonly be one that displayed the price of the assets and another that demonstrated the amount of depreciating that had been charged off against the assets' value.

Dumping

Dumping in economics refers to a country attempting to enforce its own firms' predatory pricing on other nations in the context of international trade. It also happens if a company exports its goods to a rival nation for a price that is under the one it would charge in its own domestic market or at a lower cost than the expenses it incurs to produce the goods. The reason companies and nations do this is typically to build up their foreign national market share. Sometimes they engage in this despicable practice so they can drive away their competitors.

The technical definition of dumping boils down to charging other countries cheaper prices for similar goods in their foreign markets than they do charge in their domestic market for the identical good. Many economists call this undercutting the nominal value in the act of international trade. Dumping has been officially condemned by the WTO World Trade Organization and an agreement which the member states all signed. This is especially the case when it inflicts material harm on a national industry within the nation who is importing.

There can be no doubt that the term dumping comes with an extremely negative connotation. Free market capitalist proponents consider this to be a thinly veiled kind of protectionist policy. The advocates of labor maintain that businesses must be protected from these forms of predatory practice in order to reduce the more painful consequences of trade between unequally developed economies.

International dumping has not been so successful except for in a few examples. One such case is the Chinese steel dumping dilemma. For years, the Chinese have sold steel at prices which are well below those any other nations' steel producers can match. They sell it for less than their own cost. They are also sometimes selling their steel at lower prices than they do within China. The venerable steel industry in Great Britain has been all but destroyed because of this practice. Britain was once the world's largest steel producer. Other European and American steel makers have similarly suffered from the illegal Chinese steel dumping practice.

A more controversial case pertains to OPEC's Saudi Arabian led efforts to drop the price of oil over the past several years. Because competition from American shale oil industry had become so intense and America and U.S. companies had massively increased their oil and natural gas outputs, Saudi Arabia became concerned by the excessive supplies of oil washing over the world energy markets. They decided to eliminate the U.S. shale oil company business through a covert form that might be considered dumping.

Saudi Arabia had the ability to produce oil for a substantially lower cost per barrel than the more expensive fracking process that releases the shale oil in America (and Canada). They decided to force down the prices of oil within OPEC by making the other Persian Gulf (Iraq, Iran, Kuwait, Qatar, Bahrain, United Arab Emirates, Oman) and non Gulf (primarily Nigeria and Venezuela) countries sell their oil at a lower price. They manipulated these price levels for oil down to the point that oil traded in the low $40's per barrel. At this point, the price of oil had declined to below the cost of production for several of the oil producers in the OPEC cartel, but not for Saudi Arabia.

As the Saudi's hoped, the American shale oil producers began to lay off workers and shut down production. Many of the firms in the U.S. shale industry shuttered their doors at least temporarily and some permanently. Saudi Arabia successfully dumped the Gulf and OPEC oil on world markets at prices lower than their rivals could conceivably match, permanently harming the domestic industry in the U.S. (and to a lesser degree Canada with their oil sands projects). The Saudis claim it was not dumping as they at least can produce oil for $20-$30 per barrel. So far, no action has been enforced by the World Trade Organization against either the OPEC oil cartel or Saudi Arabia for this underhanded ploy. There is still controversy regarding whether or not this particular case is technically dumping.

Economic Growth

Economic growth represents a boost in an economy's ability to create and produce services and goods. This is compared from one period of time against another. There are two ways to measure this phenomenon. It may be quantified either in real or nominal terms. When real terms are used, economists have to adjust them for the effects of inflation.

Historically and routinely, total growth in an economy is determined and expressed in the form of either the old standard of GNP Gross National Product or the more recent standard of GDP Gross Domestic Product. There are also other infrequently utilized metrics for measuring growth in an economy.

The simplest way to express such economic growth is by utilizing total productivity. Gains in productivity often correspond to an increase in the average marginal productivity. In other words, the typical worker within a specific economy becomes more productive as the economy is growing. Economies may also obtain growth even without such an average marginal productivity increase. This happens when there are more births than deaths (higher birthrate) or as additional immigrants come into an economy and begin to work. It can also result from technological revolutions. Examples of this are the Industrial Revolution, the computer revolution, or the Internet revolution.

It is always true that economies experiencing economic growth will be able to produce a higher quantity of services and goods than they did before the growth transpired. Yet there are those services and goods which command a higher value than competing goods or services. Examples of this abound. Smart phones or laptops are considered to have a higher value economically than bottles of water or a shirt. This is why growth in an economy is effectively figured up by measuring the total value of goods and services which the economy produces instead of simply the quantity.

An additional dilemma comes as different consumers put varying values on identical services and goods. For example, for residents of Alaska an effective heater would command a higher value than it would for residents of southern California. Similarly, in Florida efficient air conditioners have greater value than they do in Canada. Other individuals prefer fish to steak, or steak to fish. Value is always subjective. This is what makes measuring the value of all goods and services challenging. It is ultimately why the current fair market value is what economists employ to determine value for the purposes of measuring economic growth.

Interestingly enough, only a few means exist to create growth economically. A relatively straightforward one is through the uncovering and exploitation of better or newly discovered physical economic resources. Before gasoline was discovered to have the ability to generate energy, petroleum had very little economic value. Gasoline and hence petroleum began to create economic growth once this discovery was made. This was true for those countries with an abundance of petroleum they could export as well as for countries that utilized the gasoline to more effectively move goods across their nations.

A second means of producing economic growth is by increasing the size of the labor force. When every other factor is equal, a greater number of workers will produce additional services and goods. Much of the impressive economic growth in the United States through the 1800s came from a constant inflow of productive and inexpensive immigrant labor.

The third means of creating such growth is by developing better capital goods or higher technology. Such capital growth and technological improvements are closely correlated to the level of business investment and savings. Both are needed for firms to pursue a significant amount of R&D, or research and development.

The final method for boosting economic growth lies in better specialization of labor pools. In other words, the workers have to increase their skills at their crafts. This boosts productivity because of extra practice or through experimenting with new or improved methods. Investment, savings, and specialization are the easiest to control and most reliable means of increasing the growth in an economy.

Economic Indicators

Economic indicators are bits of economic data generally pertaining to the macroeconomic larger picture economy. Investors utilize them to decide on the investing climate as they consider the all around state of the economy. There are many different economic indicators which the government usually releases. Five of the most important are gross domestic product, consumer price index, employment indicators, PMI manufacturing and services, and central bank minutes.

Gross Domestic Product is the dollar value of every good and service a country produces in a set amount of time. It can be delivered in real and nominal formats. Real GDP makes adjustments for changes in the value of money. This indicator is one of the most anticipated by financial markets for its importance. Increases in GDP indicate an economy that is growing. Declines in it demonstrate an economy that is slowing. National growth rates like this are often utilized to judge the affordability of a country's sovereign debt. They also determine if companies operating in the country are likely to be profitable.

Consumer Price Index is an inflationary figure. It looks at the household purchased goods and services and measures their changes over time. This statistical estimate is compiled by taking prices from a group of representative items. This CPI is often used to discern how much inflation is. Markets watch CPI figures to determine if inflation is getting too high. When there is higher inflation it causes interest rates to rise and lending to decline. Deflation causes more lending and better interest rates. Inflation reduces the relative value of a currency and is bad for savers.

Employment determines the citizens' wealth and economic success. This makes employment indicators like unemployment and payroll data, income trends (earning more or less), total labor force, and percentage employed telling. These numbers are particularly important in developed countries that see most of their national income created by consumer spending. Declines in consumer spending often lead to an increase in unemployment. This in turn feeds into lower GDP numbers.

PMI manufacturing and services is part of the Purchasing Manager's

Index. Markit Group developed this with the Institute for Supply Management. They survey businesses every month to learn about business purchasing manager's activities in acquiring input goods and services. The most crucial of these surveys are the PMI Services and PMI Manufacturing indices. These are considered to be important leading economic indicators. When demand for business products declines then companies will decrease their buying of raw materials instantly. This gives a picture of problems in an economy long before consumer spending or retail sales figures will.

Central banks play such an important role in any nation's economy that their releases are very important. Markets study every word that comes from central bankers to learn what is in store in the future. Central bank minutes prove to be the official information releases that give out useful commentary on the economy and signal what actions the central bank will take in the future.

The United States has the Federal Reserve. It provides its well known beige book. In this book are economic conditions related anecdotally by each of the branches of the Federal Reserve Bank. These types of notes are also released by a great number of other central banks. Among these are the Bank of England, European Central Bank, and Bank of Japan. They are released publically on a routine schedule. Central bank minutes releases also give a clue as to when the group will raise or lower the national interest rates which affects everything from consumer and business lending activity to savings deposit rates.

Economic Output

Economic output refers to the amount of goods and services which a nation, industry, or company creates over a set time period. These might be utilized in later stages of production, traded, or otherwise consumed. The idea surrounding national economic output is a critical one in the world of economics. This is because economists opine that it is not enormous quantities of money which truly make nations wealthy, but rather their national output amount.

Other phrases that analysts and economists often use interchangeably with economic output include output and gross output. This should not be confused with GDP Gross Domestic Product. Value which is added on a national scale is the definition of GDP ultimately. On a local level, this is often called gross regional product or even gross area product. While the two ideas of GDP and output bear some similarities, they are not identical. Both concepts do measure the productivity economically of a particular nation or region for a given time period.

Economic output itself quantifies the total value for all services and goods. The problem with this idea is that it involves a double counting of all intermediate purchases. Looking at an example of this dilemma helps to clarify the issue at hand. If a furniture maker purchases its wood directly off of a saw mill at $150, they might then increase the value of it to $450 by creating an article of furniture. The output involved would be measured as $600. This represents all value in every sale involved for this particular chain of economic activity. The problem is that this method includes the wood value two times. It becomes doubly counted when it is the intermediate stage good and again in the final price or value for the article of furniture.

GDP on the other hand concentrates on only the services' and goods' additionally added value. Another way of defining this lies in the economic output minus the intermediate inputs included. When economists take out the goods' value which already came through the market once before, it allows for a more accurate assessment regarding the output. The strict GDP formula is then GDP equals the gross output minus the intermediate inputs. In the example above with furniture, the GDP equaled up to merely

$450 because the formula takes out the $150 in wood inputs from the final sales price of $600.

In the real world, the overwhelming numbers of companies produce products which they make utilizing many materials that go through a few different suppliers hands in the production process. Each supplier will add its own value. Only in the end would this value be tallied into the cost of the ultimate product. The important take away from this is that there is a significant difference between GDP gross domestic product and economic output.

One of the great economic questions of all time that economists wrestle with pertains to why the national output for a given country will constantly fluctuate, sometimes dramatically. There is no one easy answer on which economists have consensus opinion unfortunately. Instead, economists generally concur that there are a variety of factors which cause output to rise and fall. With growth, the majority of economists can agree on there being three principal sources of economic growth.

These are labor increases, factors of production efficiency increases, and capital increases. This is a two-edged sword though. Growth to the factors of production inputs can also be negative. In fact when any factor leads to a decrease in the efficiency of production, capital, or labor, then the growth rate will subsequently decline. This finally translates to a drop in economic output as well as in GDP.

Employees

Employees are individuals who work in the service of a business endeavor or trade. They do this by contributing their expertise, abilities, and labor to another individual's small business, a corporation, for the government, or in their own self employed business. Employees are also a critical component of the factors of production that include land, capital, and labor. In this capacity, they contribute the labor to a business enterprise.

In particular, an employee proves to be an individual who is engaged by some employer in order to perform a specific job or task. Within the majority of advanced nations and their economies, this word pertains to a specifically spelled out relationship that is established between companies and individual persons. This relationship is markedly different from that of a client or customer.

Attaining the status of employee generally results from undergoing a job interview with a certain business or corporation. Assuming that the person in question matches up well with the organization and their position, then she or he is made a formal employment offer for a given initial salary and place in the company. Such a person then attains all of the privileges, responsibilities, and rights as other employees. These commonly include vacation days and medical insurance benefits. Human Resource departments typically manage the actual relationships between such employees and major companies. This department works with new employees' coming on board and integrating into the organization, as well as handling the set up of their new benefits to which they are entitled. HR departments also commonly resolve any problems or grievances that employees experience.

Employees may group themselves into labor unions that can come to represent the positions and demands of the majority of an organization's work force. These labor unions are then capable of bargaining as a whole on behalf of the employees with a company's management. They do this to make demands for the members concerning payroll, benefits, and working conditions.

Employers are quick to point out that these offers of employment never assure employment for any future specified amount of time. Either the employer or the employee is capable of ending this particular relationship whenever it suits them. This capability is known as at will employment. Many professions expect a two week notice when an individual employee quits his or her job. This is a customary courtesy that the law does not require. It may be necessary in order to obtain a satisfactory job reference for future employment opportunities.

Equifax

Equifax today is an agency that reports consumer credit within the U.S. Analysts number it among the big three American credit bureau agencies alongside rivals Trans Union and Experian. The company proves to be the oldest of the three main credit bureaus in the country as it became established back in 1899.

The firm gathers and keeps information on more than 800 million consumers and over 88 million businesses around the globe. They are headquartered in Atlanta, Georgia and remain a worldwide data services provider that has annual revenues of $2.7 billion. They have over 7,000 staff operating in 14 different countries. The company is listed on the NYSE New York Stock Exchange. One of their many divisions (Equifax Workforce Solutions) is among the 55 national contractors which the United States Department of Health and Human Services hired to help develop the federal government's HealthCare.gov website.

The original company which later became Equifax was Retail Credit Company founded in 1899. The firm rapidly expanded and already counted offices around both the United States and Canada by 1920. In the 1960s, this Retail Credit Company represented among the largest of the credit bureaus. It contained files for millions of American and Canadian citizens.

While the firm engaged in some credit reporting at the time, the main part of their business came from providing reports to the many insurance companies throughout the U.S. and Canada as consumers applied for insurance policies such as auto, life, medical, and fire insurance lines. Back in the day, every one of the significant insurance firms relied on Retail Credit Company to gather their information on health, morals, habits, finances, and the utilization of cars and vehicles. Besides this, the firm investigated various insurance claims and also gave employment reports out to companies as consumers sought new jobs. The majority of their credit reporting work at that time they delegated to a subsidiary company called Retailers Commercial Agency.

In 1975, the company changed its name to be Equifax because of image problems they had earned by keeping shady and intimate personal details on all American's lives and selling them to anyone willing to pay. It was after this that the new company Equifax expanded its operations into commercial credit reporting on firms located in the United States, the United Kingdom, and Canada. Here it engaged in competition against such firms as Experian and Dun & Bradstreet. In the 1990s, they began to phase out their insurance reporting operations and spun off their division which gathered and sold specialist credit information to insurance companies. Among this was the CLUE Comprehensive Loss Underwriting Exchange database they had developed, which they included in the Choice Point spinoff back in 1997.

Throughout the vast majority of its company history, the firm engaged mostly in the B2B sector. They sold insurance and consumer credit reports and associated analytics to businesses which operated in a variety of industries and segments. Among these were insurance firms, retailers, utilities, healthcare providers, banks, credit unions, government agencies, specialty finance companies, personal finance operations, and various other kinds of financial institutions.

Since they divested from their insurance reporting primary operation, the company sells information which includes business credit and consumer credit reports, demographic information, analytics, and software. Their credit reports offer a wide and detailed profile on the payment history and personal creditworthiness of individuals and businesses. This reveals how well these groups have honored their various financial obligations, including paying back loans and bills.

Starting in 1999, Equifax started offering its vast services into the consumer credit sector. They also began consumer operations with such important services as protection from identity theft and from credit fraud. The company along with its other two main rivals is required to offer American residents a single free credit file report once per year. The data from the U.S. Equifax credit records becomes incorporated into the Annual Credit Report.com website.

Equity

Equity represents the homeowner's total dollar amount of ownership in their property. Determining equity is a simple calculation. It is found by taking the home's assumed fair market value and subtracting out the balances of liens and debts secured by the property along with the mortgage balance that is still unpaid. As a home owner pays down the mortgage, reducing the outstanding principal balance, the equity of a home owner goes up. It similarly increases as the property gains in value. To obtain one hundred percent equity in their property, home owners have to pay down both any outstanding debts that are secured by the property and the full mortgage.

Associated with the equity value of a home is the LTV, or loan to value ratio. This loan to value ratio proves to be a means of stating the property's value as against the total dollar amount of your actual loan. The loan to value ratio is simply figured up by taking the amount of your loan and dividing it by your property value. Alternatively, you could divide the amount of your loan by the purchase price or selling price, whichever of the two is the lower amount.

An example helps to illustrate the concept. If you were to purchase a $300,000 house, you might put down a $60,000 down payment using your money. The remaining $240,000 would be covered by taking out a mortgage. Dividing the $60,000 amount by the $300,000 home value yields equity of twenty percent. If you divide the $240,000 by the $300,000 home value, then you will get the loan to value ratio that amounts to eighty percent.

Should you determine later that you will sell this house, then the equity that you have will be concretely and accurately figured up for you. This will simply prove to be the fair market value of your house minus the loan that you still owe the bank on the house. Using the example from the paragraph above, consider what would happen if you lived in and made payments on your house for five years following the purchase.

In this time frame, your monthly mortgage payments lower the balance that remains on the loan to the tune of $10,000, diminishing it from $240,000 to

$230,000. Besides this, over those five years, your home value goes up. This allows you to realize a selling price of $330,000. Since the balance that you owed is still $230,000, then your equity is simply figured by taking the $330,000 selling price and subtracting the $230,000 from it. This leaves you with a final equity value of $100,000. Once all selling costs and realty commissions are figured up and taken out, you would be able to utilize the $100,000 equity in order to invest or to put down the down payment on the next house that you purchase.

Naturally, this home value can cut both ways. Should the value on the home drop from $300,00 to $250,000 in the time that you own it, then your remaining equity would be only $50,000, less than the original $60,000 that you put into it upfront.

Exchange Rate

In finance and business, exchange rates are also known as Forex Rates, foreign exchange rates, or FX rates. These exchange rates are the rates that are valid between two currencies. They are stated in terms of one currency's value in the other currency. Such an exchange rate is also the foreign nation's currency value as stated in the currency of the home nation.

There are various distinctions within the category of exchange rates. Present day exchange rates are termed spot exchange rates. Exchange rates which are quoted to you and traded today but available for payment and delivery in the future on a particular date are called forward exchange rates.

It is instructive to look at some examples. If the GBP/USD rate is 1.60, then it means that the exchange rate of the British Pound garners $1.60 in US dollars. Alternatively, a USD/CHF rate of .97 would mean that only .97 of a Swiss Franc will buy one U.S. dollar.

Exchange rates are determined on the foreign exchange market. This is the largest single market on the whole planet, trading literally trillions of dollars in currency values every single day. It is estimated that this market exceeds three trillion dollars in U.S. valued currencies on a given trading day. This market trades six days a week, and is only closed from Friday at 5PM New York time until Sunday afternoon at 3PM New York Time.

Exchange rates can be freely trading on the world exchange markets. Some countries choose to instead peg the value of their currency to another proven, more responsible, and reliable currency, such as the Euro or the dollar. In these cases, the exchange rates are constant against those that they peg to, and only fluctuate against other currencies on the market at the same pace as the currency that they are pegged to does.

Exchange rates on FOREX can be pursued for hedging purposes or for investment opportunities. Businesses that have operations in two or more countries are often interested in locking in their exchange rate in order to protect themselves from possibly violent currency swings. By buying forward exchange rates, they can lock these in for any given day that suits their needs. Alternatively, they can take on FOREX spot positions in the currency totals that they anticipate needing, so that as the price rises and falls, it will be canceled out as they repatriate their foreign currency back into home currency.

Investors can participate in the exchange rate markets for investment opportunities. Besides buying these spot currency positions or forward positions, they can purchase options contracts on these pairs. The advantage and disadvantage to these markets is the leverage that they provide, which is commonly one hundred to one. This signifies that an individual investor is able to control one hundred thousand Euros against the dollar with only a thousand dollar account value. Major gains, as well as substantial losses, become possible with only small moves, since every ten cent price change in this case represents a hundred dollars literally gained or lost.

Expense Ratio

Expense ratio relates to the costs that a mutual fund incurs as it trades and does normal business. Typical mutual fund expense ratios include a number of different costs. Among these are management fees, transaction costs, custody costs, marketing fees, legal expenses, and transfer agent fees.

Management fees comprise those charges that the fund pays to the company which handles the portfolio management. They invest the fund's money as per the direction of the mutual fund board of directors. Management costs are typically the largest single portion of the mutual fund's expenses.

These fees commonly range from as little as .5% to as much as 2%. Lower fees are usually more advantageous for investors. This is because every dollar that goes to the management of the fund is not increasing the share holders' wealth. Some mutual fund types charge a higher amount in fees. International or global mutual funds will usually cost more than simple domestic market mutual funds. They justify these greater charges by the difficulty of managing an international portfolio.

Transaction costs include the fees that the fund pays to stock brokers. These are negotiated to extremely low rates such as a penny per share or even lower thanks to the enormous volumes that mutual funds trade. Those funds that are constantly purchasing and selling investments create significantly greater transacting costs for themselves and their investors. Higher turnover rates like this also can lead to larger capital gains taxes and other costs.

The investment holdings of a mutual fund must be kept by a custodian bank. This creates custody costs where these banks register the bonds, stocks, and other investments for the fund. Some of the banks do this electronically and others keep actual stock certificates in their vault storage.

Custodian banks also collect interest and dividend payments, maintain accounting for the various positions so gain/loss info is readily available to management, and handle stock splits and other transaction issues. These custodian costs prove to be a less significant percentage of expense ratios for the mutual funds.

Marketing fees for mutual funds come out of the money that the investors pool. This money is utilized to advertise the fund so they can raise additional investment dollars. More money in the fund means more management fees for the portfolio managers. These 12b-1 marketing fees are money that does not benefit an investor after the fund exceeds $100 million in net assets. A very small number of brokers actually refund such fees to their investors.

There are some legal expenses that mutual funds must incur in the course of normal operating business. These include for paperwork they are required by law to file for regulators like the SEC, specific licenses, incorporation, and other legal procedures. The majority of funds count such costs as a small amount of their overall expense ratio.

Transfer agent costs cover the expenses that arise when a shareholder cashes out or buys into the fund. Transfer agents must handle various account statements, paperwork, and money in the process. These agents take care of all the mundane daily paperwork for purchases, redemptions, and processing which keep the fund and other capital markets working.

There are various other costs that are not included in the mutual fund expense ratio but many experts feel should be. These include mutual fund sales loads. These fees are simply commissions that go into the pocket of the institution, company, or stockbroker that persuaded you to buy the mutual fund in the first place. Because of these and other high costs of many mutual fund expense ratios, some people prefer low cost index funds that involve very low management costs.

Expenses

Expenses refer to costs that business undergo in order to conduct their daily business operations, expand and grow their business, and acquire additional assets, property and factories. Firms are capable of investing their cash into a few different kinds of investments. They might buy a new building or some real estate. They could similarly purchase office or computer equipment for their premises. They might update older technology for the firm or aging machinery for production so that the business gains a higher level of productivity. These companies might also acquire vehicles for their traveling staff, such as executives, sales people, or for their delivery personnel. Any of these various types of investments would be for capital assets, which would make them capital expenses (sometimes also called expenditures).

Such expenses represent payments that a firm makes to acquire or increase the performance of longer-term capital assets such as equipment, factories, and buildings. These are generally expensive and substantial purchases which companies pursue for a corporate investment. Another way of thinking about this is that such capital expenses increase the overall business value. In consequence, as the asset values gain, so too does the net worth of the owner or stake holders. Yet at the same time the expenses incurred in acquiring the asset will similarly increase the liability of the owners.

Another expense that businesses realize analysts call depreciation. This simply means that assets decline naturally in value with time. It diminishes the company's value as it inevitably occurs. Such costs of capital expenses thus can be depreciated or capitalized throughout a given amount of time. This time equates to what the business world refers to as the useful life of the asset in question.

It always helps to consider an example of difficult concepts like these. When companies acquire equipment in the office for $20,000, they can depreciate this expense amount over a period of five years. It means that they will be allowed to take their depreciation of capital expense to the tune of $4,000 per year. Sometimes, this depreciation can be accelerated so that businesses realize the expense benefits quicker. There are also accountants who choose to include such intangible assets as copyrights, trademarks, and patents in the capital expenses category. Such assets become amortized, which is not unlike the process of depreciation in many ways.

It follows that companies should be able to expense the costs to keep a given capital asset up, in service, and working properly and efficiently. While this surmise is true, it cannot be done under the capital expense categories. Instead, they are treated as operating expenses in many cases. Yet with repairing equipment, this would likely increase its value. In that instance, this would represent a capital expense. This is why tax professionals have to help firms with figuring up the appropriate categories and depreciating.

Some other types of assets cannot be depreciated at all. Land is one of these. Because real estate does not lose value, the IRS considers that it possesses an indefinite value. This means firms may not depreciate real estate like they can with capital expense and operating costs.

When all else is equal, companies would rather obtain their tax deductions for asset purchases sooner rather than later. Yet the Internal Revenue Service has something to say on the subject. They maintain the rigorous rules on what may or may not be expensed out immediately. Startup costs are a good example of this. They will certainly boost the firm's value but they are spent upfront. The IRS permits just a certain quantity of such startup costs to be expensed out during the first year of business. The rest of these have to be amortized. In 2015, the government passed new legislation that permitted for more liberal benefits of corporate depreciation for those companies that buy capital assets.

Fed Funds Rate

Fed Funds Rate refers to the most key interest rate benchmark in the United States. Such a benchmark rate is the one which the banks charge one another in order to borrow money from each other overnight. The Federal Reserve similarly deploys this rate as a tool in order to meaningfully impact monetary policy within the country. This is not the only benchmark rate in America today, yet it has no rival for importance.

The way the Federal Reserve is able to influence banks with it is somewhat complicated. The commercial banks must maintain a minimum level of money either in cash funds or with their particular regional branch of the Federal Reserve on deposit. The idea behind this is that it allows banks to meet customer withdrawals from their current accounts, including both checking and savings.

Sensible banks hold more than this bare minimum. They keep an excess of the reserves that the regulations and rules pertaining to the banking universe require. These are appropriately referred to as excess reserves. It is such excess reserves that the Fed Funds Rate directly affects.

As the better prepared banks keep plenty of excess reserves available, they are able to overnight loan out to the less prepared banks so that they can end business day operations at their legally required minimum obligation. This unsecured overnight loan occurs at the Fed Funds Rate. It represents the effective rate that the lending bank will charge the borrowing bank.

In nearly all cases, this Fed Funds Rate proves to be the lowest practical interest rate in the nation. Since the financial crisis, it has remained at slightly higher than zero percent. The Federal Reserve began increasing it with their first rate hike in December of 2015, both slowly and gradually.

This rate matters for more reasons than just the price at which a lending bank will charge a borrowing bank to utilize its excess reserves. The reason is that the Federal Reserve is able to set their monetary policy with the rate. As an example, they might decide they need to cut the effective rate of unemployment in the U.S. This is one of their two reasons for existing (along with keeping inflation low). In order to increase employment opportunities, the Fed will push down the Fed Funds Rate through purchasing securities off of commercial banks. As bank reserves go up, the price for them declines. This is their means for pushing down the federal funds rate.

A lower Fed Funds Rate means that banks try to find better opportunities to engage their excess reserves. They might do this by loaning out the money to individuals who seek to purchase a house. They could also lend the cash to companies interested in expanding their business. Either of these actions will boost the economy in some meaningful way. A more active economy will create more jobs and drive down the unemployment rate.

Besides this, the banks also employ the Fed Funds Rate as their basing benchmark from which they determine their other key interest rates. Once the Federal Reserve boosted their federal funds rate target back in December of 2016 as an example, each of the main banks in the country instantly increased their prime loan lending rates. These represent those rates which they offer to their best customers who are extremely creditworthy. The best customers are usually the large and economically powerful MNC multinational corporations.

This means that the effective Fed Funds Rate is not simply the one that the banks are paying each other when they borrow excess reserves from one another. Instead, it has a dramatic and literal connection to the rate of interest any individual will pay for a car loan, home equity loan or line of credit, and mortgage. It also impacts the price that companies will pay to build and grow their business using bank loans.

Federal Reserve System

The Federal Reserve System is the United States' central banking system. It is made up of the Federal Open Market Committee, the Federal Reserve Board, 12 regional Federal Reserve Banks, and state and national member banks.

Seven members make up the Board of Governors. These the President appoints to 14 year terms upon approval by the Senate. The reason this system became established was to manage the movement of credit and money in the U.S. Congress set up this system in 1913. The U.S. had experienced a variety of central banks since 1791. The country needed a more stable banking system to help encourage a stronger economy.

Practically every bank in the U.S. participates in the Federal Reserve System. The program requires these institutions to keep a set amount of their assets deposited with their area Federal Reserve Bank. The Board of Governors determines how much these reserve requirements will be. The Board of Governors changes these required reserves in order to significantly influence the money supply that is circulating in the economy.

This Federal Reserve System provides a few different functions to the country. It is a bank for all the banks. A great number of interbank transactions go through this system. Banks may also borrow money from the Federal Reserve if they can not get credit from anywhere else. The system only gives them credit in emergencies or as it is unavailable on the open markets.

The Federal Reserve also functions like the bank of the government. The inbound and outbound payments of the tax system process via a checking account at the bank. The Fed further supplies the currency of the United States even though they do not produce it. They also purchase and sell government securities like Treasury Bills and Bonds.

Among the more important functions of this system is its purpose as a regulatory agency. They act as policeman to the banking sector to protect consumers' rights and to ensure smooth functions. They are also the main resource for banks and the public in times of financial crises or a panic surrounding the banks.

National banks have to be members of the system. In order to qualify, they are made to deposit the reserve requirements from their customer checking and savings accounts in their regional Federal Reserve bank. They must also keep mandatory reserve levels with this bank. Every nationally chartered bank has to be a member of the system. State chartered banks are also encouraged to join as members of the system.

The need for this Federal Reserve System became apparent after several failed attempts at establishing a uniform banking system in the United States. The first central bank was the First Bank that existed from 1791 to 1811. The Second Bank took over this role from 1816 to 1836. These two outfits proved to be the U.S. Treasury Department's only official representatives. This meant that they were the only organizations issuing and promoting the official U.S. currency.

Every other bank in the country ran under private auspices or as a state chartered organization. Each bank had its own bank notes which competed against the two U.S. banks as currency that could be redeemed for face value.

The first National Bank Act that Congress passed in 1863 allowed for a regimen of National Banks that would be supervised. Banks had to abide by certain operating practices, rules for making and issuing loans, and capital amount minimums kept in the banks. The Act effectively killed the non national individual bank currencies by creating a 10% tax on all state level banknotes.

Fedwire

Fedwire represents an RTGS, or real time gross settlement system. This settling system pertains to central and commercial bank funds which are utilized within the United States. The Federal Reserve Banks employ it to electronically settle all of their final payments between the various member institutions. All final payment settlement is performed exclusively within U.S. dollars.

Fedwire is actually operated and owned by all 12 of the American Federal Reserve Banks. This networked system of payments and electronic processing works exclusively between the member of the Federal Reserve system banks and the regional 12 Reserve Banks. The participants in the system, which are Fedwire member banks, can also use it between each other as well.

Fedwire members include two groups. The first of these are the financial institutions of the U.S. which are depository banks. Besides this, American branches of many approved foreign financial institutions and also allowed government groups are members. They must keep an active account with one of the Federal Reserve Banks to maintain their membership as either foreign or domestic entities.

The actual Fedwire system has been newly designed in recent years. Now this national clearing system works in high technology and automated real time for all of the businesses which are involved in the Federal Reserve financial network. This includes nearly 10,000 banks. The system allows a single bank to wire funds over to a fellow domestic bank practically instantly. The Federal Reserve has its own uses for the system of course. They deploy its cutting-edged technology in order to ascertain credit. They also orchestrate the effective movement of capital throughout the nation with it.

Many people think of the Federal Reserve as a branch of the U.S. government, yet this is not truly the case. It is a private company which delivers the centralized banking system to the United States. As the directors and board members are appointed by the President though, this makes it more like a GSE government sponsored enterprise. Many critics have complained about the private nature of the United States central bank over the years. The ones who are closest to it refute these objections by declaring it to be a one of a kind mixture that is at once private and public administration which no single private entity owns and controls.

The 12 regional Federal Reserve Banks serve a vital function for the nation in helping to oversee and implement the financial policy of America. All of the commercial banks which are federally chartered financial institutions are required to hold stock in the various Federal Reserve banks.

Thanks to the new Fedwire setup, banks can count on a true real time gross settlement of their funding transfers. It means that the automated financial transfers are not only seamless, but they complete rapidly. There are many effective uses to the impressive system.

Financial institutions are able to effect payments to the SEC Securities Exchange Commission using it. Since banks and other financial institutions have to regularly remit fees to the SEC for its oversight of Wall Street and the stock market, this is a convenient means of transferring payments to them. Many of the banks choose to use the system for just such a purpose.

The member banks utilize various protocols and "tags" to ensure that they are creating standard transactions on the electronic network. Part of what makes this system so technologically advanced is it even searches out problems in resulting syntax which might delay a transaction between member banks or with the 12 regional Federal Reserve Banks in the system.

This electronic funds settling system of the Federal Reserve proves to be much like those deployed in other nations around the world. A number of countries already had their own financial networks like this. Still others are in the process of being created, designed, and developed. Such financial settlement systems drag antiquated financial regimes into the current century. This is appropriate since a huge amount of wealth and cash are already handled by automated and digital electronic systems and technologies worldwide.

FICO Score

FICO Score refers to the overwhelmingly most popular and heavily utilized credit score in the United States. The company which created, owns, and manages it to this day is Fair Isaac Corporation. Financial institutions that loan out money employ this FICO score for an individual to assess any credit risk and decide whether or not they will offer the person credit. Sometimes they also consider specific information on the credit report of the borrower, but this is increasingly uncommon.

The reason for this is that the FICO score contemplates a well-rounded set of risk parameters for the would-be borrowers. These five areas it considers and draws upon to issue a credit score for credit worthiness include the individual's payment history, present amount of debts, types of credit utilized, amount of credit history, and new credit inquiries and issued accounts.

Ninety percent of financial institutions in the United States that offer loans rely on the FICO score for assessing the creditworthiness of an individual. These scores vary from as low as 300 to as high as 850. Generally speaking, scores over 650 represent desirable credit history. Individuals who boast less than 620 conversely typically find it hard to get decent financing offers approved at reasonable interest rates. Financial institutions claim that they also consider various other details besides FICO scores. These include history of time at a job, applicant's income, and the kind of credit they are seeking.

It is interesting and illuminating to understand how the three main credit bureaus calculate this FICO Score. Fair Isaac Corporation has its proprietary model in which they weigh all categories differently for every individual. This makes it more difficult to say with certainty what percentages in each of the five categories they consider.

Yet generally speaking, payment history represents 35 percent of the total. Amount owed on accounts comprises 30 percent generally. Amount of years of credit history equals approximately 15 percent. Credit mix equates to around 10 percent. New credit inquiries and accounts represent about 10 percent.

Payment history is the simple answer to the question, "does the individual borrower pay the accounts in a timely fashion?" Thanks to the exhaustive nature of credit history, the bureaus clearly demonstrate the payments which have been made for every single line of credit. The reports make special note if any of the payments came in 30, 60, 90, 120, or still more days later than due.

Amounts owed on accounts pertains to the dollar amounts individuals owe on their various accounts as a percentage of the total available credit. This does not mean that possessing a great amount of debt ruins a credit score. What the Fair Isaac Company is considering is the ratio of amount owed to amount available. A clear example shows that when Ringo owed $100,000 yet was not near his limits on any of the accounts, he had a higher credit score than George who only owed $25,000 yet had nearly maxed out his credit card accounts.

Credit history length is a complex category. FICO considers the age of the oldest account as well as the age of the most recent one. They then compile the average account age and come up with a value for this category. Those with shorter credit histories can still get a good credit score.

Credit mix pertains to the variety in types of credit accounts. Higher category credit scores go to those people who have a strong and varied mix of credit cards, retail accounts, and installment loans like mortgages, vehicle loans, and signature loans.

Finally, the Fair Isaac Company does not like recently opened accounts in much of any quantity. When borrowers take out a range of new credit lines and accounts in only a brief amount of time, this tells them that the person is becoming a credit risk and thus decreases the total FICO score.

Fiduciary

A fiduciary is an organization or individual which owes its trust and good faith to another person or group. It means that one party takes on the most serious legal responsibility to the other party. Fiduciaries are ethically and legally required to carry out their activities in the best interest of the other person or organization.

This could involve another's well being, but it usually revolves around finances. People who manage another individual's assets or finances are good examples of fiduciaries. This means that a fiduciary could be a board member, banker, accountant, money manager, estate executor, or corporate officer.

The responsibilities and duties of a fiduciary turn out to be not only ethical but also legal. After a group or individual willingly takes on such duties for another, they must carry out the tasks with the very best interests of that party at heart. This means fiduciaries have to manage any assets for the benefit of those individuals instead of to benefit themselves or realize personal gain. This level of responsibility is called a prudent person standard of care that came out of court ruling in 1830. This prudent person rule means that the individual functioning in the fiduciary's role must always carry out the duties with the beneficiaries' needs foremost.

Conflicts of interest are not allowed to arise between the principal and fiduciary. Per an English High Court ruling on the case of Keech versus Sandford in 1726, fiduciaries are not allowed to profit from holding such a position of trust. Because of this, the only exceptions are when the beneficiary grants specific consent when the relationship starts. When the principal gives such approval, fiduciaries are allowed to enjoy any benefits received, whether they are monetary in nature or opportunities.

Where business relationships are concerned, there are many different kinds of fiduciary duties. The most typical of these occur between trustees and their beneficiaries. There are also a number of other kinds of relationships where this can occur. Some of these are between executors and legatees, company board of directors and shareholders, stock promoters and stock subscribers, guardians and wards, investment corporations and investors, and attorneys and clients.

As the trustee and beneficiary relationship is the most common for fiduciaries, it is important to understand. Trustees handle arrangements for estates and also implement trusts. The beneficiary is the one whom they are serving. The fiduciary in this case is the person who will be the estate trustee or the trust. The beneficiary is also the principal.

In this type of arrangement, the trustee commands legal possession of the assets and/or property. The trustee is fully empowered to manage assets in the trust's name. Because the beneficiary has equitable title of the property or asset, the trustee has to engage in best interest decisions. Such a relationship as trustee and beneficiary is critical in effective and all inclusive estate planning. This is why the trustee should be chosen with great care and thought.

Blind trusts are those where the trustee who has authority over the investment does not allow the beneficiary to be aware of the way the assets are being invested. The trustee still has the legal duty to use the prudent person conduct standard, especially because the beneficiary is unaware of what is happening. Politicians and other public figures create such blind trusts so that they can stay away from scandals involving conflicts of interest.

Financial Mentor

A financial mentor is a trusted guide or counselor that helps a person in the arena of business, personal finance and investments. Mentors can be many different people, but they typically have several characteristics in common. They are all loyal advisers who have the person's best interests at heart.

Mentoring is most widely used in business. Other settings that use it include medical fields and educational settings. Business experts will tell you that among the most useful, helpful, and valuable career assets that you can have in your business career is a helpful and experienced mentor.

Financial mentors are commonly older individuals who have more wisdom and experience to share with the individual than he or she already possesses. Though they do not have to be older in every single case, they must always have more experience than the person whom they are mentoring. These mentors both guide financial development and assist the person with their overall financial and business goals. They do not engage in this process with the expressed intent of making money or benefiting financially from the arrangement usually.

With financial mentors, you as the person being mentored have some preparation that you can do. You should listen carefully to the mentor and what he or she has to tell you. This is most easily accomplished by coming to the meeting with the financial mentor with some sort of recording means prepared. This might be a voice recorder, PDA, laptop, or even pen and paper. If a mentor made specific recommendations in the prior discussions, then you should have both noted and tried to apply them. Be ready to review any steps that you have taken specifically with the mentor.

You should also allow a mentor to be a part of your big picture goals and plans, and not only the particular details. The overall goals for you who are being mentored should be set together, in conjunction with the mentor. They should talk not only about present challenges and difficulties, but also concentrate on long term and short term goals together.

Good financial mentors will also do more than simply hold official meetings. They will take the time to get to know you. This does not have to be extensive amounts of time, but it should be quality time spent. This might involve a fifteen minute friendly chat over coffee or a quick bite to eat out some night. The key is not to take up too much of the financial mentor's time until you get to know him or her better. Then as the relationship broadens out into a friendship, more opportunities to get together will naturally arise.

Financial mentors can help out with many areas of your life. They can make helpful suggestions for getting out of debt. They can guide you with good concepts for practical and smart investing. They can share personal, actual experience for navigating through difficulties with a business that you own. They might suggest advice to assist you in your career development. Whatever help that you specifically request from a mentor, you should always remember to be appreciative and take the time to write thank you notes.

Financial Statement

Financial statements are official records of a business' or personal financial activity. With businesses, financial statements present any and all pertinent financial activity as usable information. They do this in a clear, organized, and simple to comprehend way.

Financial statements are commonly comprised of four different types of financial accounts that come with an analysis and discussion provided by the company's management. The Balance sheet is the first of these. It is known by several other names, including statement of financial condition, or statement of financial position. The balance sheet details will outline a corporation's ownership equity, liabilities, and assets on a particular date. This will give a good picture of the general strength and position of the company.

Financial statements similarly include income statements. These can also be called Profit and Loss statements too. They outline numerous important pieces of company information, such as corporate expenses, income, and profits made in a certain time period. This statement explains all of the relevant financial details to the business' operation. Sales and all associated expenses are included under this category. This section of the financial statement proves to be the nuts and bolts of the whole document. It provides a snap shot of the company's ability to generate sales and turn profits.

A statement of cash flow is also a part of a complete financial statement. As its name implies, this section will share all of the details regarding the company's activities pertaining to cash flow. The most important ones that will be outlined include operating cash flow, financing, and investing endeavors.

The last element of a financial statement includes the statement of retained earnings. This section of the document makes good on its name to detail any changes to a corporation's actual retained earnings for the period that is being reported. These four sections of a financial statement are all combined together to make the consolidated financial statement, once they are combined with the analysis and discussion of management.

With large multinational types of corporations, such financial statements are typically large and complicated, making them challenging to read and understand. To assist with readability, they may also come with a group of notes for the financial statement that also covers management's analysis and discussion. Such notes will go through all items listed on the four parts of the financial statement in more thorough detail. For many companies, these notes for financial statements have come to be deemed a critical component of good and complete financial statements.

Financial statements are used by several different groups of people who are looking at a company. Investors use them in order to determine if the company and its stocks or bonds make a sound investment with a chance of providing good returns on investments and profits in exchange for limited risks. Banks utilize these financial statements to decide if a company is a good credit risk for their loan dollars. Institutions and other groups that may be considering a cash infusion or buyout of the company use such financial statements to decide if the company is a viable investment or acquisition target.

Fire Sale

A fire sale is a phrase with a variety of interesting meanings. The term originated in reference to the reduced sales price for goods which were damaged in a fire of a shop or business. Since then, it has come to refer to any event which forces a business to move its assets or inventory goods for prices that are substantially discounted. The reason the business would be forced to engage in such a practice is because they are in a bind through some type of serious and often-times fatal financial distress.

Where financial markets are concerned, the phrase fire sale also refers to any securities (stocks, bonds, or other financial instruments and investments) which trade at a deep discount to their intrinsic value. This could occur in extended and painful bear market phases in the equities markets.

There are a number of examples which help to clarify the several different meanings of this concept of a fire sale. Take a department store as a prime example. When the department store company has to close its doors because of a bankruptcy event, the store might offer such a sale. In this specific scenario, the department store will offer its inventory of goods at what would normally be considered ridiculously low prices.

They do this so that they can liquidate the entirety of their in stock inventory. Since the store is closing up for good, they must be rid of each item in the store's inventory. The only means of effectively accomplishing this lies in providing prices so drastically reduced that bargain hunters will be lured in to purchase the stock. When the prices offered on the merchandise are so good as to be irresistible, then this qualifies as a fire sale.

Where securities are concerned, there are always examples of a fire sale of a given stock issue. Any time a particular equity security sells for far less than the value it is perceived to be worth, this qualifies as such a sale. Look at a clear example to consider. When the Dow Jones Industrial Average cratered by a full thousand points within the day, Proctor and Gamble (ticker symbol PG) crashed and burned by a quarter of its value on a temporary basis. This led investors and analysts to declare that there had been a real fire sale on the share of Proctor and Gamble that particular day. In this particular scenario, the phrase for this kind of a sale signifies that the asset in question possesses significantly greater value than the price for which its owner is suddenly willing to sell it.

These stock or bond securities which appear to be offered for this dramatic sale often provide an appealing risk to reward payoff possibility for the types of buyers known as value investors. This is because the asset is not likely to experience significantly further deterioration in valuation, yet the profit potential to the upside could possible prove to be impressive. The truth is that there is no single set of metrics for valuing whether or not a particular stock is actually selling for a ridiculously low price. One factor that many analysts can agree on is that if a stock is being valued at multiple year lows in the price, then it is generally considered to be a huge bargain.

As an example, stocks which are trading continuously for 14 times earning multiples would likely be fire sales when they trade for a far lower multiple of earnings of a mere seven. For this to be true in all scenarios though, the fundamentals for the given company and its stock must remain more or less unchanged. In other words, they can not simply have deteriorated appreciably in the meanwhile.

Fiscal Year

The fiscal year refers to an accounting period which governments or companies choose to use for their own accounting and in developing financial statements. Fiscal years are not necessarily the same as the calendar years. The U.S. government employs a different starting and finishing point for its own fiscal year.

The IRS Internal Revenue Service permits companies to choose whether they will use calendar years or fiscal years in their tax computations. When individuals or companies discuss budgets, they often invoke fiscal years. They prove to be a useful reference point when contrasting corporate or government financial results over the medium to long term.

The IRS has its own definition of fiscal year. To them these are comprised of 12 contiguous months that conclude on the final day in any month besides December. This means that where tax reports are concerned, a fiscal year could run February 1st to January 31st. American taxpayers also have the opportunity to utilize either 52 or 53 weeks long fiscal years instead of a 12 month one. In the case of the weeks' version, the years will rotate back and forth between 52 and 53 weeks in length.

Because the IRS automatically uses a calendar year system, those who employ fiscal years will need to adjust their own deadlines for turning in specific forms and getting in different payments. The biggest difference concerns the tax filing deadline. For the majority of American households and businesses, this will be no later than April 15th after the year in question for which they file. Those taxpayers working with the fiscal year system instead must file no later than the 15th day in the fourth month that comes after the conclusion of their fiscal period. This means that a business choosing to have fiscal years that span from May 1st to April 30th will need to turn in all tax returns no later than August 15th.

The U.S. tax code makes it relatively easy for companies to use fiscal years in their income tax reporting efforts. All that they are required to do is to turn in on time their tax return which covers that particular fiscal period. The companies also have the right to opt back to using calendar years whenever it suits them. To make the change from fiscal back to calendar years, they need to obtain individual permission by asking the IRS. Otherwise, they will have to measure up to the criteria that they outline in their Form 1128 called the Application to Adopt, Change, or Retain a Tax Year.

These fiscal years have a particular way of being addressed. Individuals who are discussing them reference them either by the end date or alternatively the end year. This means that one would refer to the American federal government fiscal year that starts on October 1st and ends on September 30th by saying the government fiscal year which ends on September 30th, 2016. If instead they were referencing spending by the government that happened in November of 2015, they would have to call this expenditure one that occurred in the 2016 fiscal year.

Five Year Plans

Five year plans are economic and social roadmaps that China began issuing in 1953. These were based upon the old Soviet central planning procedures. The Soviet Union collapsed in the early 1990s. Its plans are now a historical footnote. China continues to implement these plans every five years like a clock. They consistently show the world what China is attempting to focus on and accomplish. China has a history of meeting many if not most of its five year plan goals.

The government drafts and implements its plans on many levels. These include the district, local, provincial, and central government sectors. Industry regulators are also a part of the process. Most of these government divisions have their own five year plans as well. The NDRC National Development and Reform Commission draft the central government's plan. In these are detailed economic goals that include GDP growth rates.

Social development focuses on improvements in other important areas like education and healthcare. They come up with these specific targets after consulting with a variety of ministries and experts in industry and academia. Chinese regulators on all levels utilize these targets as they work through the implementing the period of the plan.

China spends years preparing these plans. They started talking about the goals of the 13th five year plan to run from 2016 to 2020 back in April of 2013. These plans set directions for the government priorities and policies. China met the majority of both economic and social goals they set out in the 12th FYP that concluded at the end of 2015.

These attained goals included average growth rates of seven percent, GDP services share at four percentage points higher, and seven percent annual increase to rural and urban incomes. Areas they struggled in were reducing carbon targets, raising non fossil fuels energy production, and increasing energy efficiency.

China relaxed its 35 year old one child policy as the biggest change in its current 13th FYP. This showed how the government is concerned about maintaining economic growth in the future as its population ages. For main economic targets, they set a GDP growth rate of average 6.5% per year. They also want to raise disposable income per capita by 6.5% each year. The leadership felt that this would make them into a "moderately prosperous society."

The plan also continues on its path of reforms. Markets will have more influence and the state owned industries will be retooled. They will shift the economy to services from heavy industry. Services will represent a greater contributor towards GDP. The goal is for them to contribute 56% of the total GDP by 2020. China has also committed to lessen the state interventions into everything from account interest rates to gas prices.

They aim to increase the capacity of nuclear power to 58 gigawatts and the high speed rail network to 30,000 kilometers or 18,600 miles. The country is to build minimally 50 new airports for civilians. The government wants to develop a new 50 million urban area jobs. In support of this they want to see their urban residency rise to 60% of the whole population by the year 2020.

For other social changes China intends to significantly address the pollution problems of the past. They hope to limit energy consumption to less than five billion tons of coal equivalent. They also want to reduce their total energy consumption by 15 percent and cut carbon dioxide emissions by 18%. All of this working together is supposed to improve their sometimes horribly polluted air. The goal for city air quality is to see it rated at a minimally good rating for 80% of the time.

Forced Liquidation

Forced liquidation involves a business or other organization selling its securities or assets in order to produce liquidity because of a deteriorating financial position and scenario. It is also referred to as forced selling. This activity is commonly pursued involuntarily, as a response to a series of economic or financially devastating events, business regulations, or court imposed legal orders.

Where stock securities and investments are concerned, this type of forced liquidation can happen if an investor possesses a margin trading account. Should the investor be negative with the account balance and refuse or be unable to raise the account value back over the mandatory margin requirements once a margin call has been issued, then the broker has the rights to begin forced selling of the account securities and positions. Typically, the brokerage will provide one or more warnings that an under-minimum margin situation has occurred before pursuing this drastic option. If the holder of the account refuses to respond to the repeated calls for margin leveling, then the broker can simply force sell off all positions.

It is helpful to consider a few real world examples in order to better understand this forced selling in a brokerage margin trading account. This could be the case with stocks, bonds, commodities, or futures holdings. Assume that brokerage Jean Paul Brokers enforces a minimum margin level requirement of $1,000 for all of its account holders. Gwen's personal margin trading account had a stock portfolio originally valued at $1,500. Meanwhile, Jean Paul Brokers adjusted their margin requirements up to $2,000. They begin to issue margin calls to Gwen. She is instructed to either sell some stocks or deposit additional funds to raise her account value up to the new margin amount of $2,000. If Gwen refuses or ignores the order for the margin call, Jean Paul Brokers has the legal authority to force sell off at least $500 of her account position stocks.

In another scenario with the same account, Gwen has her account net value at $1,500 while the margin requirement remains at the original $1,000. Her stocks begin to plunge in value and are now only worth $800 all together. Jean Paul Brokerage will now send her a margin call demanding that she raise the account value by depositing an additional

$200 cash to reach $1,000 in the account. Should Gwen not react by raising the now- delinquent account to this amount so that it is in good standing, then Jean Paul Brokerage will force liquidate her stock positions and shares so that it is able to decrease the amount of leveraged risk to which is it ultimately exposed as the broker responsible for the positions.

There is also an opposite of forced liquidation in such margin accounts. This is called forced buy-in. It happens in the event that the short sold shares of a margin account of a short selling trader are recalled by the broker or holder from whose account they were originally borrowed. In the unusual event when this triggers, the brokerage will buy back the shares to return them to the original owner and thus force close out the short position in the account. In such a case, the brokerage is not required to notify the account holder before performing such an account action. They must alert the account holder once they have done this.

With hedge funds and mutual funds, portfolio managers sometimes run into unanticipated financial crises. In this case, they may be required to sell off some of their holdings in order to cut their losses and free up cash. A real world example of this is Valeant Pharmaceuticals International. In May of 2016, the drug maker experienced a 90 percent stock price crash from its prior 2015 high. A number of hedge funds had poured in literally hundreds of millions of dollars into the pharmaceutical firm stock. They force liquidated their long holdings of the stock in order to salvage what remained of the investment and to safeguard their funds and clients from any further deterioration in the underlying share price.

Foreclosure

Foreclosures represent houses or commercial properties that have been seized by a bank or other mortgage lender. These properties are then sold to recoup mortgage loan losses after an owner and borrower has not made the payments as promised in the mortgage agreement.

Foreclosure is also the legal procedure in which the lender gets a court order for the termination of the mortgagor's right of redemption. This is the case since most lenders have security interests in the house from the borrower. The borrower will secure the mortgage using the house as the collateral.

Borrowers fall into home foreclosure for several reasons, most of which could not be predicted in advance. Owner might have been let go from their job or forced to take a job transfer to another state. They might have suffered from medical problems that prevented them from working. They might have gone through a divorce and split up assets. They could have been overwhelmed by too many bills. Whatever the reason, they are no longer able to make their promised monthly mortgage payments.

Foreclosures represent potential opportunities for investors. They may be purchased directly with a seller in advance of a bank completing foreclosure proceedings. Many investors who concentrate on foreclosures prefer to deal with the owners directly. They have to be aware of many laws pertaining to foreclosures, which are different in every state. For example, while in some states home owners can stay in their properties for a full year after defaulting on payments, while in others, they have fewer than four months in advance of the trustee sale.

Practically all states also allow a redemption period for the delinquent homeowner. This simply means that a seller possesses an irrevocable ability to catch up on back payments and interest in order to retain ownership of the house. The owner will likely be required to pay any foreclosure costs experienced by the bank up to that point.

Another means of purchasing a foreclosure home is to buy it at the Trustee's Sale. When this means is pursued, it is better to bid on a house that allows you to look it over in advance of putting up an offer. This is helpful so that you can determine how many repairs will be needed to make it salable and even possibly habitable. It is also worth knowing if the occupants are still living in the house and will have to be forcefully evicted. The process of going through an eviction can be both expensive and time consuming.

Many Trustee Sales will have certain rules in common that have to be followed for a foreclosure house to be purchased. They may demand sealed bids. They could require you to demonstrate your proof of financial qualifications. They might similarly insist on you putting up a significant earnest money deposit. Many of them will state that the property is being purchased in its present condition, or as is.

Franchise

A franchise can be defined in many ways. The definition from the International Franchise Association describes franchising as a means to expand a business so that goods and services can be distributed more effectively via a licensing relationship. The word itself legally means a specific kind of license. Ultimately, franchising refers to the personal relationship which a franchisor maintains with its franchisees.

In this arrangement, the franchisor licenses out its trade name as well as its operating methods, or systematic way of doing business, to a particular franchisee. In exchange for this arrangement, the franchisee pledges to run the business as per the terms of this license. The operating method here refers to the franchisor's system and way of doing business.

Franchisors guarantee their franchisees will have their support and help. They also maintain a certain level of control over specific parts of the franchisee business. This is critical for the franchise owner to safeguard its intellectual property rights as well as to be certain that the franchisee keeps to the guidelines of the brand itself. The quid pro quo of this is that the franchisee typically delivers a one time start up fee (known as the franchise fee) to the franchisor. The franchisees also pay a royalty fee to the franchisor, which is periodic and continuous. This enables the franchisee to utilize the franchisor's operating system and trade name.

The franchisor itself carries little responsibility for involvement in the daily management of the business of the franchisee. This is because franchisees exist as independent operators. Neither are they joint employers with their franchisors. This gives the franchisees a free hand in hiring employees, paying them according to their wishes, scheduling their shifts as they see fit, arranging their employment rules and practices, and even disciplining their own employees, all without requiring any approval from their franchisor. However, the uniforms which the employees wear will be stipulated by the brand and operating system of the franchisor.

Franchising is about a contractually defined relationship between the two parties. The franchisees and franchisor will share the brand in common. Despite this, both are distinctly separate businesses in both real terms and legally. The role of the franchisor is simply to build up its business and brand as part of supporting the various franchisees. The part which the franchisees play is to operate and manage their own business according to the specific terms of the franchise agreements.

It is interesting that definitions of franchises range from one state to the next according to the various laws which different states enforce. Some states include among the various elements of franchising the responsibilities of the franchisor to deliver a marketing plan to its franchisees. Others insist that the franchisor maintain an interested community of the business jointly with the franchisee.

Business Format Franchises are the most readily recognizable types of these arrangements for the everyday individual. These relationships typically cover the whole of the business and its format, not only the products, services, and trade name of the franchisor in question. In this common type, franchisors are expected to give their franchisees training, operating manuals, standards for the brand, a marketing plan and strategy to carry it out, quality control monitoring, and more.

Examples of the idea make these distinctions clear. Pizza Hut does not license out pizzas or breadsticks. Burger King does not license out hamburgers or chicken sandwiches. The two mega franchise operations instead license out components of their intellectual property. In this case it includes both their business systems and their trade marks, or their ways of producing these food items and company-described premises and atmosphere.

The history of these and other brands demonstrates that both services and products have changed significantly over the decades. Among the various advantages to these types of business format franchises and their arrangements is that they have the flexibility to do so effectively.

Today there exist numerous kinds of franchises throughout a constantly expanding array of industries and market segments in not only the United States and Canada but around the globe. Estimates state that more than 120 separate industries utilize the concept and practices of franchising now. The greatest share of franchising by far is still the food and restaurants businesses. Nowadays even medical services and home based health care rely on franchising though.

Franchise Model

Franchises are businesses where the owners sell the rights of their business to third parties. The owners of the franchise are known as franchisors. The third party operators who buy the rights are called franchisees. The franchise model is the precise way the business is run to insure uniformity among the different regional or national franchise outlets.

This model of business offers advantages to the sellers and the buyers of the franchise. Franchisors who sell their rights gain the ability to grow their business brand faster than they might with their own capital or by using the help of lenders or investors. They are able to harness other individuals' money to build up the business footprint faster than they can alone. They still maintain control over the brand.

Franchisors receive both an upfront franchise fee and continuous royalties. They avoid the deadlines of loan repayments with this model. With the royalties and fees that the franchisors gain, they are able to run the corporate headquarters operations, advertise and market the business brand, support and train their franchisees, build up their brand in the industry, and make improvements on the service or products that their business provides.

Franchisees also gain many benefits. Their franchise has a greater likelihood of succeeding than if they start up their own business. This is evident in many ways. They receive upfront training and continuous support. The time to open is less. Buyers also receive the recognition of a brand that is known, help in finding the best site for the new location, lesser costs because of group purchasing power, and better advertising exposure through regional and national campaigns.

Besides this, they receive leads that are generated by call centers and websites, the established franchise model, and moral support and counsel from fellow franchisee peers. A more recent benefit for franchisees pertains to help getting funding secured for startup and ongoing operation costs.

The model has been wildly successful particularly with nationally known franchises such as McDonald's, Subway, and Panerra Bread. Yet there are still downsides to the franchise model. These disadvantages apply to franchisees. Most importantly, they have little independence. This is evident from their services and goods they provide to franchise wide promotions that might not be effective in their own individual market.

Franchisees will have to utilize the company colors and approved paint colors on their walls. They can be made to redesign their units at significant expense. Most dangerous of all is the possibility that the franchise transforms after the franchisee signs a 10 to 15 year long contract. The ownership or management could completely change and force the brand to go in a different direction that the franchisee does not like or at all want.

The franchise model is all about following the system. This idea is central to the success of a franchisee's efforts. The reason that a franchisee purchases the franchisor's model and system is because they have confidence in it. Franchisees feel they can succeed and make money if they follow the system perfectly.

A good franchisor considers appropriate regional variations and suggestions for some changes. They also know that if they leave the system without gaining approval from the franchisor first, they may violate the franchise agreement. This could cause them to have their rights to use the franchisor's name and business model revoked.

Franchisees are also required to keep confidential any trade secrets or proprietary methods of business. They are also made to sign and abide by a non-compete clause agreement.

Free Market

Free Market is the term that refers to a system of exchange and trading that takes place voluntarily in a given economic jurisdiction. These markets have the characteristics of decentralization and spontaneous arrangements whereby the people involved are able to make real economic choices with their money. No country in the world has a completely free market. The degree of its freedom depends heavily on the legal framework and political rules. In some nations where markets are centrally planned or at least tightly regulated by an oppressive government (such as in the pariah state of North Korea), the only free markets may be enormous black markets which the government can not or chooses not to control or shut down.

The phrase Free Market is often utilized in place of the French idea of laissez-faire forms of capitalism. This phrase translates to "hands off." When the majority of individuals and investors refer to free markets, they are describing economies where competition is relatively unhindered and transactions are done on a generally private basis between willing sellers and buyers. A better definition would be a market in which economic activity is voluntarily and not coerced or heavily restricted by oppressive governmental authority.

With this more inclusive definition, both voluntary socialism and laissez-faire capitalism are real examples of the free markets. It does not matter that the socialism involves public ownership of the factors of production. So long as a central government is not restricting or impeding the free exchange of goods and economic activity, it is still Free Market capitalism. Coercion can be allowed in free markets in the cases of mutually agreed to terms as part of voluntarily signed contracts. This is how tort law and lawsuits operate under free market capitalism, though legal cases are certainly coercive obstructions to free economic activity.

It is the free market that makes it possible for goods from all across the globe to be made available to consumers in different countries. It similarly provides the greatest possible opportunities to entrepreneurs and business people. They put their personal capital at risk in order to meet the desires (both now and in the future) of the many global consumers as effectively and price-efficiently as they can. These free markets allow for savings and investment to produce capital goods while boosting the productivity of the workers (and hopefully their wages as well). It usually increases the standard of living of the employees as part of the process. Freely competing markets encourage and foster technological process and innovation which helps the inventors to satisfy the future desires of consumers across the world in creative and groundbreaking new ways.

Free markets allow for and cause the development of financial markets over time. Such markets provide for the finance and capital needs of those individuals and businesses which require greater capital resources for their business ventures than they can fund alone. While some businesses may save money through thriftiness, others actually deploy their savings in an effort to make money by expanding or incubating a new business. Securities can then be traded on secondary markets to encourage both activities.

As an example, individuals and investors who save are able to sink their resources into either the bonds or stocks of corporations. When they buy bonds, investors are providing their current savings to the businesses and entrepreneurs in exchange for the contractual agreement to repay these savings along with interest. When they purchase stocks, they are selling their savings in exchange for future claims on earnings not yet realized by the corporation.

There are many constraints that central governing authorities and regulating agencies impose on the free markets. These all come with either a verbal or implied threat of force if they are not heeded. Some of these constraints include taxation, licensing requirements, price and wage controls, quotas on exports or production, employee hiring regulations, sourcing of goods regulations, fixed exchange rates, and general regulations of many different kinds. When these restrictions become too repressive, voluntary exchange usually still occurs outside the government's knowledge in a black market. The problems with such markets is that oligopolies and monopolies often form in these underground free markets as competition is often ineffective and the prices are heavily impacted.

Gross Income

Gross income can be several different things in the United States. In tax law for business, gross income signifies all proceeds realized from every source minus the cost of goods that have been sold. It is also used for individuals and pertains to all income earned from any and every kind of source.

As such, it is not simply cash that has been realized, but it can also be income received in kind, as property, or as services. For a taxpayer, gross income is commonly believed to be all of the monies and values received. Although most income is tallied into this figure, a few kinds of income are excluded deliberately.

For companies, individuals, trusts, estates, and others, gross income is necessary for figuring up the mandatory income taxes within the United States. Taxes are figured up using a taxable income number that starts with gross income and then subtracts permissible tax deductions. Taxes are then calculated based on the resulting taxable income.

Many different types of income are considered to be a part of the gross income category. Wages are the earnings for work performed payable as tips, salaries, and related income. Income made as a result of such personal service is always tallied up in a person's gross income. Gross profits made from selling an inventory of products are also considered gross income. Gross profits result from sales prices of items minus the cost of the goods actually sold.

All interest received is also considered to be a part of gross income. Dividends, along with distributions of capital gains from companies or mutual funds are similarly a part of gross income. Gains on property that has been disposed of are also tallied into the gross income total after the extra proceeds beyond the adjusted cost in the property is determined. Also included are royalties and rents from intangible and tangible items.

A number of other non traditional types of income are also considered to be a part of this. Pensions, income from life insurance, and annuities income are counted. So are alimony, child support, and other maintenance payments. Shares of partnership income that are distributed fall under this category. Even the proceeds from national and state tax refunds are considered to be gross income.

The Internal Revenue Service claims that such gross income includes all forms of income from any source of which they are derived. As such, gross income can result from any gains having to do with labor, capital, the two together, or profits having to do with the sale of anything or a capital asset. A notable exception to gross income includes gifts and inheritances. While these could be taxed under the category of estate taxes or gift taxes, they are not deemed by the IRS to be a part of gross income.

Gross Margin

Gross Margin is also known as gross profit margin. This concept represents a business formula that companies compute. It is best expressed as the firm's total revenue less its cots of goods sold which is then divided by the total revenue. This provides the answer as a percentage. In other words, Gross Margins are the percentage of revenues the corporations keep after paying their direct expenses of creating both their services and goods. Higher percentages mean a company keeps a larger amount of every dollar worth of sales. This greater amount of retained income provides it with more money for servicing debt, making new investments, retained earnings, and paying out dividends to shareholders.

Gross margin equates to the amount from every sales dollar that the firm is able to keep for their gross profits. Consider a concrete and tangible real world example to better understand this idea. If HSBC Bank has a gross margin in a quarter of 30 percent, then this means it keeps 30 cents from every dollar in revenue it creates. The other 70 cents would go into the Cost of Goods Sold (COGS) category. Since all of the bank's COGS are already considered, the other 30 cents per dollar in revenue may be applied to general overhead, paying down any debt, expenses on interest, and shareholder dividend distributions.

Corporations utilize this gross margin in order to ascertain how their costs of production are measuring up against their revenues. When a corporation's gross margin is declining, it will try to find ways to reduce its costs of suppliers and labor costs. The supplier costs can be slashed by finding alternative suppliers who will supply the goods at lower prices. The other solution is to try to raise the prices on the company goods and services so as to increase the value of the corporate sales revenues.

Another effective use of gross margins lies in predicting the amount of money which they will retain towards general operating costs. Companies with 45 percent gross margins know they will have to work with 45 cents on each dollar of revenue they collect in order cover their remaining administrative and operating costs. The measure also allows for firms to measure up their efficiency as a company. Investors and analysts are able to compare and contrast two or more corporations of varying sizes against one another with the metric as well.

Gross margin should never be erroneously confused with net profit margin. Gross margin simply considers the connection between the cost of goods sold and the sales revenue. On the other hand, net profit margin covers every expense a corporation has. Calculating up the net profit margins requires firms to start with their revenues and subtract out their cost of goods sold and other expenses. This includes sales rep wages, distribution of product costs, taxes, and various operating costs.

Another way of looking at the differences between the two related but still different concepts is that the gross profit margin allows firms to determine the level of their manufacturing operations' profitability. Alternatively the net profit margin assists firms in considering their level of all around profitability.

Consider another example for calculating up gross profit margin. If a company brings in two million dollars in sales revenue, it might spend $800,000 on its labor expenses and another $200,000 on the manufacturing inputs. Once these costs of goods sold of one million dollars are subtracted out, a full million dollars remains in total gross profits. When individuals take the gross profits and divide it by the total revenue, the result is 0.5. Turned into a percentage, this equals a gross profit margin of 50 percent.

Holding Company

Holding Company refers to a parent company, limited partnership, or limited liability company. The firm controls a majority of the voting stock shares in the subsidiary company to dominate its management and corporate decisions. The sole purpose of a holding firm like this is to control other companies. These held firms might also be limited partnerships, corporations, or limited liability companies. Such a holding enterprise does not produce and market its own services and/or goods.

This type of Holding Company could alternatively be involved in buying and holding property assets. These might include stocks, real estate, trademarks, and patents, among other types of tangible and intangible assets. Those businesses which a holding enterprise owns fully (as in 100 percent of the company stock) are known as wholly-owned subsidiaries. In point of fact, a great number of the best known and most profitable operations around the globe are actually such Holding Companies.

There are various advantages which exist in creating this type of operation to hold other firms. The parent company gains protection against losses or lawsuits from its subsidiaries. For example, if a firm owned by the Holding Company suffers a catastrophic event like a bankruptcy or severely punitive lawsuit, the holding parent will suffer from deterioration in its net worth and sustain capital losses for sure. Yet the creditors, debtors, and judgment holders of the financially impaired subsidiary firm are not allowed to go after the holding operation in an effort to recover their capital losses or judgments.

This explains why a huge corporation might decide to establish itself as a holding operation. Perhaps a single subsidiary might possess the firm's trademarks and brand names. A second might control all of the parent corporation's real estate and real property assets. The parent company could create a third set of corporations to operate each of the various company franchises or business lines. Another one might be utilized to own all of the operating equipment of the parent firm. The end result would be that every subsidiary and the holding parent also would maintain both limited legal liability and limited financial losses.

This also permits the parent firm to reduce its overall tax liabilities. They do this by deliberately choosing to headquarter particular subsidiaries of the operation in lower tax rate national jurisdictions, such as Great Britain and Ireland.

Another brilliant feature of these Holding Companies is that they permit individuals involved in or owning a corporation to safeguard their own personally held assets. Instead of possessing such business assets personally, which would make them liable for any and all debts, risks, and possible lawsuits, the holding parent is able to hold the assets in such a way that the assets of the individual will not be placed at risk. Only the assets of the holding parent would be on the line, and not the assets of the individual owner this way.

The entire operations and business of such a Holding Company center on managing the firms it controls. The holding parent might fire or hire managers and staff as it wishes, yet the managers it engages will be the ones who bear full operational responsibility for their companies' day to day and strategic business. While the holding parent may not engage in daily operational control over these firms, it will still be involved as it may from an oversight position in order to ensure that the business prospects and performance remain strong for the foreseeable future.

There are many successful and well-known holding company operations around the globe today. The most widely recognized by investors might be Berkshire Hathaway, the holding parent of investing and insurance company legend Warren Buffet. Another prominent one is leading global bank (as measured by balance sheet assets) HSBC, which is jointly based in London and Hong Kong.

Johnson & Johnson is a final well-known example for consumers. The consumer products and health care giant owns wholly or controlling interest in 265 distinct companies which carry out the three major business lines and operations of the holding firm in pharmaceuticals, consumer healthcare, and medical devices. These numerous subsidiaries are found in practically every country on earth and are each staffed by locally based employees and managers.

Holdings

Holdings refer to the asset contents in a given portfolio which an entity or individual possesses. Pension funds and mutual funds are good examples of organizations that have holdings. These positions can include all sorts of different investment assets and classes. Among these are stocks, mutual funds, bonds, futures, options, ETF exchange traded funds, and private equity assets.

It is both the kinds and amounts of such holdings in any portfolios that determine how well-diversified the portfolio actually proves to be. Well-diversified portfolios often include various sectors of stocks, bonds from a range of maturities and companies, and a variety of other investments that do not correlate with either stocks or bonds. Alternatively, only a few positions in several stocks that come from only one sector would be indicative of poorly diversified portfolios.

It is actually the mix and amount of various asset classes in any portfolio that will substantially determine what its total rate of return will be. The biggest positions will exert a larger impact on the return of a portfolio than marginal or tinier holdings in such a portfolio will. Many investors make it a practice to closely scrutinize the lists of positions which the world's most successful money managers maintain in an effort to follow their trades.

Such investors try to imitate the trading prowess of these superior results money managers in a variety of ways. It might be the manager has purchased stocks, in which case the imitating investors will try to stake out a similar company position. If these managers sell out of a stake, the investors will similarly sell off their assets in the company. The problem with such a follower strategy is that there is often substantial lag time between that point where the money managers make their moves and when this information becomes public domain knowledge.

There is another variation on the idea of mutual funds, hedge funds, and pension funds. This is the concept of holding companies. Such organizations are groups where the investors organize their positions and assets as an LLC Limited Liability Company. The reasons for this are varied. It might be they wish to decrease their own risk exposure, pool their investment dollars with fellow investors, and/or reduce their taxes as much as possible. Such companies rarely operate their own businesses directly. Instead, they are generally only a vehicle utilized to own various investments and companies.

Probably the best-known example of such an LLC company is the internationally followed Berkshire Hathaway, Inc. This Warren Buffet-dominated Omaha, Nebraska- based corporation originally began as a clothing textiles' manufacturing firm. Over the last numbers of decades, the corporation has solely existed as Warren Buffet's personal vehicle to buy out, maintain, and sell out his numerous and wide-ranging investments in various companies. Among the greatest and most significant positions which Berkshire owns are large stakes in the Coca-Cola Company, Dairy Queen Inc, and their wholly controlled subsidiary GEICO Government Employees Insurance Company.

The simplest way to envision these holdings is to mentally picture a large bucket, which represents the mutual fund. Every rock within the bucket stands for an individual bond or stock position. When analysts add up all of the rocks (as stocks or bonds), this equals the aggregate numbers of all holdings.

Figuring out the best mix of these holdings is the challenge that mutual funds, pension funds, and hedge funds all grapple with on a regular basis. It all comes down to the type of fund which they represent. Those bond funds or index funds would anticipate having many positions. This could mean from hundreds to thousands of different bonds and stocks. With the majority of other funds, too many or too few positions is risky and dangerous. Those funds that hold merely 30 positions would be subject to extreme volatility and single stock risks. If they had 500 to 600 different stocks or bonds then the fund would be as large as many indices like the S&P 500.

Household Income

Household Income refers to the total income earned by all family members living in a single house. They must be fifteen years or older for their income to count. An interesting point is that the individuals living together do not have to be related at all to be considered a part of the overall household. This is a crucial measurement of risk that many lenders employ for underwriting loans. It also proves to be a helpful economic metric for grasping the standard of living in a given area.

The statistic of median household incomes is a commonly cited and released economic statistic within the United States. It can be misleading though, since a great number of American households are actually made up of only one person. This is why the statistic consistently plays second fiddle to median family income, which is similarly often reported as a leading economic indicator. Households which only consist of one person are not factored in to the average family income formula. This is why considering household income statistics can be constructive when analysts are attempting to do comparative measurements of living standards and true wealth from one state, city, county, or even country and the next.

Yet this household income remains among the three most frequently cited metrics for individual wealth in America today. The remaining two are per capita income and family income. These use a bit different means of approaching the standard of living for people in a certain jurisdiction and determining their overall financial wellbeing.

In fact, household income takes into account all incomes of any individual within the home who is at least fifteen years old. The weakness of the measurement lies in the fact that it similarly considers a single person dwelling alone to be an entire household as much as it would a family of seven. With the competing metric of family income, only those households which at least two people who are related via marriage, birth, or adoption are considered to be a true household.

Contrast this with per capita income, the third related measurement of individual and household wealth and standards of living. With per capita income, the measurement is the most true and accurate, since it considers only every individual person who dwells in a prescribed region, city, nation, or other area along and as themself. This means that two individual income earners within the same household or even family will always be counted distinctively under the formula for deriving per capita income.

Modern-day economists and analysts like to deploy household income all the same. They prefer it for drawing up a raft of conclusions regarding the overall economic health of a certain population group or regional area. As an example, economists will frequently compare the median household incomes from one nation of the world to many others.

This delivers a big picture as to what quality of life the citizens of various countries enjoy as compared to their compatriots living in other nations. It helps them to determine which country's citizens boast the best quality of life. In 2013, Luxembourg enjoyed the highest median household income in the globe at a staggering $52,493. Surprisingly, the United States came in at only sixth with $43,585.

Another practical application of the household income figure pertains to the regional prices for real estate. This can tell analysts much about whether or not the housing market could be overheating. Experts in household finance continuously maintain their claim that homebuyers can only afford to pay as much as three times their yearly incomes on a home.

This means that the ratio of median household income as measured against median home sales pricing will tell the tale on if a given home price is too expensive for the typical area household's income. In the housing bubble of the first half of the 2000s decade, the median home prices across many regions of the nation, including Southern California and Miami in South Florida especially, proved to be as much as five times higher than the local area median household income, making them unaffordable for the average household to all intents and purposes.

Import

In simple terms, imports are goods that are utilized in one country that were produced in another country. The term import refers to the idea of bringing goods and services into a nation. It originally came from the concept of bringing these things into a port via ships. A person who is engaged in the practice of bringing these goods and services into the other country is called an importer. Importers live and are based in the country into which they bring these goods and services.

Export is the opposite of import. It refers to sending the goods made in one country abroad to the importing country. Exporters are based overseas from the importer and importing country.

Imports are then any items, such as commodities or goods, or alternatively services that are brought to a country from a different country in legitimate means. They are commonly used for trade purposes. Such goods are then put on sale to people in the importing country. Foreign manufacturers make such goods and services that are then offered to the domestic consumers of the importing country. Imports for the country receiving them are the exports of a country that sends them.

International trade is actually based on such imports and exports. Importing any goods commonly means dealing with customs agencies in both exporting and importing nations. Imports can be subjected to trade agreements, tariffs, or quotas much of the time.

Imports can refer to more than simply services or goods that have been brought into the country. They can also be the resulting measured economic worth of any goods and services that are being imported. Such imports' values are measured over periods of time, such as monthly, quarterly, or yearly. The abbreviation of I represents the value of such imports in macroeconomics.

From an economic strength point of view, imports are considered to be somewhat negative. Exports are nearly always regarded as positive, since they represent produced items that are being sold to others for currency consideration. When a nation's imports are greater than their exports, this leads to a trade imbalance, or trade deficit. Such trade imbalances must be paid for with something eventually. Much of the time it ends up being debt instruments that are exported back to the countries from which the imports come. Countries like the United States and Great Britain are guilty of having significantly greater values of imports than exports. They commonly run large trade deficits.

Import Quotas

Import quotas are numerical restrictions which a government of one country imposes on the imports of another competing nation. The main purpose of such quotas lies in decreasing imports while simultaneously boosting a country's own inherent domestic production. With the numbers of such imports restricted, the price of these imports will increase. This then fosters the production, purchase, and consumption of more domestically-produced goods and services by a nation's own consumers.

Import quotas prove to be among three of the most common foreign trade policies utilized to discourage imports while encouraging exports. Besides these are export subsidies and tariffs. National governments undertake to enforce these quotas as foreign trade policies. They are enacted with the intention of defending domestic production through limiting foreign competition.

Quotas in general are typically quantity limitations which a group slaps on activities, services, and goods. Employers typically run into hiring quotas for different national groups of people. Sales representatives also face such quotas in their sales activities and endeavors.

This is why import quotas as an extension of this idea are simply the foreign sector amount of imports which a domestic government will permit in a given industry or service sector. By increasing the numbers of domestically-produced goods in an economy while discouraging the numbers of competing imports, a nation's consumers are prompted to buy home-produced goods and services instead of foreign-based and -produced ones.

There are five principal reasons why import quotas are sometimes imposed on foreign imports of goods and services. The political pressure is such that domestic employment has to be protected and encouraged. Many domestic jobs proponents fear the competition of low foreign wages. By decreasing the number of imports from such countries, governments are able to lower the playing field for higher and better paid domestic employees.

Governments can also be concerned about unfair trade practices and infant industry worries. Unfair trade means that the foreign-created imports could be dumped at prices which are lower than possible production costs. Foreign exporters would do this temporarily in a market in order to reduce the ability of domestic producers to effectively compete and remain in business at the same time. China has been a major practitioner of dumping and unfair trade practices in industries such as steel around the world in the past. Infant industry refers to a comparatively new domestic industry which has not grown up sufficiently in order to benefit from the necessary economies of scale. Import quotas serve to safeguard this infantile industry while it develops and grows from cheaper and more efficient competition overseas.

A final motivating factor for import quotas revolves around the quite complex idea of national security. These quotas could be employed to discourage imports while encouraging domestic production of those goods which are called crucial for the nation's security and ultimate survival of its national economy. The military hardware production industry is one such example of a sector which many nations are eager to protect from less expensive foreign competition.

Economists are divided on the net effect and overall effectiveness of import quotas as they pertain to foreign trade and government policies. They do tend to help out the domestic economy for which they are the most advantageous. Domestic firms which are struggling against competition from stronger foreign competitors are most likely backers of such policies. The national companies see benefits from greater sales and profits, as well as additional income for the owners of the resources and factors of production. The problem with boosting domestic prices by restricting consumers' access to foreign imports is that such foreign trade policies will hurt the domestic consumers by increasing prices in stores and reducing both the ultimate quality and available choices offered.

Inflation

Inflation proves to be prices rising over time. It is specifically measured as the increase in a given basket of goods and services' prices. These goods and services are taken to represent the entire economy. Inflation is also the going up in cost of the average prices of goods and services as measured by the CPI, or consumer price index. The opposite of inflation is known as deflation. Deflation turns out to be the falling of an average level of prices. The point that separates the two from each other, both deflation and inflation, is price stability, or no change in the costs of goods and services.

Inflation has almost everything to do with the amount of money available. It is inextricably tied to the money supply. This gives rise to the popularly remarked observation that inflation is actually an excessive number of dollars chasing too small a quantity of goods. Comprehending the way that this works is easier when considering an example.

Pretend for a moment that the world possessed only two commodities: oranges that are gathered up from orange trees and paper money created by government. In seasons where rain is limited and the oranges are few as a result, the cost of oranges should go up. This is because the same number of printed dollars would be competing for a smaller number of oranges.

On the other hand, if a bumper crop of oranges are seen, then the cost of oranges should drop, since the sellers of oranges have no choice but to cut prices to sell off their large inventory of oranges. These two examples illustrate inflation in the former and deflation in the latter. The main difference between the real world and this example is that inflation measures changes in the price movement on average of many or all goods and services, and not simply one.

The quantity of money in an economy similarly impacts the amount of inflation present at any given time. Should the government in the example above choose to print enormous amounts of money, then there will be many dollars for a relatively constant number of oranges, as in the lack of rain scenario. So inflation is created by the number of dollars going up against the quantities of oranges that exist, or overall goods and services existing. Deflation, as the opposite of inflation, would be the numbers of dollars dropping compared to the quantity of oranges available.

Because of this, levels of inflation result from four different factors that often work together in combination. The demand for money could drop. The supply of money could expand. The available supply of various other goods might decline. Finally, the demand for other goods increases.

Even though these four factors do work in correlation, economists say that inflation is mostly a currency driven event. This means that in the vast majority of cases, it results from governments tampering with the money supply. Generally, they do this by over printing their own currency to have money to pay for spending, resulting in higher inflation.

Inflationary Bias

Inflationary Bias refers to the opposite of deflationary bias. Both of these are government monetary and/or fiscal policy prejudices. Governments are forced to take one of two positions with reference to their monetary policy and interventions in an economy. Inflationary bias turns out to be the one which the vast majority of central banks and sovereign nation policy makers pursue for several important reasons.

Such an Inflationary Bias results from discretionary policies of national governments. If they are utilized properly with regards to the labor market, these biases cause a higher than ideal inflation level without leading to any transitions in income increases. At the same time, this bias results from the goals of those nations which are saddled with public debt levels. They would pursue these policies with a goal of fostering inflation over the medium to longer term.

There are economic theories that persuasively argue governments have a natural affinity for and tendency towards Inflationary Bias policies. The Barro-Gordon model demonstrates that the government's ability to manipulate the economy will cause it to skew towards a bias that is inflationary by nature. According to such a model, countries will try to maintain the country's national unemployment rates at lower than the naturally occurring levels. This causes a wage and price inflation that is higher than their normally occurring level. In the end, this will lead to an aggregate inflationary level that proves to be greater than the normal level of inflation.

The economic theories that are more traditional also suggest that this Inflationary Bias will be present any time that fiscal and monetary policies become enacted at the discretion of the policy makers and central bankers instead of being rules based. Still other economists argue that this bias will even be present if the policy makers are not bent on reducing unemployment to lower than normal levels and even if the policies operate off of rules instead.

As there are so many perils from such Inflationary Biases, economists have suggested a variety of measures to stop it from occurring. Some of them have argued for appointing only conservatively ideological central bankers. According to these arguments, the countries ought to set out aimed for inflationary targets and goals. When these rates of inflation are surpassed by real economic data releases, there could be a punishment of some type given out to the central bankers.

In truth and point of fact, the majority of important countries now do state their optimal inflation rate targets in their policy setting meetings, press conferences, and notes from closed door meetings alike. For most Western nation policy makers and central banks like the United States Federal Reserve, Great Britain's Bank of England, the Euro Zone's European Central Bank, and the Japanese Central Bank, this level amounts to a desired two percent inflation target over the medium to long term time frame.

For those nations that opt to go with the opposite of an inflationary bias, the only other choice is the deflationary bias. The problem with deflationary biases is that they only work for countries, businesses, and consumers which are not saddled down with enormous debt levels. This is because a deflationary bias will cause debts to progressively cost more in real terms over time even as they reward savers and creditors. Governments are especially afraid of this policy bias as they are mostly running budgetary deficits year in and year out. Only a handful of countries run government budget surpluses in point of fact.

Insolvency

Insolvency refers to the point where an individual, business, or even governmental organization is not able to cover its various financial obligations any longer. This means that it is unable to settle debts with its creditors and lenders as they are due. Many times, before such an indebted individual, company, or government becomes embroiled in any type of insolvency or bankruptcy procedures, they will try to enter into informal negotiations with creditors. This could involve setting up other payment schedules and arrangements.

Insolvency can happen for a variety of reasons. Among these is a decrease in cash flow and profitability forecasts, poor management of cash resources, or a rapid expansion in costs and expenses. Where businesses are concerned, this type of insolvency is classified according to one of two separate categories. The first of these is Cash Flow insolvency. This happens as a corporation or company simply can not pay the business debts as they become due. The second form is Balance Sheet insolvency. This type results from a company reaching the point where it possesses a negative net asset position. It simply means that the corporation's aggregate debts are greater than its total assets.

It is entirely possible for firms to be solvent by balance sheet figures but at the same time be insolvent by cash flow. The opposite scenario could also occur. If a company is bankrupt according to its balance sheet while still solvent by cash flow, it simply means its incoming revenues permit it to cover its current financial obligations. There are numerous companies which possess longer term debt obligations that continuously operate in this balance sheet-bankrupt status.

Technically, insolvency and bankruptcy are not exactly the same thing. The former is a condition of being in financial trouble or at least difficulties. Bankruptcy is instead a court order. It describes the ways in which a debtor which is no longer solvent will continue to meet its obligations or instead have its assets sold off to settle with the creditors.

This means that it is entirely possible for a company, individual, or government entity to be no longer solvent but not yet be officially bankrupt.

This could result from a temporary or sometimes fixable problem. The reverse is never the case. An entity can not be bankrupt yet still be solvent. Such a lack of solvency often translates into an eventual bankrupt state when the debtors are not able to improve their financial conditions.

Corporations and firms that have become insolvent are able to improve their financial state. They might slash costs, borrow money, sell their assets, renegotiate the terms of their debts, or seek out a bigger corporation to acquire them. The buyer could settle their debts as part of the assumption of their services, products, technology, and proprietary trademarks.

Several unfortunate events can lead to a company becoming insolvent. If they do not have enough management in human resources or accounting departments, this could contribute to the problem. A lack of qualified accounting staff could cause a company's budget to be either ignored or misappropriated.

There might also be sharply increasing vendor prices which the company is powerless to stop. Higher prices for their goods and services mean that companies will have to raise their prices in an effort to pass these along to the consumer. The problem arises when customers then shop another company or product to get a better price. Lost clientele nearly always translates into a drop in cash flow. This means that they no longer have the cash coming in to cover the bills due to the company creditors.

There could also be lawsuits brought by employees or customers that break a company's finances. The firm could be forced to pay enormous bills for both defense and in settlement damages which make it impossible for them to continue ongoing operations. As operations cease and revenue naturally drops, the ability to pay bills disappears quickly.

A final reason centers on the lack of evolution in a company product line. It might be customers simply change their needs and therefore purchasing habits. This could lead them to rival firms which offer a broader product range or line. The company which could not or did not adapt its products will find its revenues and profits decreasing to the point where they are unable to cover their expenses with their remaining income.

Intangible Assets

Intangible assets refer to the possessions of a company that are not physical. They are difficult to quantify for several reasons. These types of assets can not be physically measured. They also represent an unknown or undetermined cash value to a company. Several criteria for intangible assets are that they are invisible and can not be touched. Despite this interesting characteristic they are intrinsically valuable. These assets prove to be critical to the overall success of any business.

Intangible assets are typically classed in two categories. These are legal assets and competitive assets. Legal assets are easier to understand than are competitive assets. Legal assets include the wide varieties of intellectual and creative property. In this category are such important holdings as patents, copyrights, brand names, trade secrets, and trademarks.

Each of these can be owned and has value, though it is not easy to assign a value to these elements. Patents are the rights to inventions. Copyrights give ownership of writings and similar creative property. Brand names are a company's physical name or product, such as Coca Cola, McDonald's, or Big Mac.

Trade secrets refer to a company's ways of making things that are not known to rivals and competitors. The formula for Coca Cola is a well-known example of a trade secret. Trademarks are the ownership of popular company or product slogans or phrases as used in advertising.

The second category of intangible assets is the competitive intangible assets. These are more abstract and difficult to grasp. Competitive assets refer to reputation and the knowledge of how to do things for the business. Such assets as these can be obtained with experience mostly. These types of assets include human capital, know how, leveraging, reputation, and collaboration. Naming such ideas is hard enough, but assigning them values is a matter of conjecture.

There are reasons why coming up with values on such intangible assets is so incredibly hard. Valuing properties means that an analyst must gaze into a company's future to determine the ways that these assets will impact its bottom line in the coming years. In the process they take the assets' cost and allocate it through the expected life of the asset. Some intangible assets are valued in legal terms. An intangible asset will never be given a longer life span than forty years. When the analysts and accountants do this allocation, it is referred to as amortizing the intangible assets.

Another division of intangible assets is the category of either definite or indefinite assets. With definite assets, individuals are referring to those that will endure for a specific amount of time. Contract agreements are good examples of these types.

Indefinite assets can last for an indefinite time span. A well-known example of this is a company's brand name. Such an asset will endure so long as the enterprise keeps making the products.

Intangible assets may be hard to value, but they are still valuable for a company. Clearly an intangible asset can not have the same easily assessable value that a physical plant or other equipment would. Such intangible assets are often of great value to the company though.

There are many cases of such a property being instrumental in the company's eventual success or failure. McDonald's is so wildly successful because of the tremendous value it gains from consumer recognition of its brand name. This recognition can not be physically touched or seen.

The results of its impact on the company profits are unquestionably valuable to McDonald's. The strength of their global brand pushes sales around the world on every year. These intangible assets like brands are so powerful precisely because they make an impact on customers' choices. This allows companies to charge higher prices for their products.

Intellectual Property

Intellectual property, also known by its acronym of IP, is the concept having to do with creations from a person's mind. The ownerships of such property are recognized as rights that can be possessed, bought, and sold. As such, they have also given rise to relevant fields of law.

As a result of this intellectual property rights and law, creators and owners of many intangible assets obtain exclusive rights to them. This includes literary, musical, and art works; inventions and discoveries; and also phrases, designs, symbols, and words. The most prevalent forms of intellectual property are then trademarks, copyrights, trade secrets, patents, and industrial design rights.

Intellectual property rights go back to the 1600 and 1700's in early modern Great Britain. The Statute of Monopolies from 1623 is viewed as the origin of patent law, while the Statute of Anne from 1710 is looked at as the basis for copyright laws. The phrase intellectual property arose in the 1800's. It finally became common in the U.S. in the late 1900's.

Intellectual property rights are believed to create economic growth and a flourishing free enterprise system. This is because such rights of exclusivity permit the creators and owners of these intellectual properties to realize financial benefit from their creation. It gives individuals and businesses motive to develop and invest in intellectual property. With patents, such businesses are willing to come out of pocket for the development and research costs because of this incentive.

Because of this, the creation and maintenance of these intellectual property laws are given the credit for major contributions made to great economic growth in the Western World like the United States and Great Britain. Many economists point out that around two thirds of big businesses' value lies in intangible assets. It is also said that industries that use intellectual property intensively create as much as seventy-two percent more added value for every employee than do those industries that do not use intellectual property intensively. This is to say that a great deal of economic growth is generated by intellectual property rights and associated industries.

Critics of intellectual property rights do exist. Those in the free culture movement hold up intellectual monopolies as examples of things that hold back progress, damage health, and concentrate ownership to the disadvantage of the common people. They argue that the public good is hurt by monopolies that constantly grow out of software patents, extensions of copyrights, and business method patents.

Besides this, some claim that intellectual property rights that are strictly enforced slow down the transfer of technological advances and scientific break through to poor countries. Still, developing nations are beneficiaries of developed nation technologies like vaccines, the Internet, mobile phones, and higher yielding crops. Critics claim that patent laws come down too hard in favor of the people who develop innovations versus those who employ them.

Interest Rate

Interest rates are the levels at which interest is charged a borrower for using money that they obtain in the form of a loan from a bank or other lender. These are also the rates that individuals and businesses are paid for depositing their funds with a bank. Interest rates are central to the running of capitalist economies. They are commonly written out as percentage rates for a given time frame, most commonly per year.

As an example, a small business might require capital to purchase new assets for the company. To acquire these, they borrow money form a bank. In exchange for making them this loan, the bank is paid interest at a pre set and agreed upon rate of interest for lending it to the company and putting off their own use of the monies. They receive this interest in monthly payments along with repayments of the principal.

Interest rates are also used by government agencies in pursuing monetary policies. Central banks set them to influence their nation's economic performance. They impact many elements of an economy such as unemployment, inflation, and investment levels.

There are several different interest rates to consider. The most commonly expressed one is the nominal interest rate. This nominal interest rate proves to be the amount of interest that is payable in money terms. If a family deposits $1,000 in a bank for a year, and is paid $50 in interest, then their balance by the conclusion of the year will be $1,050. This would translate to a nominal interest rate amounting to five percent per year.

The real interest rate is another type of rate used to determine how much purchasing power is received. It is the interest rate after the level of inflation is subtracted. Determining the real interest rate is a matter of calculating the nominal rate and removing the amount of inflation from it. In the example above, supposed the economy's inflation level is measured at five percent for the year. This would mean that the $1,050 in the account at year end only buys what it did as $1,000 at the beginning of the year. This translates to a real interest rate of zero.

Interest rates change for many reasons. They are altered for political gains of parties in power. By reducing the interest rate, an economy gains a short term boost. The help to the economy will often influence the outcome of elections. Unfortunately, the short term advantage gained is often offset later by inflation. This reason for changing interest rates is eliminated with independent central banks.

Another main reason that interest rates change is because of expectations of inflation. Since the majority of economies demonstrate inflation, fixed amounts of money will purchase fewer goods a year from now than they will today. Lenders expect to be compensated for this. Central banks raise interest rates to fight this inflation as necessary.

International Bank Account Number (IBAN)

IBAN is an acronym which stands for the International Bank Account Number. This standardized numbering system for identifying bank accounts around the world with precision was first conceived of and implemented by the banks of Europe. They wanted to make simpler the means of transacting between bank accounts of financial institutions based in different countries.

This internationally agreed to system for identifying the world's banks and bank accounts was critically needed for banking across international borders. European banks found it necessary to come up with a way to effectively process the cross border transactions. They wanted to dramatically lower the dangers of errors in transcription and subsequent transmission problems which sometimes resulted.

It was the ECBS European Committee for Banking Standards that first adopted the IBAN concept. It later evolved into a global standard under the auspices of ISO 13616:1997. This standard became updated with ISO directive 13616:2007 that now utilizes SWIFT as the official registrar. The system originally arose as a means of facilitating payments made throughout the European Union. It has now been put into place by the majority of European nations along with many countries throughout the globe, especially in the states of the Caribbean and Middle East. Sixty-nine different nations utilized the IBAN account numbering system as of February 2016. More sign up all the time.

The IBAN account number is made up of several components. The two letter national code comes first. This is followed up by the two check digits which enable an integrity check of the IBAN number to be sure it is correct. Finally come as many as thirty alphanumeric characters which are also called the BBAN, or Basic Bank Account Number. Each national banking association decides which BBAN will become the standard for their own national bank accounts. In general, the remaining thirty characters include such information as the domestic bank account number, branch location identifier, and additional routing information.

While the IBAN concept has taken hold effectively throughout the continent of Europe, it is not a universal global standard yet, though it is the closest thing to one. The practice of working with such standardized account numbers as these is growing and gaining in popularity in other countries of the world. This is proven by the fact that nearly forty non- European countries now employ the International Bank Account Number system for themselves on only the twentieth anniversary of the concept being introduced originally.

Before the rise of the IBAN, every country utilized its own national standard to identify bank accounts within their own borders. This proved to be confusing in Europe, particularly as the borders between the 27 different EU countries began to blur thanks to the EU. Free movement of people, capital, and goods meant that money was being drawn from and transferred back and forth between the banks and bank accounts of different European states on an increasingly common basis. Sometimes important and even critical routing information was simply missing from transfers and payments.

SWIFT's routing information does not require transaction specific formats which identify both account numbers and transaction types specifically. This is because they leave the transaction partners to agree on these. SWIFT codes also lack check digits, meaning transcription errors can not be detected nor can banks validate the routing data before they submit the payments without these two digits. Continuous costly routing errors were creating delays on payments and transfers as the receiving and sending banks were also working with intermediary banks for routing.

The ISO International Organization for Standardization overcame these problems in 1997 by creating the IBAN in association with the European Committee for Banking Standards. Because the ECBS simplified and better standardized the original format proposed by the ISO, an update was issued with ISO 13616:2003 and then again in ISO 13616-1:2007.

As of 2017, the United States' banks do not employ IBANs themselves. Instead, they utilize either Fedwire identifiers for the banks or the ABA Routing Number.

Inventory

Inventory refers to a collection of items that are an important part of any firms' assets. These finished goods, products which are being built, and even raw materials constitute items that the company will sell. As such, analysts often consider inventory to be among the most crucial assets of companies since it is the sale of such goods that constitutes the main revenue generating sources. This leads to the corporate earnings which ultimately accrue for the good of the company stake holders.

Such inventories can be in a range of stages of completion, so long as the corporation keeps them on its company premises. It is also possible to have this on consignment. Consignment refers to a deal where the firm holds its goods at locations that are third party owned and operated. The company still maintains the ownership all the way to the point where it sells the goods.

Corporations report their inventories on their balance sheets. They do this beneath the category of current assets. Inventories are the intermediary stage standing in between order fulfillment and manufacturing. As these inventories become sold off, their carrying cost moves under the category for cost of goods sold found on the income statement.

Three different parts of inventories are broken out beneath this account on the statement. These are finished goods, works in progress, and raw materials. The finished goods prove to be those final products which have completed production processes. The business can put them up for sale. There are so many examples of this type of goods. Finished trains, boxed up electronics, and available to ship airlines are some of them. When retailers purchase such goods to resell them, they utilize the name of merchandise. Merchandise covers countless items which stores sell such as jewelry, clothing, and electronics that the retailers decide to stock.

Under the category of works in progress are a range of goods. These would still be under the manufacturing process to change them into soon to be completed goods. Examples of this include a ship under construction, sweaters which are half knit, and cars that are partially assembled.

Raw materials are those items which become a component in the production process. They are the source materials of the finished goods. Airline manufacturers would purchase steel, refineries would buy crude oil, and chocolate companies would buy sugar and cocoa.
There are also three different ways to value inventories as accountants measure them. FIFO First In, First Out means that their cost basis for the goods relies on the materials which the firm bought first. The last inventory would have carrying costs that relied on the last bought materials for its basis. There is also a LIFO last in, first out method. This does just the opposite. Goods' costs depend on the pricing of the materials bought last, with other inventory having earliest purchased materials as the cost basis. The last methodology utilizes a weighted average for cost basis. Goods' cost sold and inventory alike become based on the materials purchased average cost for the entire period.

Inventory management is a critical concept for any business that wishes to be profitable. Those companies which hold a great quantity of inventory will run afoul of expensive storage costs, spoilage possibilities, and their goods gradually becoming outdated. It is similarly a problem to not have sufficient inventories of goods. Companies can miss sales and possible market share gains when they do not possess enough goods to sell. This is why the near-science of inventory management attempts to predict and strategize so that these costs can be minimized and goods may be constructed and obtained as they are required. One of these effective management process systems is called the JIT just in time inventory system.

Joint Venture

Joint ventures are businesses or projects that two or more companies create together. They typically have shared risks and returns, ownership, and control structure. Companies form joint ventures for a primary reason. Usually they are trying to combine their various resources in order to achieve some specific goal. It could be for an existing or a new project. Each of the JV owners is ultimately liable for the losses, profits, and costs that come with it. The joint venture itself is a separate company that has different objectives from the main interests of the owning companies.

Companies form joint ventures as a means to pool their expertise in the industry, their business reputation, their technology and abilities, and their separate human resources. This gives them the advantage of combining resources on a project as they are able to share the costs, liabilities, and risks associated with the job.

Joint ventures are most often temporary partnerships between two or more companies. They draw up contracts that spell out the joint project terms for which every participant will be responsible. At the end of the joint venture, every participating party gets its shared percentage of the losses or profits. They sign an agreement that the joint venture is over and dissolve the original JV agreement. These are among the advantages for forming such joint ventures.

There are many disadvantages to these joint ventures as well. Because of these, as many as half of the JVs ever formed end with conflict in under four years' time. Among the problems that plague joint ventures are greater liability, reduced outside opportunities, and unfair divisions of resources and work.

Greater liability is a serious and real issue for the owners of joint ventures. Most joint ventures become set up with structures of limited liability companies or partnerships. Each of these types of business structure comes with its own liability. Only if they form a business entity that is separate can they avoid this increased liability for the JV. All participating owners equally share responsibility for any claims that are filed against the JV. This is true regardless of how much they are involved in the activity that instigated the claims.

Contracts with joint ventures also typically reduce the amount of outside opportunities for all of the companies participating. This lasts so long as the joint venture project is ongoing. There are often non-compete agreements and exclusivity arrangements made in the process. These agreements will impact their business dealings with vendors and customers alike. The idea is to keep all parties focused on the joint venture's success and to reduce conflicts of interest between their various businesses. These limitations will end after the project concludes. In the meantime, they can negatively affect the main business and operations of the various partner companies.

Unfair divisions of resources and work are a final problem that haunts many joint ventures. The parties involved all share control and ownership. This does not mean that the employment of resources and amount of work done will be fairly divided. One company might only have to put people to work on the project while another has to provide facilities, technology, or access to distribution. This may mean a lot more work and resources are committed by the one partner.

Despite this unfair burden, the shares of the profits are the same for all contributors. It does not matter that one partner often contributes much more to the project. Such unfair distributions of work and resources often cause conflicts among the owners of the JV project. Conflicts like this can create a lower rate of success for the project in the end.

Key Performance Indicator (KPI)

Key Performance Indicators are measurements that aid companies and other organizations in assessing the progress they are making towards their key goals. It is important for any organization to start out by deciding on its mission and determining its goals. Once they have done this effectively, they can decide on the best means of measuring their incremental progress to reaching the goals.

A characteristic of Key Performance Indicators is that they are measurements that are quantifiable. They must also be relevant to the organization's particular benchmarks of success. These will be different for various organizations. A business and a community service organization will not have the same KPIs.

Businesses could have KPIs that relate to their total profits or amount of income that they derive from repeat customers. Customer service departments could use KPIs that measure the number of calls they answer in under a minute. Schools' Key Performance Indicators could center on the percentages of students who graduate. Community service organizations might look at a KPI that revolves around the number of individuals they are able to assist in a given year.

There is no one right or wrong Key Performance Indicator. KPIs only need to be measurable, relevant to the goals of the organization, and a core part of the group's success. As an outfit's goals evolve or are met, the KPI goals may shift as well.

Key Performance Indicators have to be definable and measurable to be useful. It is no good setting a KPI that is subjective or a matter of opinion. Their definitions also should be consistent year in and year out. This is the only way that the targets set for each KPI will be meaningful.

If a company sets a goal to be the best employer, then they might use their company Turnover Rate each year as a Key Performance Indicator. This will work so long as they are using the same turnover rate definition and measurement each year. Reducing turnover by a certain percent annually is an understandable goal that different departments can act on and address.

Another important attribute of these Key Performance Indicators is that they have to be relevant to the organization and its goals. A business whose goal is to become the most profitable company in the sector will need to use KPIs that address profits and relevant finances. They might choose profits before taxes. Schools that are not interested in turning profits would not utilize such KPIs.

For Key Performance Indicators to be helpful they also need to be a core part of an organization's success. KPIs are only practical so long as they relate to the elements that the organization needs to work on so that they can attain the goals. Another important facet of these KPIs is that there should not be too many of them.

The idea is for the members of the organization to be able to focus on the identical Key Performance Indicators. It is possible for the organization as a whole to have three to five KPIs while departments have several others that help to support the overall goals. So long as these goals can be neatly categorized under the company's larger ones, this is acceptable.

Key Performance Indicators make a good tool for performance management. When everyone in the organization is aware of the goals, then they can take appropriate steps to help reach them. KPIs can be posted on company websites, in employee break rooms, and in company conference rooms. All of the activities of the members of the organization should be focused towards meeting or even surpassing those KPI goals.

Leverage

Where business and finance are concerned, leverage pertains to the concept of using investment capital, revenue, or equity to multiply any gains or losses realized. Leverage can be affected in various ways. Among the most popular means of achieving it are through purchasing fixed assets, borrowing money, or utilizing derivatives.

There are several important examples to the use of leverage. With investments, hedge funds work with derivatives to leverage their capital. They could do this by putting up one million dollar cash for their margin and using it to control twenty million dollars of crude oil. They then realize any and all gains or losses achieved by the twenty million dollar crude position.

Businesses may similarly achieve leverage on their revenue by purchasing fixed assets. In so doing, the business would boost its proportion of fixed costs. Any change in revenue would then lead to a greater change in the associated operating income.

Publicly traded corporations are also able to obtain leverage on their stock share holder equity through borrowing money. The greater amount of cash that they borrow, the lower amount of equity capital they will require. This translates to all profits and losses being distributed out to a smaller share holder base, making them proportionately bigger in the end.

There are formulas for the four main types of leverage. Accounting leverage is found by taking all assets and dividing them by all assets minus all liabilities. Notional leverage is found by taking all notional quantities of assets, adding them to all of the notional liabilities, and then dividing the result by equity. To find the economic leverage, the equity volatility has to be divided by the identical assets' unlevered investment volatility. Finally, operating leverage can be calculated through taking the revenue in question and subtracting out the variable cost, then dividing the operating income into the result.

Leverage entails significant benefits and also substantial risks. While it does allow potentially great amounts of money to be made when investments go the way of an individual or organization, it can also involve devastating losses when the investments move against the entity. As an example, a stock investor who purchases stocks with fifty percent margin will double his losses when a stock goes down. Companies that borrow excessively to increase their leverage can experience collapse and bankruptcy in a downturn in business at the same time as a company with less leverage could survive.

Not all uses of leverage entail the same degree of risk. Corporations that borrow money so that they can engage in international expansion, increase their line up of products, or modernize their plants and equipment gain additional diversification. This could provide more than just an offset for the extra risks that result from the leverage. Not all highly leveraged companies are risky either. Public utilities commonly include high levels of debt, but they are generally considered to be less risky than are technology companies that lack leverage.

Liabilities

Where a business is concerned, liabilities prove to be amounts of money that are owed by the company at any given point. These liabilities are displayed on the firm's balance sheet. They are commonly listed as items payable, or simply as payables.

There are two types of liabilities. These are longer term liabilities and shorter term liabilities. Long term liabilities turn out to be business obligations that last for greater than the period of a single year. Mortgages payable and loans payable are included in this category.

Short term liabilities represent business obligations that will be paid in less than a year. There are many different kinds of short term liabilities. They include all of the items detailed below.

Payroll taxes payable are one of these. They represent sums automatically collected from the employees and put to the side by the employer. They have to be given to the IRS and any state taxing agencies at the pre determined time.

Sales taxes payable are another short term liability. The business collects them from its customers when sales are made. They hold them until it is time to give them to the proper revenue collecting department within the state.

Mortgages and loans payable are another short term liability. These represent payments made every month on mortgages and loans. They are not large single payments or the total amount of a loan that is eventually owed, but instead represent recurring monthly obligations.

Liabilities for individuals are another type of liabilities altogether. They also represent money that has to be paid out. For people, they are debts owed, as well as monthly cash flow that goes out of the individual's accounts.

Liabilities and assets are the opposites of each other, yet people often get them confused. While assets are things that contribute positive cash flow to a person's finances, liabilities are those that create negative cash flow, or money that leaves an individual's accounts every month. For example, a house that an individual owes money on and makes monthly payments on is a liability, not an asset. The house takes money from the person in the form of monthly mortgage payments each month. For a house to be an asset, it would have to be completely paid off. Even still, if monthly taxes and insurance payments are being made, then technically it would still be a liability. Houses can only be assets really and truly when they are rented out and the rental income that a person receives is greater than all of the expenses associated with the house every month, including any mortgage payments, taxes, insurance, upkeep, and property management fees. When the net result of a property is money coming in, then it is an asset and not a liability.

Liability Insurance

Liability insurance is a commercial insurance product that protects businesses and other enterprises from accidents and injuries that occur on their premises. Accidents in a business can cause various types of injuries that create financial, physical, or psychological problems for customers. Business owners are ultimately at risk of law suits and claims from any individuals who deal with the business in any capacity. These issues can range from business contracts that are unfulfilled to medical injuries that require money for treatment.

Business liability insurance practically helps businesses to survive difficult scenarios in this way. It provides for the expenses involved in the legal defense and damages that the business owner may be required to cover. The maximum amount that can be paid out by the insurance company is the policy limit of the liability insurance policy. Owners of the business would then be responsible for any claims beyond these limits if there were any remaining. In general, business liability coverage limitations are sufficient to cover expenses in the claims and lawsuits.

There are a variety of different scenarios where this type of insurance proves to be useful for a business. Operations and premises are a first potential area of business liability. This covers accidents such as slips and falls in a business. It would pay for hospital bills that the customer incurred because of the accident. It could also be used to pay for legal bills that resulted from a negligence lawsuit.

Completed operations and products are another area of concern. A job that the business performed or the products which it sold may turn out to be flawed. This could lead to financial and other repercussions for the injured customer. Liability insurance would take care of the legal defense costs. If the business loses the case, it will also cover the financial damages for which the company is responsible.

Data breaches and cyber liability are a growing area of concern for countless businesses with online presences. Any business with a computer is potentially at risk for this type of cyber crime. Customers' names, addresses, phone numbers, and sensitive credit card information can all be stolen this way.

Important sensitive business information can also be taken. Fixing the problems in the hacked computers and websites is the easy part. Making sure the customers and even business itself do not become victims is the complicated issue. Cyber liability insurance provides hacked businesses with important security and risk management services for the business and its customers at no charge. It also aids with needed forensic and legal help to track down the source of the breach and to prosecute where possible.

Another area that liability insurance assists business owners with is employment practices. Businesses that operate in a segment which has significant turnover will have hired and lost numerous full or part time employees. Any employees that have been let go can file legal action against their former employer without warning. Employment practices liability insurance protects business owners as well as officers, directors, and employees from these suits. It deals with lawsuits involving discrimination, harassment, wrongful termination, and other offenses while employed.

Business liability insurance is also important for another reason. Many individuals structure their businesses as partnerships or sole proprietorships. It may be that the business income and assets are insufficient to pay for all of the expenses of a lawsuit and associated claim. If they do not have business liability insurance any other expenses can be taken from their own personal income and assets. Owners of companies who are unprotected may also be sued for personal liability in certain cases. This is why every business should have the full coverage of business liability insurance.

Limited Liability Company (LLC)

A limited liability company is often referred to by its acronym LLC. These business setups combine the best in both worlds of proprietorships and corporations. They offer the sole proprietorship or partnerships' advantages of pass through taxation. At the same time, an LLC provides the same limited liability for the owners which a corporation receives.

With a limited liability company, the owners will file their business losses or profits with their individual tax returns. This is because an LLC is not considered to be its own taxable structure. When lawsuits against the company are involved, it is only business assets that are at risk of seizure.

Creditors and lawsuit parties are not usually able to get to the LLC owners' personal assets, like cars or houses. This is not absolute protection. If the owners of the LLC engage in unethical, illegal, or irresponsible behavior, then they can forfeit this level of security.

Setting up a limited liability company is harder than establishing either a sole proprietorship or partnership. Once this hurdle is cleared, it is much easier to run the LLC than it is a corporation. Officers of corporations are not completely protected from actions they undertake in the business.

LLC owners must be careful not to behave like the entity is a mere extension of their own individual activities. Should the owners not act as if the LLC is its own separate business concern, then courts can determine that the business LLC does not really exist. In these cases, the judge could decide that individuals are masquerading their business affairs and conducing business as a personal venture. They can became liable then for these actions if this determination is made.

Taxes are another major reason that individuals opt to set up a limited liability company. As pass through entities, the income from their business passes on through the entity directly to the members of the LLC. This means that they must report all financial gains or losses from the enterprise directly on their own tax returns. They do not have to file separate business tax returns. The IRS does require that LLC owners make an estimated quarterly tax payment four times per year.

LLCs which are owned by more than one individual do have to file the informational return Form 1065 every year with the IRS. This form clearly states every owner's share of the limited liability company profits or losses. The IRS goes over these to be certain that the owners are all appropriately reporting their share of the earnings.

Limited liability company management is specific in how it has to be conducted. There are two forms of this. Member management involves an equal participation of the owners in the operating of the business. This is the way that the majority of smaller LLC owners run them.

The alternative form of management is called manager management. In this type of business operation, the collective owners of the LLC must choose someone to handle the daily responsibilities of managing the company. This could be an owner or several of the owners. It could also be someone who is not a part of the LLC ownership who professionally manages the business on their behalf. In this arrangement, the owners who are not managing are only tasked with sharing in the profits or losses of the business. This is often the case with family members or friends who invest in a limited liability company.

Liquidation

The meaning of liquidation depends on the use of the word. In financial terms, there are three different definitions of it. In economics or finance it refers to a failed company. A company that is insolvent is unable to pay its bills when they are owed. Liquidation is the process of winding up the company. The operations of the company cease at this point. The assets would then be divided up among its creditors and stock holders. This is done based on whose claims have priority.

Insolvent companies that choose to go into liquidation generally do so under U.S. bankruptcy code Chapter 7. This legal statute gives the rules on liquidation of companies. Companies that are still solvent but are in trouble may also file a Chapter 7 bankruptcy. This is less common. There are also bankruptcies for companies that do not force liquidation. One such provision that covers this scenario is Chapter 11. In a Chapter 11 filing the trustee saves the company and restructures its debts.

When the process of liquidation occurs, the company halts all operations. All of its assets are tallied up and then distributed to the various claimants. After this is finished, the trustee finally dissolves the business. The debts actually have not been discharged in this process. They still exist to the point where the statute of limitations on the debts expires. There is no debtor in existence to pay off these debts. Creditors simply write them off in practice.

The assets in this liquidation process are handled in a certain methodical way. The Department of Justice appoints a trustee. This individual supervises the process. Assets are distributed to those who have claims based on their priority. Secured creditors are first in line. This is because their loans are backed up by collateral.

The lenders are allowed to seize this collateral and then to sell it. Many times they receive far less than the actual asset value because there are limited time frames. Sometimes the assets are not enough to cover their debt. These creditors are compensated from any other liquid assets in this case.

Unsecured creditors come next in the process. In this category are holders of bonds, the IRS, and employees. Bond holders are a form of unsecured creditors. The company may owe the IRS taxes. Employees may be waiting on payroll or other money they are due. The last category to receive compensation is shareholders. If any assets are left they receive them. Preferred stock investors receive priority before the common stock holders. Usually there is nothing left for either class by the time the creditors are paid.

Another definition of liquidation surrounds huge sales. Sometimes a company needs to close out a great deal of inventory. They would do this by liquidating their inventory at deep discounts. Any company can do this. They do not have to file for bankruptcy in order to sell off inventory.

A third definition of liquidation involves closing out an investment. This generally occurs when an investors sells their holdings in exchange for cash. An individual might also liquidate out of a one position and into an opposite one. If he or she held long shares in a stock, they could instead take on the identical number of short shares.

Brokers can force liquidate trader positions in certain cases. Traders who have acted or traded recklessly with risk can have this happen. If traders' account values drop below the minimum margin requirements they can suffer from forced liquidation as well.

Liquidation Value

Liquidation Value represents the full value of a corporation's complete range of physical assets if and when it declares bankruptcy or actually goes out of business. This value is compiled when every asset on the company books and balance sheet becomes tallied up. This value then includes real estate, equipment, factories, fixtures, and inventory. Those assets that are intangible would never be a part of the firm's final liquidating value.

This is one of four key types of value assigned to a corporation or company's various assets. These include book value, market value, salvage value, and liquidation value. With every category of value, this delivers an alternative view point for both analysts and accountants alike to classify the total value of all assets. For individuals and investors who engage in workouts and bankruptcies, this Liquidating Value is absolutely essential to know.

Book value and market value generally vie for the crown of largest assets' category valuation. In cases where any group of assets' market value has deteriorated because of decreasing market demand instead of the business using it up, this proves to be true. With book value, the asset value equates to the one declared upon the corporate balance sheet. Since the company balance sheet declares these assets for their historical price and cost, this means that the book value could equate to more or less than the relevant market prices which apply on a given day. When the all around economy is growing and prices in general are rising, then this book value is traditionally less than the relevant market value.

With liquidation value, the sum represents the anticipated price for the asset after it has been sold, generally for a loss as compared the original price. Salvage value refers to the one assigned to the assets once they reach the conclusion of their natural and useful life. This then would represent the scrap value of assets. Liquidation value typically proves to be less than the book and market values yet still higher than basic salvage value. Liquidating assets are still valuable, they just sell for less than they otherwise should and would because of the proverbial fire sale in a shortened time frame. It causes them to be sold for losses versus their listed book value.

There are reasons why such liquidation values never include any intangible asset prices. Such intangible assets comprise the goodwill, intellectual property, and brand recognition of the company or corporation. When firms are sold off instead of being liquidated, the firm's value will include both intangible assets' value and liquidation value. This is why traditional value investors will consider and contemplate the variances between the ongoing concern value and the market cap value. They are able to decide this way whether or not the stock of the corporation represents a good value.

It is always useful to consider an example in order to clarify the concept of liquidation value. A given corporation the Snappy Pop Company has $550,000 in liabilities. They also possess book valued assets of $1 million on their company balance sheet. The auction value of these assets might be $750,000, which represents three-quarters of their fair value. At the same time, the salvage value is $75,000. To determine the liquidation value, analysts simply subtract out any liabilities (in this case $550,000) off of the auction value (in this case $750,000). This gives a value of $750,000 minus $550,000 for a grand total of $200,000 liquidating value.

Liquidity

Liquidity refers to the point that a security or asset is able to be sold or bought in a given marketplace without interfering with the price of the asset. Good liquidity is demonstrated through a great amount of trading activity. Liquid assets prove to be the kinds that are simply and quickly able to be purchased and sold. Liquidity can be summed up in a single sentence as the capability of rapidly turning an asset into cash.

Although no single means of determining liquidity exists, liquidity can be figured up through utilizing liquidity ratios. It is generally accepted that investing money in liquid assets proves to be safer and more accessible than placing your money into illiquid ones. The reason for this is that you are able to withdraw your money from a liquid investment quickly and without obstacles.

There are many types of assets that prove to be simply convertible into cash. Money Market accounts are some of the most liquid assets. Blue chip stocks turn out to be the most liquid of stocks traded.

Liquidity also has other meanings for businesses and economics. A business' capability of fulfilling its payment responsibilities is referred to as its liquidity. This is figured both with regards to the company having enough liquid assets that they are able to get to in a timely fashion.

The most liquid asset is money in your hand. This can be utilized right away for all economic functions. Among these are selling, buying, taking care of immediate needs and desires, and paying down debts.

In general, liquid assets possess many or at least a few of a number of features in common. These assets that have good liquidity are able to be sold at any point during market operating hours, quickly, and with as small a loss in value as possible. Markets with liquidity possess numerous sellers and buying who are both willing and able to transact at all times that the market is open. For markets to have deep liquidity, eager and willing parties in great numbers have to be present in a market all of the time that it is open.

The liquidity of a market has much to do with its market depth. Market depth is able to be quantified as the number of individual units that may be purchased or sold for a certain price impact. The opposite of this related term market depth is market breadth. Market breadth is quantified as the amount of price impact for every unit of such liquidity.

A given item's liquidity is measurable in terms of how frequently it is sold or purchased. This is called volume. Investments in markets with great volume like futures markets and the stock markets are generally understood to have far greater liquidity than do real estate markets. This is simply a function of stocks and futures' capability of being rapidly transacted.

There are assets that possess even liquid secondary markets. These offer greater advantages for traders, and because of this, buyers will pay a greater price for such an asset than for an asset that is similar but does not possess a liquid secondary market. This liquidity discount proves to be the lowered anticipated return or guaranteed yield on these kinds of assets.

An example of this is the variance between just issued U.S. Treasury bonds and treasuries that are no longer recently issued. Both may have the same amount of time until they mature, but investors are more interested in purchased the ones that have only just been issued. Because of this, these newest ones have a higher price and lower yield.

Market Trends

Market trends refer to the idea that financial markets tend to move in a given direction. Among the different types of these trends are secular, primary, and secondary kinds. Secular ones refer to longer time periods. Primary trends are those which happen over medium time frames. Secondary trends turn out to be those that occur over shorter time frames.

Traders try to figure out and predict such trends with the study of technical analysis. This study provides a means of characterizing such trends in the market as predictable patterns, especially when prices reach resistance and support levels, which vary with time. The dilemma with predicting trends is that they are only truly knowable after they have begun. This is because future prices can never be fully predicted with accuracy.

Secular markets actually cover those longer term trends which run from five to 25 years in duration. They are made up of a group of primary market trends. This means that a secular bull market would be comprised of bigger bull markets and smaller intervening bear markets. Conversely, secular bear markets are comprised of bigger bear markets and smaller intervening bull markets.

An example of a secular bull market was the period in U.S. markets from 1983 through 2000 (or sometimes considered to be through 2007). The intervening bear trends would be considered the Black Monday Crash in 1987 and the dot-com crash from 2000 to 2002.

Primary market trends are those which instead last only a year to several years. They generally enjoy significant and broad based support in the whole market while they are happening. In a primary bull market, the prices are generally rising. The bull market begins with a great deal of pessimism which is nearly universal. Somehow the despondency gives way to first hope, then belief before finally peaking out at irrational exuberance. At that point, the bull market has finished.

The average bull market has lasted around 8.5 years, according to the market data Morningstar compiled from 1926 through 2014. Annual gains in these types of markets averaged between 14.9 percent and 34.1 percent.

Important bull markets in the U.S. occurred from 1925-1929, from 1953-1957, and from 1993-1997. Two of the three ended badly in the Great Depression and the Dotcom crash, an ominous warning to investors.

In primary bear market trends, the markets are deteriorating over a given amount of time. Vanguard defines these as minimally twenty percent price declines in a given two month period. Bear markets followed the great Wall Street Crash of 1929, occurred from 1937 to 1942, and following the Arab Oil Embargo crisis from 1973 to 1982. More recent examples were from 2000 to 2002 and from 2007 to 2009 in the wake of the Great Recession and Global Financial Crisis.

Secondary trends are those which are short term in nature. These generally last for several weeks to several months. Market corrections are actually a kind of secondary market trend. Such corrections are defined as a shorter term decline in market indices by from around ten percent to around twenty percent. From April 2010 through June 2010, the S&P 500 dropped from 1,200 to around 1,000. Investors at the time believed this was the end of the bull market and the start of a bear market. In fact it was only a correction as the markets turned and continued going back up afterward.

There can also be bear market rallies within the secondary market trends. These are better known as dead cat bounces. They are comprised of a price run in the markets amounting to from ten percent to twenty percent before the bigger bear market trend continues again. Such a dead cat bounce actually happened in 1929 after the initial Black Friday crash. The markets then descended into the ash can through 1932 and more or less through 1942. Another such false bounce occurred in the latter years of the 1960s and early 1970s.

Merger

A Merger refers to a financial transaction which combines two preexisting companies into a single larger resulting firm. A few different kinds of mergers exist today. There are a variety of reasons for why companies engage in such mergers. These mergers and acquisitions often go through with an eye to extending a firm's customer base and product reach, increasing its market share, or moving into new markets and industry segments. In the end, the ultimate motivation is to make shareholders happy by adding shareholder value.

These combinations occur as two firms join forces into a new larger single company. They are nearly identical to takeovers and acquisitions. The main difference lies in the stock shareholders of each firm holding on to an interest in the share of the new corporation. With acquisitions though, a single company buys out all of or a controlling interest in the stock of the target company. This leads to an unbalanced ownership within the newly formed corporation. Practically the whole process of such mergers is generally kept under wraps so that the members of the investing public are completely unaware of it until after they are announced.

Most personnel at both companies are kept in the dark as well. In fact, the lion share of such merger efforts fail. With the majority of them completely secret, it is hard to say with any accuracy the number of possible mergers that become discussed and considered any year in question. The number ought to be extremely high as the quantities of successful ones prove how desirable such mergers are for a great number of corporations.

There are so many different explanations for why two firms wish to combine. Some of these are ideal for shareholders while others are actually not. A profitable company could be combined with a loss-making firm. This would allow the profitable company to employ the losses of the losing target as a tax write off against its own considerable profits. It would simultaneously grow the entire new corporation.

A good reason for these types of combinations is to boost the market share of a given firm. This is especially helpful with bigger corporations which cannot easily grow their market share organically any longer because of their sheer scope and size. When major competitors combine, the new company might be able to overwhelmingly dominate the industry, providing it with a wide range of choices in setting prices and buyer incentives. In these cases, the Sherman Clayton Anti-Trust laws often come into play to stop the merger and prevent the formation of a new monopoly.

There is another popular motivation to combining two existing companies. When they make products which are distinctively different yet still complementary, it presents an opportunity for cost savings. It could be that the acquiring firm wants to obtain the assets of a target firm which is a part of its product supply chain. As an example, there could be significant manufacturers who wish to obtain control over the warehousing chain. This would enable the buyer to save considerable costs on warehousing and to earn profits from the business it buys out at the same time.

A real world tangible example of this type of merger occurred when PayPal merged with eBay a few years ago. eBay became capable of sidestepping the considerable fees it had to pay PayPal previously. The complementary product line was actually a good match also.

It is usually investment bankers who handle the particulars details of and arrangements in a merger. They help with the transfer of ownership of the company itself via stock sales and strategic issuance. This does give incentive to investment banks to encourage mergers between existing clients. It could happen even when a merger would not be in the best interests of the two companies' underlying shareholders.

Monopoly

Monopolies refer to markets where a single producer or supplier controls all or nearly all of the market. This means that they have the ability to set prices for the good or service they produce. For there to be a true monopoly, there can not be any near substitutes for the product in question. The term monopoly has also come to represent the company which dominates the market of the good or service. Monopolist is another better name for the supplier who controls the market.

When a monopoly exists, there is no competition in the price of the good or service. The monopolist is able to set the price. They will usually choose to make it as high as the market will bear.

Monopolies usually occur because there are particular factors that prevent other companies from competing effectively against the monopolist. These factors are called barriers to entry. There are a number of different barriers to entry which can cause a monopoly to arise.

Sometimes a company exclusively owns a critical resource that companies need to produce the product. This can help it to become a monopoly. Exclusive knowledge of a process to make something would also count as sole ownership of a critical resource. This is what makes pharmaceutical companies monopolies in various types of medicine which they develop and first release.

Government protected ideas can also create monopolies. This can exist in the form of copyrights and patents. In these protections, the government guarantees these companies a minimum period of time to produce the goods or services without any competition. This creates a temporary monopoly until the intellectual property protection expires.

Markets where a good or service is new typically see these types of monopolies. Governments justify copyrights and patents as the means to encourage invention and innovation. Without this temporary protection, many companies would not invest resources needed to create new inventions and products.

A related monopoly is a government franchise. Governments create these types of monopolies when they give the exclusive ability to operate in an industry to a single business. This could happen with a business that is owned by the government or a private company. Train operators and mail delivery companies like the postal service are good examples of this type of government franchise.

Natural monopolies sometimes arise on their own without government help or intervention. This is most often the case when the costs are lower for a single company to service the whole market. Numerous smaller companies competing against each other could actually raise costs and prices in these instances.

Some companies have limitless economies of scale. This means that they are so large and powerful in an industry that no new players could compete with their prices. This could be because the costs to enter the industry are so high that no one will bother. They also represent natural monopolies. There are a number of technology infrastructure companies in this position. Some of the more common industries where these types of natural monopolies occur include telephone operators, Internet service, and cable television providers.

It is not always clear if a company possess a monopoly in a given industry. Some people consider certain brands to be monopolies because of how popular they are. This is true even when they do not control all of the product market share.

The Coca Cola Company has a monopoly on producing the soft drink Coke. This is not the only soft drink on the market, but there is no exact substitute for it. Even though rivals Pepsi Cola and Dr Pepper Snapple Group control a large share of the soft drink market, neither of them produces Coke. This is why the debate for monopolies continues to rage on about what constitutes a close substitute. Anti-monopoly regulators constantly wrestle with the question.

Negative Income Tax

A negative income tax is a tax regime that is considered to be extremely progressive. In this system, those individuals who earn less than a minimum specified amount obtain additional income from their government rather than have to pay the government taxes into the system at all.

This type of forward thinking system has been bandied about by various economists over the years and yet never fully realized in a developed economy. In the 1940's, British politician Juliet Rhys-Williams became among the first to make the political discussion serious. In the 1960's in the United States, American legendary free market economist Milton Friedman became a major proponent of the idea.

The function of a negative income tax can be two fold. It can institute a minimum income level. It might also be utilized to provide supplemental income to families earning too little to survive. In this capacity, it would serve the function of providing a system with a guaranteed income minimum.

In such a negative income tax regime, those individuals who bring home a particular income amount would not pay any taxes. Others who earn over this threshold would then pay a percentage of the income they earned over that pre-determined level. Those individuals on the margins of society who realized incomes lower than this amount would receive payments to supplement at least a part of their income shortfall. The amount of money by which their income was below that pre-set level would equal in theory the amount of payments they received from the government and its taxing authority.

In 1962, renowned American economist Milton Friedman first seriously put forward the plan for a guaranteed minimum income in the United States. He envisioned a nation where subsidies provided in the form of federal income would be dealt out to families or individuals whose income was lower than a minimum level.

This negative income tax would ensure that potential claimants could simply and easily obtain the money by filling out their annual tax returns instead of having to apply for and receive welfare benefits. The advantage to such a system would be that it eliminated more or less the requirements of having a complicated welfare system bureaucracy.

Despite the income distribution benefits for the poor that a negative income tax system offers, it is not without its substantial share of vocal critics. This main critique stems from the fact that some low income workers would be discouraged from working at all when on this system. The reason is because if the government will provide one with $2,500 per year without working at all when the individual might only earn $5,000 annually in working dozens of hours per week, many consumers would opt instead to not work at all. They would prefer to enjoy the leisure time which they could spend working, even if this means that they ultimately might have a smaller amount of money which was insufficient to cover their essential costs of living.

Another criticism centers on accountability and potential abuse of such a negative income tax system. These critics argue that it is impossible to completely eliminate a large and costly welfare system infrastructure by doling out negative income tax payments. The other taxpayers who are in effect paying for the subsidies will insist on accountability being instituted for those citizens who are receiving what are ultimately subsidies from their income. Such a demand would necessitate a complicated combination of oversight and rules that were necessary to stop possible abuses of the negative income-welfare system.

Negative Interest Rates

Negative interest rates are those that fall below 0%. In the past, negative interest proved to be only a theoretical discussion that economists played around with for the sake of argument. In 2010 Sweden's central bank put these rates into practice as a means of stemming the flow of outside money into the country. Denmark followed suite in 2012. Since then, minor to major central banks have moved into the mostly uncharted waters of these negative rates.

The reason that central banks would be interested in such negative interest rates is that they help the economy. Central banks cutting the rates into negative territory creates a similar effect as simply lowering interest rates. Lower rates help consumers to spend and businesses to invest more.

They also boost prices in the stock markets and other risk assets. They reduce the level of the nation's currency. This helps exports to be more competitive against other country's goods. Finally lower rates cause people to expect higher inflation rates in the future. This encourages consumers to spend their money now as opposed to later when it will be worth less.

The world has many decades of knowledge of what happens when central banks influence economies by reducing rates from 3% to 2% because of downturns in the economy. In theory this shifting to negative interest rates is similar with the difference of a starting point at or below zero.

Such NIRP negative interest rate policies are called unconventional monetary tools. The idea is to move benchmark interest rates into negative territory. Doing so means breaking the centuries' long barrier of 0%.

Deflation is what caused desperate central banks to pursue these negative interest rates and policies. In times where deflation pervades an economy, the businesses and consumers tend to hold their money rather than invest and spend it. Eventually this creates a reduction in total demand that in turn causes prices to fall even more. Output and production slow down and unemployment increases as a result.

Stagnation like this is typically avoided when central banks pursue a loose monetary policy. The problem arises when the deflation becomes so powerful that dropping interest rates to zero is no longer enough to encourage lending and borrowing.

The result of negative interest rates is profound. Central banks charge their commercial banks money (negative interest) in order to keep their deposits at the bank. Commercial banks then pass along these costs to their larger account holders as they are able. The financial institutions have not much stooped to official negative rates on their depositors. Instead they charge fees for keeping money in these current accounts. This amounts to negative rates under the guise of a different name.

Central banks hope that the commercial banks will loan out money instead of paying to hold it. Instead many banks have been paying the fees themselves, and this has impacted bank profits. Banks fear passing along fees to small deposit account holders who may withdraw their money instead.

As of 2016, the negative interest rate policy has been adopted by the European Central Bank, the Swiss National Bank, and the Bank of Japan besides the Scandinavian Central Banks. Early evidence suggests that the Euro zone did manage to reduce interbank loans with the negative interest rates. Companies have not so far much benefited from the negative interest rates. This is because the risk is perceived to be higher with corporations who borrow than with governments. One notable exception is with Nestle the Swiss food conglomerate that has issued negative interest rate corporate bonds.

Net Asset Value

The Net Asset Value refers to a mutual fund and its per share value. It is also known by its acronym NAV. Exchange traded funds, or ETFs, can also be referenced by the NAV. These values which the companies themselves compute for investors only provide a snap shot of the NAV at a particular time and date. In either security type, the fund's per share dollar value arises from the aggregate value of every security within its portfolio minus any liabilities the fund may owe. Finally this is expressed over the total number of outstanding shares in order to arrive at the shares' ultimate NAV.

Where mutual funds are concerned, the Net Asset Value is derived one time every trading day. They utilize the closing market prices for every security within the fund's holdings in order to determine this. Once this is done, the fund is able to settle all sell and buy orders which are outstanding on the shares. These prices will be set by the NAV of the mutual fund in question for the value per the trade date. Investors will always be required to wait to the next day in order to obtain their actual trade-in or trade-out price.

Because mutual funds do pay out nearly all their capital gains and income, such NAV changes are never the optimal gauge for the performance of the given fund. Instead these are better determined by looking at the yearly aggregate return, or total return.

With ETFs, these are actually closed end types of funds. This means that they actually trade more like stocks do. The shares of these Exchange Traded Funds therefore constantly trade at the market value. It might be a literal value which is higher than the NAV. This would be trading at a premium to the Net Asset Value. It could similarly trade under the NAV. This would mean the prices were trading at a discount to the NAV.

With these ETFs, the Net Asset Value becomes computed once at the markets' close so that the fund can correctly report the ETF values. During the day however, these are figured differently than the mutual fund computations. This is because the ETFs will compile the during-the-day NAV in real time at numerous points in every minute of the trading day.

It is helpful to consider an example of how the mutual funds compute their Net Asset Value calculations. The formula is actually very straightforward. It is simply that the NAV is equal to the mutual fund's assets less its liabilities with the difference divided by the total number of shares outstanding. The assets in the case of mutual funds include cash equivalents and cash, accrued income, and receivables. The main portion of their assets commonly are their investments, which will be priced per the end of the day closing values. Liabilities equate to the complete longer-term and shorter-term money owed, along with each accrued expense. Among these expenses will be utilities, salaries of the staff of the fund, and various operational costs for running such a fund.

Consider that the fictitious Diamond Stocks Mutual Fund counted $200 million in investments, figured utilizing the end of day closing prices of all their assets. Besides this, it has $14 million in cash equivalents and cash and another $8 million in receivables in total. The daily accrued income amounts to $150,000. Besides this, Diamond Stocks owes $26 million in its shorter-term liabilities and has $4 million of longer-term liabilities. The daily accrued expenses amount to $20,000. With 10 million outstanding shares, the net asset value would equate to $19.21 in the case of the Diamond Stocks Mutual Fund.

Net Operating Income

Net Operating Income can refer to two different concepts. It may be used in regards to companies and corporations, or to properties and their annual incomes. Where companies are concerned, Net Operating Income, also known by its acronym NOI, is the income after deducting the company's operating expenses. It is figured up in advance of taking off interest and income tax deductions.

When this number proves to be a positive number, it is called net operating income. If the number turns out to be a negative value, then it is referred to as a Net Operating Loss, also known by the acronym of NOL. Many analysts like to look at the Net Operating Income as a realistic picture of how a company is performing. They feel that this number is more difficult for management to manipulate than are other numbers in the income statements of a company.

Pertaining to properties, Net Operating Income equals the annual gross income minus the expenses for operating. In this respect, the gross income is comprised of real income from rentals as well as other incomes like laundry receipts, vending receipts, parking charges, and every type of income that is related to properties. Operating expenses prove to be the expenses that are encountered in the typical maintenance and operating of the property in question. Among these expenses are insurance, maintenance, repairs, utilities, management fees, property taxes, and supplies. Some costs are not deemed to be operating expenses, such as capital expenditures, interest and principal payments, income taxes, depreciation, or amortization of the points on a loan. So, calculating the Net Operating Income on a property involves first taking the various forms of annual gross income and adding them all up. Then the operating expenses should be taken and added up. Finally, the operating expense total is subtracted from the operating income total to achieve the Net Operating Income figure.

In real estate, Net Operating Income is utilized within two critical real estate ratios. The Capitalization Rate, also know as the Cap Rate, is employed to come up with an estimate of the actual value of properties that produce income. For example, maybe a property being considered for purchase possesses a market capitalization value of ten. Coming up with the market cap rate is achieved by considering the financial information from the sales of properties that produce income and are similar in a particular market.

The other important real estate ratio that relies on Net Operating Income is the Debt Coverage Ratio, also know as the DCR. The Net Operating Income proves to be a critical component of this DCR ratio. Investors and lenders alike utilize the debt coverage ratio to determine if a property has the capability of covering both its mortgage payments and operating expenses together. A result of one is deemed to be the break even point. The majority of lenders want at least a 1.1 to 1.3 ratio in order to contemplate making a commercial loan to a given property. The higher this debt coverage ratio works out to be in a banks' opinion, the safer the loan will ultimately be.

Net Operating Profit After Tax (NOPAT)

Net operating profit after tax is also called by its acronym of NOPAT. This refers to the potential earnings (in cash) of a corporation working under the pretense that it has no debt. This NOPAT metric is often utilized in so-called EVA economic valued added calculations. The formula for determining NOPAT is as follows: the operating income times the result of one minus the tax rate. For companies which are debt leveraged, this NOPAT proves to be a more precise and exact way of examining their operating efficiencies. As such it does not factor in the tax advantages which a number of corporations enjoy from their debt load.

Analysts and accountants consider a number of varying performance metrics when they are evaluating a corporation in which to invest. The two most frequent performance measures turn out to be sales (or revenue) and net income growth. With the revenue/sales figures, this delivers a top line performance metric. It does not say anything about the company's operating efficiency value though. Similarly the net income does include the operating expenses of a firm, yet it also factors in the net tax benefits and savings from the company's particular debt leverage.

This is where the Net operating profit after tax comes in as a useful hybrid form of alternative calculation. It permits the analysts to compare and contrast a company's performance against past metrics and other companies by removing the effects of debt leverage from the equation. This allows analysts to truly fairly measure one company against another, regardless of the two firms' net debt positions.

It always helps to consider a real world, concrete example with these complex terms. If a company's EBIT Earnings Before Interest and Taxes was $12,000 and their tax rate was 25 percent, then the calculation for NOPAT would translate to $12,000 times the result of one minus .25,(or .75). This equals $9,000 as a NOPAT. It is an after tax cash flow estimate that does not include the tax benefits of debt. For those companies without debt, Net operating profit after tax equals the same amount as does the net income after tax.

It is worth noting that analysts prefer to compare and contrast firms within the same industry when utilizing the NOPAT metric. This is because every industry has its own normal range of operating costs. Some industries' typical expenses turn out to be dramatically lower or higher than others' do.

For example, cable utilities would have extremely high operating costs associated with initially putting in, continuously upgrading, and maintaining their technology and physical hard-wired distribution networks. Soft drink businesses like Dr. Pepper/Snapple Group (DPS) have relatively low costs since they generally license out their products to other companies which produce and distribute them on their behalf.

Net operating profit after tax has other uses besides the helpful view of a company without its debt leverage being considered. Those analysts who follow and predict mergers and acquisitions utilize this NOPAT value all the time. It helps them to figure up the FCFF free cash flow to firm. This is equal to the NOPAT less any changes to working capital. It also equates to the net operating profit of the firm after taxes less the firm's capital.

These two metrics NOPAT and FCFF are commonly utilized by those types of analysts who hunt down targets for acquisition. The reason for this is that the financing of the acquiring firm will then substitute in for the present financing arrangement (their corporate debt).

Net Profit

Net Profit refers to the remaining sales dollars which are left over after a firm pays for all of its operating costs, interest on debt, preferred stock dividends, and taxes. Common stock dividends are not included in the amounts deducted from the firm's aggregate sales revenue. Sometimes analysts call this type of profit the net income, the bottom line, and/or the net earnings.

A simplistic (but useful) way of thinking about this form of profit is that it is all of the money which remains after all of the expenses of the going concern are paid in full. Calculating the net income is done when aggregate expenses are subtracted from total revenue. Because these net earnings traditionally occur on the final line in an income statement, companies often refer to it as their "bottom line."

It remains true that this Net Profit is still among the most closely watched business indicators in the world of finance. Because of this, it has a substantial part in the computations of financial statement analysis and ratio analysis. Stake holders in the corporations also scrutinize this bottom line carefully since it ultimately proves to be the way they become compensated as shareholders in the firm. When corporations are unable to realize enough profits to pay their shareholders, stock prices plunge. On the other hand, when corporations are growing and in solid financial health, the more available profits become reflected in greater stock prices.

A common mistake that many individuals make is in their understanding of what net profits actually represent. Net profit is never the metric for the total cash earnings a firm realized in a certain period. The reason for this confusing fact is that income statements also showcase a range of expenses that are not cash-based. Some of these are amortization and depreciation. In order to understand the true amount of cash which corporations actually generate, investors and analysts must carefully review the cash flow statement.

In fact any changes to net profit will be constantly and thoroughly reviewed, examined, and discussed. When firms' net profits are negative or even lower than anticipated, there are a host of issues that could be causing it. It might be that the customers' experience is negative. Sales could be decreasing for one or more reasons. Expenses at the company could be out of control or simply poorly managed and monitored. New management teams may not be performing at the anticipated or promised levels.

In the end, the Net Profit will range wildly from one firm to the next and according to which industry they represent. One industry's profits will likely be substantially different from another industry's. It is not a useful comparison to make between one corporation and another since these profits are quantified in dollars (Euros, pounds, Swiss francs, or yen). It is also a fact that no two corporations will be exactly the same size by either revenues or assets.

This is why many analysts prefer to make comparisons between corporations and industries by utilizing what they call profit margin. This is the net profit of a company as a percentage amount of its total sales. Sometimes analysts and investors will also look at the P/E Price to Earnings Ratio alternatively. This widely cherished ratio reveals to considering investors what the price is (in the form of stock price) for every dollar of net profit the corporation actually generates.

Analysts still like the metric of net profit despite these limitations. A survey conducted querying around 200 marketing managers who were senior level revealed that an incredible 91 percent agreed that they believe this measurement to be very useful.

Net Worth

Net worth is a figure that represents a business, an individual, or another group's difference between the assets that they have and the liabilities that they owe. Figuring up this net worth is done by first taking all of the entity's debts and obligations and then subtracting that number from the entire sum of assets. If the total of all of these assets is greater than the sum of all of the debts and obligations, then a positive net worth results. Otherwise, when the debts are greater than the assets, then the entity has a negative net worth.

When you sit down to determine the net worth figure, every asset should be totaled in the operation. There are many different kinds of assets. These are comprised of cash in the bank, holdings of stocks, real estate, bonds, and other types of investments, and major possessions like vehicles. Correctly figuring out the different assets' values is done with the use of the up to date fair market value, not the cost paid for the item when it is purchased.

You must also correctly add up the total of debts and obligations when you are attempting to get a correct net worth value. Liabilities cover many different obligations, like a car payment, mortgage, total of credit card debt outstanding, and any other forms of loans that have balances left on them. Both every asset and liability must be measured in order to come up with an accurate net worth.

Knowing your present net worth is very useful and meaningful. If you are able to cover all of your outstanding debt obligations simply by selling of all of your assets, then you have a financial condition that is fairly stable and in order. If your assets are more than sufficient to cover all of your obligations, then your finances are in greater shape. Most businesses and people seek to reach a point that they have actual positive net worth.

There are a few benefits from having a correct understanding of your net worth. It is essential that your present assets' value is greater than your present debt load. A person who owes more money than they actually own presents a profile of a person who is not an especially good credit risk. Without a positive net worth, many lending institutions like banks will think twice about providing you with the most advantageous loan rates offered. This is because they feel that you present more of a risk to lend money.

It is also good to know where your net worth stands because it is a helpful beginning point for your general financial planning. Should you discover that you hardly have sufficient assets with which to cover your present amount of debts, then this is a good sign that you should not engage in any other purchases until later, after you have eliminated several of your debts. This means that if you occasionally figure up your net worth, then you will comprehend not only where you stand now, but also when you will be in a better position to purchase a new car.

Operating Expenses

In the world of business and corporations, operating expenses is the term that pertains to the continuous costs of running a business. This makes operating expenses the expenses for everything happening behind the scenes. Such operating costs include any expenses incurred for the literal operation of the business.

You occasionally see the words operating expenses written as OPEX. This is especially true in internal memos and documentation that are relevant to the earnings of a company. The most frequent operating expenses are those having to do with employee benefits and salaries. These commonly make up the biggest individual expenses for a corporation. Other operating costs could be office supplies, marketing budgets, licensing and legal fees, raw material expenses, costs of research and development, accounting fees, and office utilities.

Another key operating expense is depreciation. Depreciation proves to be the quantity of value that diminishes in an asset over a period of time. This means that accounts can take equipment, vehicles, and other assets and subtract out the lower value off of the initial value to come up with depreciation as assets gradually lose value. This depreciation can be counted as an operating expense so long as the asset is still employed by the business in its operations.

Some expenses are deemed to be capital expenses instead of operating expenses. This is generally the case for single event expenses, like buying replacement equipment for completely depreciated existing equipment. This division of costs allows both the firm and its investors to have a more realistic snap shot of for what the money is used before it is able to be put to profits. When you are self employed, then you may count both CAPEX and OPEX as business expenses.

Operating expenses have to be included in the annual reports of both not for profit outfits and corporations that are publicly traded. This kind of information commonly comes with charts that compare the operating expenses of several years. In this way, a reader is able to obtain a good understanding of how the expenses are progressing with time.

By tracking operating expenses in an ongoing fashion all year long, the information is easily at hand for a company to include it in their reports. Accountants, or alternatively programs that do financial management, are generally used to help with operating expense tracking and calculation. When operating expenses go up and down every year, investors will want to know why this is the case. Detailed records provide good explanations for the final numbers to satisfy the questioning parties. Corporate treasurers are generally responsible for answering these queries and coming up with answers.

Overdraft

An Overdraft refers to the extension of credit where a bank or other lending institution allows for debits to be paid after an account has hit zero dollars. Thanks to these overdrafts, individuals are able to keep drawing down the account value below zero, although there is no money left in it or an insufficient amount to resolve the withdrawal. Another layman's definition of this term is when the bank permits its clients to borrow a given sum of money.

When individuals possess an account with overdraft facilities, the bank will courtesy cover any checks that will put it into overdraft instead of returning them unpaid (bouncing them back to the check depositor). Naturally the outstanding overdrawn balance will have interest charged on it, as with any loan. Typically such interest rates prove to be far lower than those offered by credit cards though. Sometimes there may be other fees for utilizing the overdraft protection. This would decrease the overdraft protection amount available. Some of these could be per withdrawal or per check insufficient funds assessed fees.

Such overdrafts on money market savings accounts, regular savings accounts, and checking accounts happen when the customers do not keep sufficient funds within this account to cover the incidents such as check and ATM withdrawal transactions. In order for it to equal an overdraft, the bank will have to be willing to process and cover the transaction regardless of the shortfall of funds.

Many banks will pay overdrafts on four kinds of banking transactions. These include recurring transactions of debt cards, checks and related transactions that rely on the account number, online banking transfers and payments, and auto bill payments.

Banks might decide to utilize their own corporate funds in order to pay a client overdraft. They might also have customers link the overdraft on to one of their credit cards. When banks deploy their own money in order to pay an overdraft, then this does not usually impact a client's credit score. As credit cards are utilized to cover overdrafts, this could increase the client debt to the amount where the credit score became negatively impacted.

This does not directly result from checking account overdrafts however.

The problem comes when the overdrafts do not become repaid in a prearranged time frame. The bank might opt to hand over the account into the hands of a collection agency. Such a collection activity might negatively impact the credit score if it becomes reportable to any or all of the three primary credit agency bureaus of TransUnion, Experian, or Equifax. This comes down to how the collection agency reports its accounts to the agencies. It will determine whether the overdraft protection on a checking account shows up as a problem or not.

Such Overdraft protection will deliver a useful tool to help manage the checking account on a day to day basis. For example, a person might easily forget that they drew out money for a Starbucks or Costa Coffee run. The overdraft protection will make sure that the ATM is not turned down or that the ATM Debit card purchase does not get rejected at the merchant point of sale. Banks will commonly assess an overdraft fee and use this to make money from the convenience they are delivering. This is why such protection should not be too commonly used and over-utilized. Instead it is to be reserved for emergency needs and situations.

Every overdraft protection dollar amount is not equal. Each bank and type of bank account will vary the level of protection they deliver. This could also vary on a case by case basis. When such protection is overused, the bank or other financial institution may simply elect to remove the courtesy off of the bank account. Getting it reactivated after such a penalizing move is never easy.

Passive Income

Passive income refers to money that, once it is arranged and established, does not require additional work from the person getting it. A variety of different types of passive income exist. Among them are movie, music, book, screenplay, television, and patent royalties. Other samples of passive income include click through income, rental income, and revenue from online advertising.

Activities that lead to passive income have something in common. They usually need a great amount of money, time, or both invested in them upfront to get them started. There are financial means to establishing passive income as well. You could purchase a rental property or choose to invest in a partnership or other form of company where you are a silent partner. The income that you derive from these investment activities is deemed to be passive.

Various other kinds of passive income do not need a great deal of financial investment made in them, but instead require great amounts of effort, time, and even creativity to achieve. More than a year can be required to either build up a popular website that can contribute passive income from advertising or to write a great novel. Making money from such passive income that is actually profit may take longer.

Books are a good example of how long it can take to actually make money from passive income. Publishers generally get to recover all of their printing and promoting costs, as well as any advance monies given to authors, before royalties are created and paid. Books that sell poorly could turn out to pay the author little to nothing.

Websites have a different set of challenges for their creators. There has to be more than simply good content to make money from them. They must similarly rank high in the search engine results for the necessary amount of visitors to find and go to the website. Unless a great number of visitor hits are recorded on a website, the passive income that is generated will be negligible or even none.

People are willing to put in such a huge amount of time with little assurance of results because they know that the passive income generating activity will create money for them around the clock for years to come, if it is successful. This means that passive income money is constantly being made, even when the person is asleep or on vacation. If you are able to get one passive income project up and running well, then you can attempt others. This way, you might hope to develop a few different income streams that result in a significant annual revenue which can even support you.

Many investors believe that passive income is the most superior kind that you can achieve. This is why rental properties can be so popular. Even though they can require a significant amount of maintenance work and tenant management, they can provide substantial income once several such properties are owned and made profitable.

Personal Assets

Personal assets are items of value that belong to an individual. There are many examples of such tangible personal assets. Among these are houses, real estate, cars, and jewelry. Personal assets can also be any other thing with cash value.

When individuals go to a bank or other institution to apply for loans, such personal assets and their values are often considered. These assets are also the bedrock of the formula for net worth for consumers. The value of people's personal assets can be higher than they expect and surprise them as so many different items can be included under this label.

There are many personal assets that are material and easy to measure. These include such financial assets as savings accounts, checking accounts, and retirement accounts. Assets that have a value that can not be easily accessed are also included in the personal assets category. This includes life insurance policies and annuities that have cash values. Other items of value which would be included in a list of personal assets cover such items as antiques, art collections, electronics, personally owned businesses, and other valuable items.

Personal assets can do more than simply help people get loans and count towards net worth. They are also sometimes able to create income for their owners. Bank accounts and savings accounts accrue interest. Holders of real estate are able to lease or rent it out. This brings in rent or lease fees. Individuals who have personal assets should educate themselves in the best practices for managing them so that they are able to increase their total wealth by generating the highest income possible from them.

It is important to keep a careful track of rent or other income obtained from personal assets as the money will be taxable. Income that is not properly reported to the government on the correct tax forms can incur penalties from the Internal Revenue Service.

It is also important to know the value of an individual's personal assets. There are two different methods of learning this. In the first method, individuals examine the item's market value. This is the value for which the asset would sell if a person were to put it straight on the market. Another way to determine the value of these assets is to have a personal asset appraised.

Appraised values can be substantially greater than market values. This is because an appraisal value relies on the possible future price of the item in question. This difference matter significantly, particularly when having an item insured. Individuals generally have to obtain appraised value insurance coverage. This means that they will likely have to pay for a greater amount of insurance.

When properly managed, personal assets can greatly contribute to an individual's personal financial situation. It is also true that these assets can prove to be a liability if they are not well taken care of or managed. Part of managing assets well involves asset allocation.

Financial experts warn against placing all or the majority of personal assets into a single asset type or location. This type of practice causes people to take on additional risk than is prudent. Instead, it is better to spread around an individual's wealth into a variety of different assets so that if one suffers or decreases in value, some of the other assets may offset this by outperforming or increasing in value.

Taking care of personal assets is also an important part of maintaining their value. Individuals can break expensive electronics if they are not careful. Not engaging in proper maintenance for works of art can also lead to their value declining over time.

Power of Attorney

A power of attorney is an agreement in writing that grants another individual the authority to make some choices if the grantor is not available. This person who receives the power does not have to be an attorney. Attorneys are typically only involved in drafting up or potentially witnessing such an agreement. The phrase comes from an individual receiving status as an agent or attorney in fact.

When people implement such a power of attorney they do not lose the ability to make their own decisions. Instead they are allowing another individual to act for them in matters specified within the written text. This can be very helpful if people are out of the country or in the hospital as an example. Someone else with this authority would be able to cash checks at the bank or pay bills on their behalf. It is simply a matter of sharing power with another person. The agent is only carrying out the grantor's wishes, not actually making choices for them, so long as they are coherent and mentally capable.

People who will be out of town for an extended period of time might find these arrangements particularly useful. With a power of attorney, the agent could carry out major decisions such as selling cars or other personal assets. The Internet has eliminated the need for some of these functions as computers and mobile devices make it possible for people to buy and sell stocks and handle many financial transactions from anywhere they have an online connection. There are still cases where a transaction will require an in person agent to handle them.

There is also a special kind of power of attorney that is used by individuals who lose their ability to handle decisions for their personal financial affairs. This is known as a durable power of attorney. In this case, the word durable refers to the ability of the agent to make the choices on the grantor's behalf when he or she can not mentally do them. This type of arrangement grants the agent the legal authority and responsibility to make the best possible physical and financial decisions for the grantor.

It means that the agent is able to spend the individual's money as appropriate, cash checks, deposit checks, and even withdraw money from the personal bank accounts. The agent further gains the authority to sign contracts, sell personal property, take legal actions, and file and follow up on insurance claims.

When people decide to enter a durable power of attorney arrangement, a notary public or lawyer should witness the document before they sign and execute it. If such individuals need to have a durable agreement established and are not mentally able to do it, courts can do this for them as they deem necessary.

Agents who become appointed to this position are expected to keep correct and segregated records on each transaction they perform. The records must also be easily available at all times. When the individual dies, his or her power of attorney becomes null and void. The will is responsible for the dispensation of the deceased person's estate.

Powers of attorney can be rescinded. If individuals feel unhappy in the ways that their agent is managing their personal affairs, they can simply revoke the authority back at any point. It is always wise for people to choose an individual to be agent whom they know and implicitly trust.

Prime Rate

The Prime Rate is the most typically utilized shorter term interest rate for the United State banking system. All kinds of lending institutions in the United States employ this U.S. benchmark interest rate as a basis or index rate to price their medium term to short term loans and products. This includes credit unions, thrifts, savings and loans, and commercial banks.

This makes the Prime Rate consistent around the country as banks strive to be competitive and profitable in their lending rates which they provide to both consumers and businesses. A universal rate like this simplifies the task for businesses and consumers as they shop around comparable loan products that competing banks offer. Every state in the country does not maintain its own benchmark rate. This makes a California Prime or New York Prime identical to the U.S. Prime.

Commercial and other banks charge this benchmark rate to their best customers. These are those clients who have the best credit ratings and loan history with the bank. Most of the time banks' best clients are made up of large companies.

The prime interest rate is also known as the prime lending rate. Banks typically base it on the Federal Reserve's federal funds rate. This is actually the rate that banks loan money to each other for overnight purposes. Retail customers also need to be aware of the prime lending rate. It directly impacts the lending rates that they can access for personal and small business loans as well as for home mortgages.

The federal government and Federal Reserve Bank do not set the prime lending rates. The individual banks set it. They then utilize this base rate or reference rate to set the prices for a great number of loans such as credit card loans and small business loans.

The Federal Reserve Board releases a statistics called "Selected Interest Rates." This is their survey of the prime interest rate as the majority of the twenty-five biggest banks set it. It is this publication which reveals the Prime Rate periodically. This is why the Federal Reserve does not directly set this important benchmark rate. The banks more or less base it on the target level of the federal funds rate that the Federal Open Market Committee sets and changes at their monthly meetings.

Different banks adjust their prime lending rate at the same time. The point where they change it is generally when the Federal Open Market Committee adjusts their own important Fed Funds Rate. Many publications refer to this periodically changing reference rate as the Wall Street Prime Rate.

A great number of consumer loans as well as commercial loans and credit card rates find their basis in the prime lending rate. Among these are car loans, home equity loans, personal and home lines of credit, and various kinds of personal loans.

The rates above the prime lending rate that banks charge their less then prime (or subprime) customers depend on the credit worthiness of the borrower in question. The banks attempt to correctly ascertain the risk of default for the borrower. For the best credit customers who have lower chances of defaulting, banks can afford to assess them a lower interest rate than others. Customers with higher chances of defaulting on their loans pay larger interest rates because of the risk associated with their loans not being repaid.

As of June 15, 2016, the Federal Open Market Committee voted to maintain its target fed funds rate in a range of from .25% to .5%. As a result of this, the U.S. prime lending rate stayed at 3.5%. Once per month the Federal Reserve committee meets to determine if they will change the fed funds rate.

Principal

Principal has several different meanings. It most commonly pertains to the initial amount of money that a person either invests or borrows with a loan. A secondary meaning has to do with a bond and its face value. Sometimes the word pertains to the owners of a company or the main participants in any type of transaction.

Where borrowing is concerned, this term relates to the upfront amount of any loan. It also is utilized to describe original amounts which the individuals still owe on the loan in question. Looking at a clear example always helps to clarify the concept. When people obtain a $100,000 mortgage, this Principal is the same $100,000. As the individuals pay down $60,000 of this amount, the remainder of $40,000 that is left to pay off is similarly referred to as Principal.

It is the original Principal that decides how much interest borrowers will pay. If borrowers take out a loan with an initial amount equaling $20,000 that comes with a yearly interest rate at seven percent, then they would be required to pay $1,400 in annual interest for each year that the loan remains open. As borrowers pay the monthly payments to the loan servicer, the interest charges for the month will first be paid off. What remains goes toward the initial amount which the individuals borrowed. Paying down this original amount borrowed remains the only means of lowering the interest amount that accrues on a monthly basis.

Another form of mortgage that operates differently has the name of zero principal mortgages. Bankers think of these as interest-only loans. They represent a unique form of financing where the routine monthly payments of the borrower only apply to the loan's interest. This means that the initial loan amount never gets paid down unless the borrower makes extra payments. It also translates to no equity building up in the property which backs the mortgage loan.

Because of this, financial advisors will typically not recommend these types of mortgages to home buyers as they are rarely in the true interest of the purchaser. Despite this fairly obvious assessment, there are a few unusual cases when they could work out for certain people. When a home buyer is starting out on a career path that pays very little initially but will later on earn substantially more in the not too distant future, it could be worthwhile to lock in the home price now while it is lower. Once the income increases apace, the borrowers always have the ability to refinance into a more traditional mortgage which would cover payments on the initial amounts borrowed as well.

Another scenario where these loans make sense relates to unusual and fantastic opportunities for a particular real estate investment deal. When huge returns on investment dollars can be anticipated, it is practical to go with these mortgage's far lower payments that are interest-only. Meanwhile the borrower can plow the additional monthly payment money savings into the exceptional investment opportunity.

Principal also finds use describing the first initial outlay on an investment. This does not take into consideration any interest that builds up or earnings on the investment. Savers might deposit $20,000 at a bank in a savings account with interest. After a number of years, the balance will grow to $21,500. The principal remains the original $20,000 the savers gave the bank. The additional $1,500 will be called interest or earnings on top of this initial outlay.

It is interesting to note that inflation will not change the nominal value of a loan or financial instrument's principal. Yet the effects of inflation do very much reduce the real value of the initial amount.

Profit Sharing Plan

Profit Sharing Plans are not all the same. These plans can come in a range of different formats. Many times they are utilized as a supplement to another kind of retirement account. These defined contribution plans prove to be a significant benefit with tax advantages for a number of American employees.

The reason that employers establish these types of plans is to provide valuable employees with another method of compensation. This particular one permits the employees who participate to receive a portion of company earnings from a trustee. Individuals who have the benefit of a profit sharing account will enjoy contributions made by their employers to their personal plan account. They can then invest these funds and increase them tax free. Maximum individual employer contributions per year are limited to $53,000.

There is a caveat to many of the retirement plans that are employer sponsored. They typically require the employees to become vested in the plan over a period of pre-defined years in which they participate. It might be the employees gain 20% vesting per year over five years. While Money Purchase Plans set up a pre-arranged percentage of yearly earnings which become contributed to the accounts, profit sharing works differently. These plans and their contributions are based on the profitability of the company.

The rules that are typical of these defined contribution plans apply to profit sharing as well. Withdrawals can not be taken before the account owner reaches 59 ½ years of age. If they do take distributions earlier than this, the withdrawals will be fully taxed like personal income. They will also have the standard 10% early withdrawal penalty assessed against them.

The money from profit sharing plans is commonly invested by the trustee administrators into one of several investments. These include variable annuities, mutual funds, company stock, or life insurance. In rare cases with specific job scenarios, the individual employee may be allowed to manage the investment vehicles within the profit sharing account.

Rollovers have a specific set of rules that govern them with profit sharing accounts. The only money from these accounts that can be rolled over is that which has become fully vested. It is important to understand completely the schedule for vesting before account holders think about moving retirement funds to another qualified type of account. The IRS has no unusual restrictions on transferring vested profit sharing account funds. The plan administrator will have to mail out specifically detailed explanations to the account holder of how this can be done without incurring any taxes or penalties.

This is important because if the distribution is not properly rolled over, then the disbursed funds may be treated by the IRS as an early withdrawal. In this case, they will be taxed as ordinary income and suffer the 10% penalties for being taken out ahead of minimum retirement age. This is why transfers such as these should be done as direct rollovers in lieu of indirect rollovers whenever possible. Withholding requirements apply to indirect rollovers besides the danger of experiencing penalties for accidental early distribution.

Plan providers determine what specific investment choices an account owner may pursue with the money from their profit sharing plan. Much of the time, account holders do not have the ability to determine the investments that their profit sharing money participates in at all. The IRS allows investments for these funds that include individuals stocks, government and corporate bonds, mutual funds, options, and exchange traded funds shares.

While these choices may be available to a profit sharing plan account owner, investing in physical gold bullion and the other precious metals is not. Gold ETFs and gold mining company stock shares may be an alternative option for those who wish to diversify away from dollar based assets.

Rate of Return

In the worlds of finance and business, the rate of return, also known by its acronym ROR, proves to be the ratio of money lost or gained pertaining to an investment and the sum of money that is originally invested in it. This rate of return is also called the rate of profit or more commonly the return on investment, or ROI.

The sum of money that is lost or gained could be called the loss or profit, interest, or even net loss or net income. Regarding the money that is actually invested, it is sometimes called the capital, asset, or principle. It is also referred to as the cost basis of an investment. Rate of return or Return on Investment is commonly stated as a percentage and not a fraction.

This rate of return is one measurement of how much cash is made or lost as a direct result of the investment in question. It quantifies the amount of income stream or cash flow that moves from the investment itself to the investor as a percentage of the original amount that the investor put into the investment. Such cash flow that accrues to the investor comes in a number of forms. It might be interest, profit, capital gains and losses, or dividends received. These capital gains and losses happen as the investment's sale price is greater or less than its initial purchase price. The use of the term cash flow includes everything except for the return of the original invested money.

Rates of return can be figured up as averages covering a number of different time periods. They may also be determined for only one time frame. When these calculations are being made, it is important not to mix up annualized and annual rates of return. Annualized rates of return prove to be geometric average returns figured up over several or even numerous periods. Annualized returns might be the investment return on a period less than or greater than a year, for example for six months or three years. The rates of return are then multiplied out or divided in order to come up with a one year rate of return that can be compared against other annual rates of return. As an example, if an investment possessed a one percent rate of return per month, then this might be more appropriately expressed as an annualized rate of return of twelve percent. Or, if you had a three year rate of return amounting to fifteen percent, then you could say that this is a five percent annualized rate of return.

Annual rates of return are instead returns figured up for single time frame periods. These time frames are commonly one year periods running from the first of January to the last day of December. Alternatively, they could cover any year long period, regardless of what month and day they started and ended.

Retained Earnings

Retained earnings are a component of the earnings categories of corporations. They describe the portion of a company's net earnings that they do not give out to shareholders as dividends. Instead these earnings are kept by the firm so that they can pay down debt or reinvest in their core operations and business model. Balance sheets note earnings which are retained as part of the shareholder's equity column.

There is a formula for figuring out retained earnings. It adds the initial earnings with net income or subtracts net losses from it. Dividends must then be subtracted out from these earnings as they are paid out to stockholders.

Corporations have their reasons to keep a portion of their earnings. In the majority of scenarios, they wish to invest them into segments of the market where the firm is able to build opportunities or growth. This could be by spending money for additional research and development or in purchasing new plants, equipment, or machinery. Companies can also use these earnings to purchase other firms. Such acquisitions allow them to expand their market share or product offerings in this method of non organic growth.

It is possible for such earnings to become negative. This happens when the firm's net loss is larger than the initial retained earnings. Such a case creates a deficit. The general ledger for these earnings becomes adjusted each time an entry is placed for the expense or revenue accounts.

At the conclusion of the company's accounting period, such earnings that are retained become reported. This could be in the quarterly report or the annual report. They will either continue to be accumulated and be positive, or they can shift into negative territory and be recorded as a deficit. These changes in earnings from one accounting period to the next are not directly noted. It is easy to infer them by looking at the totals of ending and beginning retained earnings for the accounting period. Increases or decreases to the accumulated totals happen because of dividend payouts and net losses or net incomes for the period.

Every period, a firm's revenues and expenses must be closed out. This is done into an income summary that shows the total net income or loss. Finally these are closed out into the retained earnings column. Net income directly boosts or decreases these earnings this way.

Dividends are the other major item that decreases the retained earnings number. Such dividends can be paid out as stock or cash. Either type reduces the earnings which are retained. This is because cash dividends come out of the net income ultimately. The greater amount of dividends that a company distributes, the lower amount of earnings it will retain. Dividend accounts are also temporary in nature and are closed out to the earnings which are retained at the end of the accounting period.

Though newly issued shares given out as dividends do not reduce the net income, they must be reconciled on the balance sheet. This is done in the accounts for additional paid in capital on the balance sheet. The earnings which are retained category decreases by the identical amount as this paid in capital column.

Return on Assets (ROA)

Return on Assets is also known by its acronym ROA. It is also sometimes called return on investment. This proves to be an indicator of a company's profitability compared to its aggregate asset base. With ROA, investors and analysts can learn about the big picture of the efficiency of an organization's management compared to the deployment of their company assets which produces earnings.

This is figured up relatively easily. To calculate the ROA, simply take the corporation's annual earnings (or income) and divide these by the firm's total assets. The final answer is the percentage amount of ROA. Other investors will do a slight variation on the formula by adding back in the corporate interest costs to the net income. This allows them to employ operating returns before the net cost of debt.

Thanks to Return on Assets, analysts and investors can learn the amount of earnings that the invested capital or assets produced. Such a figure ranges dramatically from one publically traded company to the next. Every industry's ROA varies substantially. For this reason, analysts prefer to compare and contrast the ROA primarily against the company's own prior figures or alternatively versus another company which is both similar and in the same industry.

Company assets are made up of equity and debt together. The two kinds of financing will jointly fund most corporations' various operations and projects. Because of this Return on Assets number, investors are able to discern the efficiency with which the firm converts its investable money into actual net income. Higher ROA numbers are always considered to be superior. They mean that the corporations can bring in larger revenues and earnings on a smaller amount of investment.

Consider a real world example for clarification. If Imperial Legends Strategy Games produces a net income of $2 million on aggregate underlying assets of $6 million, then it has a Return on Assets of 33.3 percent. Another company Joy Beverages may enjoy the same earnings but against a full asset base of $12 million. Joy Beverages would have an ROA of only 16.7 percent in this scenario. This means that ILSG does twice the job of converting its all around investments into profits as does Joy Beverages. This matters because it speaks volumes of the quality of management. There are not too many managers who are able to turn over significant profits utilizing small investments.

The Return on Assets provides observers with a snapshot and analysis of a business that is distinctive from the usual return on equity formula. Consider that certain industries need to pay more careful attention to the ROA figure than other ones do. In banking, some firms managed to avoid the various banking crises of the last few decades. The ones that sidestepped the problems better than others had something in common. It was that they were more conservative based on the ROA they deployed. The more successful banks did not allow their return on assets numbers to become too unnaturally high. They did this by contemplating the underlying fine details in the loan book. Too many loans that yielded too high a return indicated that management was taking excessive risks. Yet in the business of software development firms, these enterprises are not leveraged, so this ROA comparison is less important.

An important difference separates asset turnover from Return on Assets. Asset turnover specifies that companies have sales which amount to a certain amount per asset dollar on the corporate balance sheet. Conversely, the ROA explains to investors the amount of post tax profit that a firm creates for every $1 of assets it has. This is to say that the ROA compares all of the company earnings relating to the entire resource base the company claims, including both long-term debt and the capital from shareholders. This makes the relevant ROA a strict test of shareholder returns. When companies possess no debt, then their two figures of ROA and ROE Return On Equity will be identical.

Return on Equity (ROE)

Return on equity proves to be a useful measurement for investors considering a given company. This is because it takes into account three important elements of a company's management. This includes profitability, financial leverage, and asset management. Looking at the effectiveness of the management team in handling the three factors gives you as an investor a good picture of the kind of return on equity that you can expect from an investment in such a company.

Return on equity is very easy to calculate. You can figure it up by collecting two pieces of information. You will need the company earnings for a year and the value of the average share holder equity for the same year. Getting the earnings' figure is as simple as looking up the firm's Consolidated Statement of Earnings that they filed with the Securities and Exchange Commission. Alternatively, you might look up the earnings of each of the last four quarters and add them up.

Determining share holder equity is easiest by looking at the company's balance sheet. Share holder equity, which proves to be the difference of total liabilities and total assets, will be listed for you there. Share holder equity is a useful accounting construct that reveals the business assets that they have created. This share holder equity is most commonly listed under book value, or the quantity of the share holders' equities for each share. This is also an accounting book value of a corporation that is more than simply its market value.

To come up with the return on equity, you simply divide the full year's earnings by the average equity for that year. This gives you the return on equity. Companies that produce significant amounts of share holder equity turn out to be solid investments, since initial investors are paid off using the money that the business operations generate. Companies that create substantial returns as compared to the share holder equity reward their stake holders generously by building up significant amounts of assets for each dollar that is invested into the firm. Such enterprises commonly prove to be able to fund their own operations internally, which means that they do not have to issue more diluting shares of stock or take on extra debt to continue operating.

The return on equity can also be utilized to determine if a corporation is a cash generating machine or a cash consuming entity. The return on equity will simply show you this when you compare their actual earnings to the share holder equity. You can learn at almost a glance how much money the company's present assets are producing. As an example, with a twenty percent return on equity, every original dollar put into the company is creating twenty cents of real assets. This is also useful in comparing subsequent cash investments in the company, since the return on equity percentage will demonstrate to you if these extra invested dollars match up to the earlier investments for effectiveness and efficiency.

Return on Investment (ROI)

ROI is the acronym for return on investment. This return on investment is among the most often utilized methods of determining the financial results that will arise from business decisions, investments, and actions. ROI analysis is used to compare and contrast both the timing and amount of investment gains directly with the timing and amount of investment costs. Higher returns on investment signify that the results from investments are positive when you compare them against the costs of such investments.

Over the past couple of decades, this return on investment number has evolved into one of the main measurements in the decision making process of what types of assets and equipment to buy. This includes everything from factory equipment, to service vehicles, to computers. ROI is similarly utilized to determine which budget items, programs, and projects should be both approved and allocated funds. These cover every type of activity from recruiting, to training, to marketing. Finally, return on investment is often employed in choosing which financial investments are performing up to expectations, as with venture capital investments and stock investment portfolios.

Return on investment analysis is actually used for ranking investment returns against their costs. This is done by setting up a percentage or ratio number. With the vast majority of return on investment calculation methods, ROI's that are higher than zero signify that the returns on the investment are higher than the associated expenses with it. As a greater number of investments and business decisions compete for funding anymore, hard choices are increasingly made using the comparison of higher returns on investment. Many companies believe that this yields the better business decision in the end.

There is a downside to relying too heavily on the return on investment as the only consideration for making such business and investment decisions. Return on investment does not tell you anything regarding the anticipated costs and returns and if they will actually work out as forecast. Used alone, return on investment also does not explain the potential elements of risk for a given investment. All that it does is demonstrate how the investment or project returns will compare against the costs, assuming that the investment or project delivers the results that are anticipated or expected. This limitation is not unique to return on investment, but similarly plagues other financial measurements. Because this is the case, intelligent investment and business analysis also relies on the likely results of other return on investment eventualities. Other measurements should also be used along side the return on investment to help measure the risks that accompany the project or investment.

Wise decision makers will demand more from return on investment figures than simply a number. They will require effective suggestions from the person making the return on investment analysis. Among these inputs that they will desire are the means of increasing an ROI's gains, or alternatively the means for improving the ROI through decreasing costs.

Revenue

Revenue refers to the amount of money which firms generate in receivables within a certain time frame. It includes deductions for merchandise which is returned as well as any applicable discounts. This is also known as the gross income or sometimes the "top line" amount. Net income can be figured out by subtracting the costs from the revenue.

Analysts and accountants determine the amount of revenue simply by taking the price for which services and goods sell and multiplying this by the quantity of units or the actual amount which the firm sells. Sometimes revenue is referred to as "REVs."

There are a number of other definitions and synonyms for revenues. Some call it sales in layman's terms. Whatever name businesses and individuals refer to it by, revenue proves to be the total amount of cash which a company garners through its aggregate business activities. The price to sales ratio is one measurement in business that relies on revenues for the denominator. This contrasts with the competing measurement of price to earnings ratio, which utilizes the profits instead for its denominator.

Revenue can be figured up by several different means. It is really up to the method of accounting which companies and corporations choose to employ. With accrual accounting, sales which the firm makes using credit also count among the revenues so long as the customers have taken delivery of the services or goods. This is why investors and analysts must review the company's cash flow statement in order to evaluate how effectively a firm actually collects on the money which its customers owe it.

The other primary form of determining a company's revenues is through cash accounting. This form of accounting utilizes only sales for the revenues' quotient once the money a customer owes has been collected by the firm in question. When a customer gives the money to a corporation or company, the firm recognizes it as a receipt instead of the general category of revenues. Companies can actually have receipts that do not include revenues. This is possible if a customer were to pay for a service in advance of receiving it or for purchased goods which they have not yet received.

Revenue can also be called "top line" since income statements display them first on the report. Analysts then take revenues and deduct the expenses so that they can come up with the "bottom line," which is also called simply profit or alternatively net income.

Many times investors evaluate both a firm's net income and revenues independently of one another so that they can ascertain how strong a business' health really turns out to be. The reason for this is that net income can increase while revenues remain flat. Cost cutting can actually cause this phenomenon. This scenario is not a positive sign for the longer term growth potential for a firm.

Analysts and investors often further subdivide the revenues from a given company or corporation according to the groups which generate the money. Company accountants can also divide up the receipts of the firm into several categories of operating revenues, the core business of the firm's sales, and non-operating revenues that come from secondary sources. Such non-operating variants are typically not recurring or can not be forecast successfully. This is why these are sometimes known as one-time gains or events. Examples of this could be money gained through lawsuits, investment windfalls, or receipts from selling an asset.

Where a government is concerned, revenue refers to the receipts they obtain as a result of fees, taxation, fines, securities sales, transfers, intergovernmental grants, resource rights and mineral rights, or any sales of government assets or state-owned and -run companies which they might make.

In the world of not for profit organizations, such revenues are commonly referred to by the phrase of "gross receipts." Among the components that make up these receipts are donations from companies, foundations, and individuals; investment returns; grants out of governmental agencies and entities; membership dues and fees; and fundraising endeavors.

Royalties

Royalties are payments which owners receive in exchange for the use of their property. This most typically covers natural resources, franchises, patents, and copyrighted works. Royalty payments go to the property in question's legal owner. Individuals who want to utilize the owners' patents, property, franchise, natural resources, or copyrighted works will do so with the intention of creating a revenue stream or realizing a lump sum income. Royalties are typically intended to provide compensation for the licensing of the asset. As such, these arrangements become legally binding.

Much of the time, these royalties are stated in percentage of revenue terms. They can also be arranged to fit a particular scenario or environment. They are often employed as the vehicle for realizing income in instances where the owner, inventor, or natural resource holder wishes to sell the product in question in exchange for payments against future revenues that this activity might create for the third party licensor.

An example of this is Microsoft. The computer software giant earns a royalty from every installation of the internationally standard Windows operating system on almost any computer a manufacturer produces. Such an example relates to creative content, copyrights, and patents.

A royalty could also apply to resources, trade marks, art works, books and published works, copyright materials, franchises, patents, and resource holdings. Even fashion designers are able to charge a royalty to other companies that wish to make use of their designs or names. Authors, production pros, and musical artists also receive this kind of compensation when a firm or individual uses their copyrighted and produced works. Cable and satellite firms pay a royalty to the owner of a television channel so they can offer the most stations in a country.

The oil and gas business is one that is rife with royalties. Companies provide a royalty to a landowner in exchange for permission to gather the natural resources off of their private property. This might amount to so much money per barrel of oil or per cubic foot of natural gas which they extract.

A license agreement is a key component of a royalty. It represents the terms by which the property owner will receive the payments. This clearly and legally explains the restrictions and limitations of the royalty in question. As an example, it would deal with the length of time the agreement will endure, the geographic territorial limitations, and the specific amounts they will pay for the various kinds of products utilized or extracted. These types of license agreements are differently and specifically regulated depending on whether the owner of the resource or property in question is a private individual or the government.

A royalty rate represents the specific amount of payment that must be paid for a given service or product. This will naturally depend on the kind of fee the third party is providing. There are a number of different factors involved in a royalty rate. Among the most frequently cited examples are alternative option availability, rights' exclusivity, the relevant risks involved, technological sustainability, structure of the market demand, and scope of the innovation which the service or product offers.

These terms should not be confused with a royalty trust unit. Such units provide the holder of the unit with a share of the income which the properties a trust owns actually produce. These royalty trusts acquire ownership stakes in cash flows or general operating concerns. The royalty trust itself will own the cash flow or income which the company is generating. They will then pass through this money to the trust royalty unit holders. Such royalty units have often been viewed as positive and desirable investments since the income which the asset creates only becomes subject to individual tax levels. There is no so-called "double taxation" as common stocks dividends experience (on both the company earning the money and then the person receiving it again).

S Corporation

S Corporation refers to the Subchapter S Corporation type of company filing which measures up to certain requirements set by the IRS Internal Revenue Service. This status provides a corporation which possesses a hundred or fewer shareholders all of the advantages of incorporation while also keeping the benefits of only being tax treated like a partnership.

One of the many benefits to this type of incorporation is that it is able to pass all of the company income straight through to the shareholders, thus avoiding the problems of double taxation which are a real issue with shareholders of public companies. There are some particular requirements that must be met to enjoy these advantages. The firm must be domiciled as a domestic corporation. It cannot possess over a hundred shareholders, and it may only count a single class of stock.

Such S Corporations can pass all of their credits, deductions, losses, and any income straight through to the various shareholders. They may then report this loss or income directly via their own personal tax returns. It allows them to pay out their taxes at generally considerably lower individual income tax rates. There are some built in gains on which the S Corporation will pay the taxes at the corporate level, but these are few and far between.

These S Corporations have to be domestically headquartered firms whose shareholders are estates, certain kinds of trusts, and individuals. A corporation, partnership, or non-resident alien can never qualify for this category of shareholder. There are also some financial institutions, domestic international sales firms, and insurance outfits that are not allowed to incorporate as an S Corporation.

There are some significant advantages to establishing an S Corporation. It builds up real creditability with employees, possible customers, investors, and suppliers as it proves the owner is seriously committed to the firm. Employees may also be shareholders in the company, which allows them to enjoy company salaries while also receiving any corporate dividends and distributions which are tax-free as compared to the investment in the company. This is certainly beneficial for morale.

Paying out distributions in the form of dividends or salaries allows the owners to lower the self-employment tax liability at the same time as it creates wage and expense deductions for the firm. Since this S Corporation will not pay any federal taxes at company level, such losses can be utilized to offset other forms of income for the tax returns of the shareholders. It is always helpful to save money on the onerous American corporate income taxes, particularly for new firms. It is another benefit to these companies that the various interests within the corporation can be easily transferred without creating tax liability events and consequences. Complicated accounting rules do not create restrictions nor does the company have to adjust the basis of property either.

Yet there are also a few downsides to establishing a company as an S Corporation. The IRS closely examines any and all distribution payments made to shareholders in the forms of either dividends or salaries to make sure that they are really employees working in the firm. If wages become characterized as dividends, then the company will lose its compensation paid deduction. Should dividends be characterized as wages, then the company will pay a greater amount of employment taxes. It is also easy for mistakes to be made in the areas of notification, consent, election, filing requirements, or stock ownership requirements that lead to the S Corporation being untimely terminated. There is considerable money and time investment in such a corporate structuring as well.

The owner will have to begin by filling in and filing articles of incorporation to the Secretary of State, get a registered agent on board for the company, and pay any relevant fees and costs involved. Owners often have to pay yearly reporting fees and franchise taxes along with ongoing types of fees. These may be inexpensive, but they can still be deducted under the cost of doing business category. Even if the investors possess non-voting shares of stock in this form of corporate structuring, they will still get distribution and dividend rights.

Sales Tax

Sales Tax refers to a government imposed tax on consumption of both services and goods. Traditional sales taxes are collected at the appropriate points of sale. The retailers gather the money which they then pass on to the appropriate governmental agency. Businesses are also liable to pay such sales taxes to the relevant jurisdiction (state or local government) if they have what is known as a nexus in that jurisdiction. This could be an employee, physical office location, presence of some other type, or an affiliate. The laws of the jurisdiction in question determine which of these criteria apply in determining business residence.

Conventional forms of sales taxes only become charged to or are payable by the final seller of a service or a good. Since the overwhelming numbers of goods in today's economies go through a range of manufacturing points and stages, they become a part and parcel of many different entities' operations. This means that great quantities of paper work must be kept and filed in order to determine the end seller who will be finally liable for the sales taxes owed.

As an example to better understand the dilemma this poses, consider a sheep farmer. The farmer sells his wool to a firm which makes yarn. The yarn maker would be responsible for the sales tax unless it is able to gain a resale certificate from the responsible governmental agency. This certificate must declare that the yarn maker is not the final user. Next, the yarn maker will sell its yarn products to a clothing manufacturer. This manufacturer also has to get such a resale certificate. The clothing maker then sells its wooly sweater to an outlet store. It is this outlet store that must charge sales tax to its customers besides the price of the sweater.

The various jurisdictions all charge their own sales tax rates. This can be confusing as they are also overlapping on one another. In some localities, the state, the county, and even the municipality (city or town) will all levy their individual sales tax amounts.

The nexus point raises an often-confusing set of issues for many businesses. They are only resident to a particular jurisdiction (state or locality) if the government there defines the nexus in a way that will call them resident for business purposes. Such a nexus is defined usually by the criteria of physical presence. Such a presence may not only be limited to maintaining a warehouse, factory, or office though.

It could mean that a company which has an employee who lives in the state will be considered to have a nexus. Partner websites (which direct traffic over to a business' websites in exchange for cash payments), or affiliates, can also be considered to be part of a nexus. This illustrates the difficulties encountered between sales tax collection and the sprawling and growing arena of e-commerce. Bigger states like New York have enacted what they call "Amazon laws." These make all internet retailers selling goods to customers in their states pay the sales tax, regardless of whether or not they maintain a physical presence in the state. The laws were named for the giant Internet retailers like Amazon.com.

Sales taxes usually work on a percentage basis of the goods' prices. As an example, states could collect a five percent sales tax, while the county gets two percent, and the city one percent. This would mean the residents in that given city of the county would have to pay a total sales tax of eight percent.

Many necessary items can be exempt from these taxes to help the lower income earners. This includes food as well as sometimes clothing items which cost under $200 in total. Other taxes specially levied on only certain products are called excise taxes. Many of these the states refer to as "sin taxes." In essence, this kind of excise tax would cover cigarettes and alcohol, which have been historically labeled by the churches as sins. New York State levies a $4.35 excise (and "sin") tax on every pack of cigarettes, as of 2016.

Seller Financing

Seller Financing turns out to be a loan that a business or property seller offers to the buyer. When seller financing is provided, the buyer generally gives a down payment amount to the seller. The balance of the purchase price is paid to them using installment payments that are typically monthly. This is accomplished at a certain time of the month and for an interest rate that the two parties agree to, until the loan itself has been completely paid back.

Seller provided financing is not governed by any regulatory body or set of laws. Because this is the case, for a seller and a buyer both to protect their interests, a purchase agreement that is legally enforceable in a court of law needs to be drafted by an attorney. The two parties, buyer and seller, can then sign this agreement to make the transaction fully legal.

There are many benefits offered in pursuing seller financing. Both the seller and the buyer of a real estate property can realize significant closing cost savings that typically amount to thousands of dollars. The interest rate, loan conditions, and repayment schedule may also be negotiated with seller financing. Borrowers are not forced to go through a loan qualification process via a loan officer or underwriter either. Private Mortgage Insurance is also not required to be paid. Buyers are able to make specific requests as part of the condition of buying the property too, like having the appliances included in the sale.

Sellers also receive benefits when they provide seller financing. They might end up with a better return on the investment if they get their equity payments with interest. They similarly might be capable of obtaining a better selling price and interest rate. They could choose to sell the property in "as is" condition, meaning that they will not be required to cover the costs of any repairs that the property needs. Finally, the seller is capable of picking out the security documents that he or she believes best serve the interests of getting the loan paid off, such as deeds of trust, mortgages, or land sales documents.

There are some downsides to seller financing that should be carefully considered as well. While the buyer might make the payments on time, the seller could choose to not pay off more senior financing on the property, which would cause the property to be foreclosed on. Besides this, the buyer might not be given the title to the property if there are problems tying up the property title, even when he or she paid off the loan as per the agreement. The buyer also does not benefit from the safeguards offered by mortgage insurance, home inspections, or appraisals that will ensure that he or she is not paying too high a price for the house.

The seller also encounters risks with seller financing. If the seller does not get an accurate picture of the buyer's ability to pay for the property, then he or she might suffer through a foreclosure. This foreclosure can require as long as a year to complete. Finally, the seller might accept a smaller down payment and then find that the buyer later abandons the property and payments since he or she puts a limited investment into the property.

Small Business

Small Business refers to any company that has a maximum of 500 employees, per the definition set by the United States' own SBA Small Business Administration. According to this definition of small business, the majority of companies within the United States are actually small businesses. SBA states that 99.7 percent of the around six million U.S.-based business with employees fall into this category. In point of fact, fully eighty percent of all American businesses employ less than ten people. Yet despite this, the larger corporations still employ a greater share of the American work force.

Yet U.S. Presidents often refer to statistics for small businesses that include those who employ only under 50 workers. This is why when someone (like a politician for example) mentions small businesses, one should understand to which definition of small they are referring. Yet qualifying for the various federal programs does not clarify the situation of what a small business is either. This is because the legal standard of this status will vary per each and every industry.

It always helps to consider some real life examples of a challenging concept in order to better grasp it. Consider the definitions set by the BLS Bureau of Labor Statistics. According to their industry by industry cutoffs, "cookie and cracker makers" have a maximum threshold for small businesses classification of as many as 750 employees. Yet in the "cereal manufacturing business" or for those firms engaged in "specialty canning" operations the limit is 1,000 workers. "Smaller oil refiners" are allowed to employ as many as 1,500 workers to qualify for the designation. Still other industries do not possess a hard and fast limit to the numbers of employees if their average company receipts in dollars are under a certain threshold limit. With "egg or chicken producers," they are allowed to realize as much as $12.5 million yearly in receipts and still be considered as a small business under the all-important guidelines of the SBA.

Understanding whether or not they are a smaller business is similarly important because of Obama-care regulations and rules. Provisions for these companies in the health care laws will vary. Smaller businesses who employ under 25 employees with average annual wages of less than

$50,000 will receive subsidies. Those employers who maintain staffs of less than 50 employees however are exempted from all of the penalties for not offering standard health care coverage to their workers.

Forbes magazine publishes a list called the "Small Giants." In this ranking, they reveal the best of the not so big companies every year. These top ten recipients of this ranking for the year 2017 were as follows: Barefoot Books with 20 employees, Basecamp with 52 employees, Dansko with 150 employees, Dutch Brothers Coffee with 170 employees, Essential Ingredients with 66 employees, Fresh Books with 248 employees, Fusion OEM with 55 employees, Galileo Learning with 80 employees, GYK Antler with 85 employees, and H.B. McClure with 500 employees.

The criteria to be considered a small business by Forbes are obviously quite different from the various departments of the government, though it does seem to agree with the Small Business Administration limit of 500 employees or less. Forbes says about these respected companies that they opted to be great firms instead of big ones.

Stagflation

Stagflation refers to the simultaneous problems of high unemployment, stagnated economic growth, and persistently high inflation. It is an unlikely scenario, as slowing economies typically reduce demand sufficiently in order to keep higher prices in check. When workers lose their jobs, they purchase less. Businesses are then usually forced to reduce their prices in order to convince remaining customers to buy. It is this typically slower growth in market economies that prevents inflation from running away.

Stagflation policies typically lead to hyperinflation. Central banks that expand the country's money supply as the national supply is restricted do so by printing up additional currency. Monetary policies then create additional credit. This increases demand from consumers. It is the simultaneous supply restrictions that keep companies from producing enough to keep up with the rising demand.

Such a scenario happened in Zimbabwe back in 2004. Their government printed up so much currency that it pushed well beyond stagflation and evolved into ruinous hyperinflation. A stagflation in the United States only transpired in the 1970s. At the time the U.S. government expanded its dollars significantly to try to create additional economic growth. While they did this, President Nixon's wage price controls severely limited business-produced supplies.

The name stagflation actually comes from the 1973 to 1975 era recession. In those six consecutive quarters, the U.S. GDP shrank in size. Inflation literally tripled in 1973 alone, jumping from a relatively tame 3.4% to 9.6%. In the time between February of 1974 and April of 1975, inflation stubbornly remained between 10% and 12%.

Experts today look back at the 1973 Arab-led oil embargo as the crisis that triggered first oil price inflation. At this time, OPEC nations drastically cut their oil exports to the United States, forcing prices to quadruple. The inflation from oil spread to many other parts of the economy dependent on oil and gasoline, such as shipping, rail, and trucking.

The mild recession of 1970 was the precursor to the problems. President

Richard Nixon in his bid to be re-elected introduced as series of four fiscal and monetary economic policies that helped to ensure he won. These unfortunately also created the conditions for stagflation a few years later.

Nixon's first mistake was the start of wage and price controls. U.S. businesses were unable to raise their final prices even as import costs were soaring. They could only respond by reducing costs via worker layoffs. That boosted unemployment and further slowed economic growth by lowering demand. Nixon secondly took the U.S. off the gold standard to stop an international run on American gold reserves. This only crushed the value of the dollar and created still higher import prices and yet more inflation.

In order to fight off the inflation, the Federal Reserve had no choice but to continue raising interest rates. These reached their peak of 20% by 1979. Because the Fed did this in an up and down motion, businesses became confused and chose to keep up higher prices.

Though stagflation has not yet reoccurred in the U.S., Americans became worried it might again in 2011. The Fed had begun employing aggressive expansive monetary policies to save the U.S. economy from the grips of the 2008 financial crisis and Great Recession. This caused many to fear that high inflation would return. The economy only grew at low levels form 1% to 2% at this time.

Economists observed stagflation was a viable risk if inflation rose while the economy continued to struggle. Instead, deflation became the serious concern of the day. Massive increases in global liquidity were used to try to fight off this opposite kind of problem.

Subsidies

Subsidies are types of financial support or aid which a government or organization extends out to an economic industry, institution, individual, or business. These are done for the purpose of fostering particular economic or even social policies. The government is the most common provider of this type of assistance, but such support can also come from Non Governmental Organizations.

Such grants can be derived from a number of different forms of aid. These include indirect help as with insurance, tax breaks, accelerated depreciation, lower interest loans, and rent rebates. They can also be direct assistance in the form of interest-free loans or outright grants of cash or other assets. The ultimate goal of such a subsidy is to alleviate a form of financial burden. They are often deemed to be to the overall advantage of the entire public and not a specific person, business, or interest group by the very nature of the group receiving the help.

Such a subsidy grant is often regarded by governments as privileges. This is because they help with a relevant burden which was somehow unfairly levied on the receiver. They could also encourage a certain behavior or ultimate result through delivering financial support, as with farming subsidies to encourage domestic agriculture.

In general, such a subsidy will typically benefit a segment of an industry within a national economy. These can be employed to help out markets which are suffering by reducing perceived burdens from which they struggle. They might also boost additional development within an industry or research line via offering financial support for the efforts and work. Many times, these areas of production or research do not receive the necessary assistance which they require from the workings of the mainstream economy. Sometimes they are even outright disadvantaged by the actions undertaken by rival economies and nations.

There are two principal forms of subsidy aid as mentioned previously. These are direct and indirect subsidies. The direct form encompasses payments specifically directed to a certain industry or a given group. Cash is usually the medium of exchange offered to the receiving parties.

With indirect forms of a subsidy, there is no preset monetary value at which the help is limited or specified when it is provided to the individual, businesses, or industry. This might involve special goods or services which are price reduced. It could also include another form of government support to the given industry. It helps the much needed items to be bought at under the present market cost. This level of savings can vary greatly depending on the amount of the given organizations' participation in the program.

Governments, in particular the American Federal and European Union governments, provide many different types of subsidies. These are not only limited to help for domestic industry or farmers. They can also involve welfare and social assistance as with payments, student loans, grants, housing loans, and a farm subsidy. When domestic farming struggles to endure within the intensely competitive international farming arena because of their lower prices of other countries' farms, the U.S. or EU government bodies may provide actual cash subsidies to the farmers in order for them to afford to sell their products at the lower market rates. The intended goal is that they will still reap financial rewards sufficient to justify continuing to farm with this outright monetary assistance.

More recently, the government has become involved with health care subsidy to private citizens on an individual and family level. The Affordable Care Act of the U.S. allows its citizens to receive subsidies dependent on their size and income of the relevant household. Such a subsidy is intended to reduce the enormous out of pocket expenses associated with high health care premiums and co-payments for households which earn under a minimum income threshold. The funds of the subsidies go directly to the insurance company in question. This reduces the amount of money which the insurance company requires from the individual or household.

Supply and Demand

Supply and Demand refers to a law that attempts to explain the interaction between the forces involving a resource or good's demand and available supply. It is this law that determines how much of a given product will be supplied and demanded at a certain price. When supply is low and demand is high, price tends to go up, while a higher supply and lower demand leads to falling prices.

This is considered to be a foundational economic law. It impacts the overwhelming majority of economic principles in some way. Supply and demand vie with one another as the market pricing attempts to reach equilibrium. There are many factors impacting both demand and supply, which means that there is no single way that they can affect the prices of the underlying commodity or goods in question. It is this equilibrium price, or market clearing price, that determines the set price for which producers will be able to sell off all of the units they can produce and at which the buyers will be able purchase as much as they want.

It always helps to look at a concrete example when considering a highly complicated topic like this one. If a business rolls out a new product, it may choose to start with a higher price. The problem will be that only a few consumers will purchase it at these higher prices. Because the business has large warehouses stocked with the new product, they will reduce the price to move their inventory. Demand will rise apace, yet now the business' supply diminishes. The company will then raise the price back part of the way to where it originally was now until it achieves the ideal price to balance out both consumer demands with its own available supplies of the product in question.

In the real world scenarios, there is rarely only one company producing a given good or resource though. This means that the supply will depend on a range of competing factors. Costs of production, capacity of production, and the quantity of direct competitors will all impact the amount of supply that the producers can prepare. There are other side factors which include weather, availability of sometimes scarce raw materials, and dependability of the various supply chains that also have an impact on available supplies ultimately.

Demand is a more straightforward concept. It often comes down to the straight up cost of a good and the quality which is produced. There will also be close substitutes which are available, price shifts, and advertising campaigns that all have an impact on the actual demand. When video game machine prices decrease, the games (on the system) demand may rise as a greater number of individuals purchase the game machine and demand related games to play.

This law of supply and demand applies to more than simply prices. It can also be utilized to effectively explain various forms of other economic activities. One of these is that when unemployment proves to be higher, the supply of available workers is elevated. Businesses will respond by reducing wages to match the supply of workers. At the same time, if unemployment is lower, the available supply of employees will also be lower. This leads to companies providing higher salaries in order to attract top employees to their firms. This also explains stock market prices. The laws of supply and demand will similarly aid in describing why a stock price rises or falls on any given trading day.

SWIFT

SWIFT Network is the internationally relied upon system for transferring money. It underlies the overwhelming majority of security and international money transfers. This vast network for financial messaging is employed by financial institutions such as banks to rapidly, securely, and accurately receive and send information that includes instructions for money transfers. In any given day, almost 10,000 different member institutions of the SWIFT system deploy around 24 million unique financial messages throughout this truly impressive worldwide network.

SWIFT is an acronym that actually means the Society for Worldwide Interbank Financial Telecommunications. This messaging network securely transmits both instructions and sensitive information for financial institutions using a standardized operating system of codes. In order for this amazing system to work, SWIFT itself gives a one of a kind identification code to every financial institution in the world which participates. These codes are comprised of either 11 or eight characters. Names for this code range from SWIFT Code and SWIFT ID to BIC bank identifier code and ISO 9362 code. It should not be confused with the similar yet still different IBAN International Bank Account Number.

An example of one such SWIFT code for a member institution is helpful to look at in order to better understand how SWIFT puts these identifiers together. Consider UniCredit Banca based in Milan, Italy. The eight character SWFT code for UniCredit Banca proves to be UNCRITMM, which stands for UNI CREDIT ITALY Milan (Milan is identified with two Ms). SWIFT always takes the first four letters from the institution's name, making up the institute code. The second two letters are the national code. The next two characters represent the city location code. Another optional three characters stand for the individual branch within a large bank, as in using ZZZ to represent a particular branch location.

Thought SWIFT is undoubtedly a powerful institution and system in the world today, it does not ever hold or touch any securities or cash. It also never manages accounts for clients. Instead it is simply a financial transaction messaging system. Yet this service is critical in today's fast moving world of finance, business, and banking.

This is because the world before SWIFT was a ponderous place in which to do international wire and bank transfers. Before the advent of SWIFT, there was only the Telex system to send the international wire transfer message confirmations. Telex was fraught with problems. Among these were it had security issues, was terribly slow, and lacked a unifying system of standardized codes as SWIFT possesses for naming both the banks and the types of financial transactions being conducted.

A sender with Telex was forced to detail out each and every transaction utilizing sentences that had to be first interpreted then executed by the receivers on the other end. As these people often spoke other languages besides the lingua franca English, it led to countless human errors and mistakes in ultimate transmission.

In order to get around these many problems, seven of the biggest international financial institutions came together to create a cooperative society and system whose entire reason of being was to run a global financial network with would relay such critical financial messages utilizing both speedy and secure means. It only took SWIFT three years to grow rapidly from the original seven founding banks to 230 banks in five nations.

Despite the fact that competing financial messaging services such as FedWire, CHIPS, and Ripple exist, SWIFT has continued to enjoy its now-dominant market share and position. Many observers have noted that this stems in large part from the way it constantly comes up with newer message codes for various financial transactions.

Besides the simplified payment instructions SWIFT arose to deliver, the network additionally delivers messages for a significant and broad-based number of treasury and security transactions throughout the globe. Almost half of the SWIFT worldwide traffic still stems from the traditional heart of the network, the payment messages. An impressive 43 percent today pertain to security transactions. The other under ten percent deals with treasury transactions.

SWIFT has continued to evolve and grow into other related businesses. Today it also deploys its lengthy data maintenance history to deliver reference data, business intelligence, and compliance information services. An area it is addressing now is the delivery and implementation of software automation for its financial transaction messaging system. The company has successfully created and tested such software, but its use and deployment will come at a higher cost to participating banks.

Takeover

A takeover is a corporate event where a company chooses to acquire another firm in an effort to gain full control over the target firm in question. They often do this by buying a majority percentage of the firm's outstanding shares.

If such a move is successful, the company which is acquiring the target obtains control over and responsibility for its target firm's holdings, operations, and debts. If the target firm proves to be a publically traded stock company, then the company which is acquiring must place an offer to buy all of the outstanding shares of the target company.

There are several different types of takeovers in the world of business. Welcome takeovers are those like mergers and acquisitions. They typically proceed calmly as the two companies involved in the situation consider it to be a positive end scenario for all. The opposite type of takeover is known as hostile or unwelcome takeover. These often turn out to be aggressive since the receiving party does not willingly or voluntarily participate or even give its consent.

Hostile takeovers are exactly like they sound. The firm which is doing the acquiring may resort to underhanded tactics. Some of thee include a dawn raid. In this clever maneuver, a predatory firm purchases a large portion of the company's stock at the immediate opening of the market. This leads to a target firm losing control over its company before it even is aware of what is occurring. The target company's management and board of directors could choose to staunchly resist these unsolicited efforts via such defenses as taking a poison pill. Poison pills are where the shareholders of the target firm buy additional shares at a discounted price in order to dilute the holdings of the acquirer, causing the takeover to become potentially prohibitively expensive.

There are various reasons that a company would pursue a takeover. This is practically the same end result as an acquisition. Companies can perform like a bidder by attempting to build up their market share or create larger economies of scale which will aid the company in lowering its overhead so that it can boost its profits.

Firms which are the most attractive types of takeover targets are those which possess a unique advantage with a specific service or unique product. This includes smaller firms with profitable services or products but inadequate financing. Another similar company that is geographically near might decide that by combining their forces they could boost efficiency. Other examples are companies which are viable but that have to pay too high an interest on their debt which might be effectively refinanced for a better rate if a bigger and more powerful firm with superior credit ratings acquired it.

A few years ago, ConAgra tried to engage in a friendly takeover to acquire competitor Ralcorp. As the first advances were spurned, ConAgra demonstrated it would instead go the route of a hostile takeover. Ralcorp retaliated by instituting a form of poison pill strategy. ConAgra was not to be so easily outmaneuvered. They upped the ante by proffering $94 a share. This amounted to significantly more than the going rate of $65 per share for Ralcorp at the time the initial acquisition talks began.

Ralcorp declined and beat back the hostile attempts; though in the end the two companies came back to the negotiating table the next year. Eventually the deal succeeded via a friendly strategy as ConAgra paid $90 per share. At this point and time, Ralcorp had finished spinning off its division Post Cereal. This meant that the final price per share offering from ConAgra amounted to substantially more than the prior year's original offer.

Tax Bracket

A tax bracket refers to a certain income range against which the government levies a specific income tax rate. With the majority of income taxing systems in the world today, lower incomes fall under lower income rates tax brackets. At the same time, higher incomes are taxed at greater rates. The idea behind such brackets is to ensure that a progressive income tax system remains in place.

In the tax year for 2016, the Internal Revenue Service decreed there would be seven different tax brackets. Each of these offers minute variations on the theme for married filers, single filers, and head of household filers. This led to the de facto establishment of 21 real tax brackets for the tax year.

Importantly, the tax bracket thresholds did increase a little for tax year 2016. As an example, the lowest bracket proves to be under $9,325 for individual taxpayers, which was raised from $9,275 back in tax year 2015. The highest possible tax bracket for this tax year 2016 is now $418,041, itself raised from the 2015 tax bracket high of $415,051. This changes every year, so it is important to consult the IRS.gov website for current information annually.

Those individuals whose incomes are under the minimum bracket of $9,275 have income which is taxed according to the minimum 10 percent tax rate. For everyone filing singly who earns over this amount, the first $9,275 becomes taxed at the rate of 10 percent. Earnings which exceed this on up to $37,650 are then taxed at 15 percent. From $37,650 to $91,150 the earnings become taxed at a steeper 25 percent rate. Income beyond the $91,150 is taxed at still higher rates. This means that many tax filers actually fall into several tax brackets and not only the first one.

The tax bracket should never be confused with the tax rate. Tax rates represent the actual percentage at which the given income becomes taxed. All tax brackets possess their own unique tax rates. Many people simplify and call their tax rates the bracket at which they are taxed as if they were identical. The comparison is not valid since the majority of Americans have earnings which fall into more than one tax bracket.

An example helps to make the tax bracket concept clearer. Consider an individual who earns a hefty $500,000 every year. At such a lofty level as this, the filer will have income that goes into each of the single filing tax brackets. This means the person will pay many different tax rates (seven in fact). This will depend on which part of his or her income is being considered. On all earnings which exceed $406,751 the tax rate will be a punishing 39.6 percent. On the initial $9,075, the rate will merely be the 10 percent rate of the first tax bracket. This means that the actual tax rate of such an individual will lie somewhere in the middle of the two tax rate extremes of 10 percent and 39.6 percent, making it closer to 25 to 35 percent effectively.

The opposite of such a progressive income tax system as this one is a flat tax system. In these taxing arrangements, every individual becomes taxed on all income at the identical rate. It does not matter how much people make in this type of tax setup.

Those analysts and economists in favor of the tax bracket system in particular and progressive tax systems in general argue that the people who make higher incomes can bear a heavier taxing burden and still enjoy a comfortable, high standard of living. Lower income earners will struggle to cover their basic human needs at any tax rate.

The other argument is that such a system will cushion and stabilize against losses in after tax income. The reason is because a real salary decrease becomes counterbalanced out by a drop in the effective tax rate. In this way, people who suffered a pay cut would feel the blow to their post-tax income less severely since the tax rates would drop alongside the income decline.

It is worth noting that such tax brackets do not only apply to individuals who file their income taxes. The IRS also sets the rates and brackets for trusts, companies, and corporations. They adjust both these and the personal tax brackets for the impacts of inflation from time to time.

Tax Credits

Tax credits refer to different sums of money which taxpayers may deduct from their total tax bill that they owe the federal, state, or local government. The amount of a given tax credit will naturally depend on the type of credit involved.

Some kinds of credits accrue to businesses or individuals who operate (or live) in particular locales, industry segments, or specific classifications. These credits are different from exemptions and deductions that lower the amount of income the IRS considers to be taxable. Instead, a tax credit will actually decrease the amount of tax which the business or individual owes.

Governments often provide such tax credits to foster certain patterns of behavior and actions. This could be to lower the aggregate cost for certain taxpayers' housing, or for replacing appliances which are older with newer and more efficiently operating appliances.

Generally speaking, such tax credits prove to be more beneficial than an exemption or deduction since they diminish the amount of taxes the entity or individual must pay on a dollar for dollar basis. These other types of expenses and exemptions do lower the ultimate tax liability. Their limitation is that they only reduce this based on the marginal tax rate of the individual or business. This means that those individuals who are considered to be a member of the 15 percent tax bracket only receive 15 cents in tax savings for each marginal tax dollar deduction. On the other hand, the credit decreases such tax liabilities by a whole dollar.

These credits can be broken down into refundable, partially refundable, or nonrefundable tax credits. Refundable credits prove to be the most helpful form since they are refundable in their entirety. No matter how high (or low) the tax liability or income of particular taxpayers may be they will receive the full dollar credit amount. This is still the case even when such a refundable tax credit decreases the tax liability to under $0. In such a scenario, the taxpayers will receive a negative tax liability, which the IRS calls a refund.

Per the year 2016, the most typical refundable tax credit remains the EITC

Earned Income Tax Credit. There are similarly other types of refundable tax credits which taxpayers may claim for health care insurance and coverage, for educational expenses and costs, and for raising children.

Other tax credits may be partially refundable. This means that they can reduce taxable income and also decrease the individuals' (or businesses') tax liability. In 2016, a partially refundable form of tax credit proved to be the American Opportunity Tax Credit. When taxpayers manage to lower their liabilities to below zero and still have part of the $2,500 (as of 2016) tax deduction remaining, they may apply 40 percent of what is left as a refundable credit.

The final type of such a credit is the nonrefundable tax credit. These the taxpayers may deduct directly from the liability of taxes all the way to the point where the liability then equals zero. The remaining nonrefundable tax credit can not be deployed to take refunds. These types of credits have a negative effect on lower income taxpayers, since they can not gain the full benefit from the credit amount. Such credits which are nonrefundable will only be valid for the particular reporting year too. They also expire once the return has been filed and can not carry forward to future years. Specific examples of such nonrefundable tax credits for 2016 include raising children, adoptions benefits, realizing foreign income, and paying interest on mortgage.

Tax Deductions

Tax Deductions prove to be a legal method for reducing income which the taxing authorities consider to be taxable. They typically arise because of expenses, especially such costs as taxpayers or businesses experience in the course of producing income or earning profits. This differs from exemptions and credits as both exemptions and deductions actually reduce the amount of income which can be taxed, while the credits applied actually reduce the total tax individuals and business will have to pay.

Two categories into which tax professionals often divide tax deductions are above the line and below the line. Above the line deductions benefit all taxpayers regardless of how much income they earn. Below the line ones only provide value if they surpass the individual taxpayers' standard deductions. For 2016, this deduction turned out to be $6,400 for single taxpayers without families or dependents.

Tax deductions also differ according to business and personal types. For the United States, (as well as most business taxing jurisdictions), businesses may take both trade and business expenses off of their taxable income. These allowances vary widely from one type to another and are often restricted. In order to be permissible, said expenses have to be realized in the operations of the business on an activity the owners undertake in an effort to make profits.

Cost of goods sold is a nearly universally accepted tax deduction for most every system of income tax regardless of the jurisdiction. This reduces the gross income, and tax authorities typically consider it to be an expense. In the United States, the Internal Revenue Service permits "all the ordinary and necessary expenses paid or incurred during the taxable year in carrying on any trade or business" as typical business tax deductions. These will be governed by any applicable limitations, enhancements, and qualifications.

Limitations do exist with regards to these types of business deductions. This is the case even though the necessary expenses may pertain directly to the business in question. Some of these limitations apply to activities which include lobbying expenditures, key employees' compensation packages, the use of vehicles, and entertainment related to the business. Besides this, deductions which exceed the income of one enterprise can not necessarily offset income earned in other ventures. The U.S. limits those deductions from one passive activity to being used against income from another such passive activity.

Depreciation is another key tax deduction which the U.S. permits businesses and sole proprietors. This mechanism for cost recovery happens through deductions in the form of depreciation. It applies to most any tangible asset. The IRS permits such depreciation throughout the potential useful life of the asset, which they estimate.

The government assigns most depreciation (useful life) time-frames using the nature and utilization of such assets and the type of business as their guidelines. For example, they may allow three years of depreciation for tax deductions on a laptop or desktop computer. This means that the cost of the purchase can be divided by three and each resulting third of the price may be used as a specific tax deduction for three consecutive years.

Personal deductions are the other principal type of tax deductions. These pertain to individual taxpayers. Some intrinsically personal goods, costs, or services may be deducted from taxable income, per the IRS. The standard and set allowance for taxpayers and also some of their family members or dependents which they support is determined by the Internal Revenue Service and varies most every year.

The IRS calls these personal exemptions. In the United Kingdom and other British English-speaking jurisdictions throughout the world, these are known as personal allowances. In both types of systems, such exemptions and allowances become reduced and finally eliminated for those married couples or individuals whose income surpasses preset maximum levels.

Among the types of personal exemptions (which the U.S. and many other systems allow) are property taxes and local or state income taxes paid, medical costs, primary home loan interest charges, contributions to charitable organizations, contributions to either health savings or retirement savings plans, and some educational costs or interest paid on education-related student loans. The U.S. and Britain also allow payments to other individuals to become deducible in many cases, such as with child support or alimony.

Tax Exemptions

Tax exemptions are special monetary exemptions that decrease the amount of income which is taxable. This can take the form of full tax exempt status that delivers 100 percent relief from a certain form of taxes, partial tax on certain items, or reduced tax rates and bills. Tax exemption can refer to particular groups such as charitable outfits (who receive exemption from income taxes and property taxes), multi-jurisdictional businesses or individuals, and even military veterans.

The phrase tax exemption is commonly utilized to refer to specific scenarios where the law lowers the amount of income that would fall under the taxable label otherwise. With the American Internal Revenue Service, there are two kinds of exemptions which are available to individuals. One example of a tax exemption concerns the decrease in taxes the IRS gives for any dependent children who are under age 18 (who actually live with the head of household income tax filer).

For the year 2015, the Internal Revenue Service permitted individuals who were filing taxes to receive a $4,000 exemption on every one of their permitted tax exemptions. This simply means that any individuals paying taxes who count on three permissible exemptions are able to deduct fully $12,000 off of their taxable income level.

In the cases where they make a higher amount than an IRS pre-determined threshold, the amount in tax exemptions which they are able to utilize becomes phased out slowly and finally eliminated completely. For the tax year 2015, those individuals filing taxes who earned in excess of $258,250, as well as those married filing jointly couples who earned more than $309,900, received a lower amount for their exemptions. This complicated sliding scale with seemingly random numbers in place is all part of the reason why observers claim the American tax system is outdated and overly complex.

There is an important caveat for individuals filing taxes. They can not claim their own personal exemption when someone else claims them as a dependent on their tax return. This is one of the elements that separate exemptions from deductions in the world of tax terminology. Each individual filing is permitted to claim his or her personal deduction.

Looking at a real world example helps to clarify the complicated rules. Young college students who have a job while they go to school will typically be claimed by their parents like a dependent on the parents' income tax return. Since the parents are claiming them as a dependent, the students are not permitted to claim their own personal exemption. They can take the standard deduction however. This means that the students who earn $13,000 will be allowed to take the $6,300 standard deduction. This lowers their taxable income to $6,700. If their parents did not claim them, it would mean they were able to also claim the personal exemption, which would reduce their taxable earnings down to $2,700 (derived by subtracting the $4,000 exemption amount from $6,700).

In the majority of cases, individuals who file are also able to obtain a personal deduction for their husbands or wives. This does not apply if the spouse turns out to be claimed by their parents as a dependent on the parents' tax return.

There are many scenarios where the dependents of an income tax filer prove to be minor aged children of the primary taxpayer. Regardless of this fact, individuals who pay their taxes may also have other kinds of dependents they can claim for exemption purposes against their income. These dependents are typically relatives of the payer in question, such as a child, parent, sister, brother, uncle, or aunt. They must be truly dependent on the person paying the taxes in order to live for the IRS to accept them as dependents for income tax filing purposes.

It is possible for a person to have no tax liability whatsoever thanks to the combination of personal deductions, personal tax exemptions, and exemptions and deductions for his or her dependents. When this is the case, these individuals are allowed to request an official exemption from withholding tax from their employers. When they do so, their payroll department will only withhold Social Security and Medicare contributions (but not income tax contributions) from their paychecks.

Tax Rates

Tax Rates refer to the percentage of their income that corporations or individuals will have to pay in taxes to their governing authority or authorities. In the United States, this proves to be the percentage rate that both the federal government and many state governments assess against the taxable income of an individual or the earnings of a corporation. In the U.S., the system utilized is a progressive tax system. This simply means that as the amount of taxable income rises, so will the percentage rate at which taxes are levied on the income or earnings.

Another way of looking at the Tax Rate is that it is the percentage rate that a company or individuals owe form their respective earnings or income. They must pay this to at least the central authority (federal government in the United States), sometimes the state government (or provincial government), and occasionally the municipal governments as well (counties or cities). This makes the tax burden extremely high on these residents and companies. It explains why as much as more than half of earnings or income can be easily taxed in the United States today.

Another feature of these tax rates in progressive systems like the U.S. is that the tax rates are further grouped into tax brackets. There are seven of these brackets. In each of the brackets, the dollar threshold depends on the filer status. These could be single, head of household, married filing jointly, or married filing separately. The two most common statuses for tax filing are single and married filing jointly.

The seven tax brackets include 10 percent, 15 percent, 25 percent, 28 percent, 33 percent, 35 percent, and 39.6 percent. Every tax payer falls into one of these categories in the U.S. As the individuals' incomes rise, so too does their tax bracket. This means that those who make the most money should in theory pay the most taxes. Yet the way it works is that on the particular income above each threshold, they pay that specific tax rate.

As an example, consider the year 2016. Those individuals who were single filers and earned $450,000 would pay the largest bracket rate of 39.6 percent on only their income in excess of $415,050. On each lower bracket amount, they would be levied the appropriate tax rates on the money earned in that bracket.

For their first $9,275 in income, they would pay 10 percent on this. On the next income up to $37,650, they would be assessed 15 percent. The money from that point up to $91,900 would be levied at 25 percent. The next amount of money up to $190,150 would be assessed taxes at the rate of 28 percent. Money earned up to $413,350 taxes at 33 percent. To $415,050 pays at 35 percent. The remaining money up to the total income of $450,000 would be taxed at 39.6 percent, the top income tax bracket.

If the people were married filing jointly, the bracket threshold amounts would be higher in the example above. For their first $18,650 in income, they would pay 10 percent on this. On the next income up to $75,900, they would be assessed 15 percent. The money from that point up to $151,900 would be levied at 25 percent. The next amount of money up to $231,450 would be assessed taxes at the rate of 28 percent. Money earned up to $413,350 taxes at 33 percent. The remaining money up to the total income of $450,000 would be taxed at 35 percent. If they had earnings above the $466,951 threshold maximum tax bracket income level, this would be assessed at the the top income tax bracket of 39.6 percent.

If this sounds like a complicated and confusing mess, that is because it is. It explains why the United States requires over a million employees at the Internal Revenue Service alone to keep up with the most complicated tax systems in the history of the world.

Tax Refund

A Tax Refund refers to money which the IRS Internal Revenue Service gives back to a tax payer for overpayment of their taxes in a given tax year. For the eight out of ten Americans who receive them most every year, they evoke feelings of wild celebration. The truth of the matter is it simply means that this majority overpaid their income tax out of their payroll tax withholding with their employer throughout the calendar year. This is not a good thing in reality.

Self-employed people will also receive a refund if they have overpaid their estimated taxes. This does not represent free money or additional income when a tax check arrives in the mail or is alternatively direct deposited. Instead, it signifies that the recipient cheerfully agreed to loan Uncle Sam money without charging him any interest for the service.

It is also possible for tax refunds to be issued out of refundable tax credits. This can occur if any money remains from such credits after the taxes due from the federal income have been covered. After the federal government receives and processes all of the return for the tax year in question, it must formally sign off on a refund before the money will be dispatched.

The amount of time that this requires varies according to the means which individuals employ in filing their taxes. Electronically filed taxes-refund processing times are usually sent in under 21 days from the Internal Revenue Service accepting the return. It is possible for delays to hinder this by as much as 12 weeks, though it is highly unlikely that this would happen. Paper tax returns which are mailed typically take from six to eight weeks to be issued and arrive in the mail in the form of a traditional paper check.

If individuals wait until peak tax return season to file, their refunds will commonly be delayed. Tax preparers at the IRS can and do become overwhelmed as easily as any person at this busy time of the year. After all, the IRS is not guaranteeing the time frame for the refunds to be sent out, only estimating their best guess. This is why those waiting for a tax refund should never wait on such a payout to fund a critical purchase or make a time sensitive payment (on a house, mortgage, or other credit card bill).

For those who do find themselves in desperate straits to receive such a refund though, there are loans against imminent refunds which taxpayers can apply for and receive. Some tax preparers, such as H&R Block, will issue refunds against owed refunds as well, in exchange for a small percentage convenience fee. All delay liabilities then transfer to the tax preparing firm and away from the individual tax filer.

Where electronic tax refunds are concerned, individuals have three choices. They can have the IRS deposit them to a checking account, savings account, or retirement account (such as an IRA). Besides this, one could have the IRS purchase a $5,000 or less Series I savings bond if he or she fancies receiving less than a single measly one percent per year in interest.

People have up to three years from the point of filing to claim their refund. This means that now in 2017, filers could still apply for a refund from the tax year 2014. When the IRS grants an extension for any reason, the deadline for the three years starts at the end of the deadline extension.

The sad news is that sometimes people are not allowed to keep their whole refund. The IRS could make a tragic mistake and overpay a refund. They will get this back eventually one way or the other. Any individuals who owe back payments on child support will also have this seized, as they would for back taxes of overdue student loan bills. It is also possible to get a smaller than expected check. In the event that the remaining money does not show up within two weeks of the incorrect amount, it is always a recommended idea to contact the Internal Revenue Service directly.

Tax Revenue

Tax Revenue refers to money that a government collects. They do this by levying taxes on their own citizens living within their jurisdictions (and living overseas as well in the case of the U.S.). There are many different kinds of taxes collected in the present day and age. Among the most frequently levied taxes are income taxes, property taxes, and sales or VAT taxes.

The revenues from taxes finance government spending. They also go towards maintaining and developing new public works projects. Taxes pay for a variety of other important programs. Some of these are for education, defense, and social welfare expenditures. Practically all governments have laws in effect that provide them with the authority to tax their citizens legally.

Income taxes come from many sources of income which people earn. This might be comprised of commissions, wages, or royalties. There are governments around the world which also tax money earned on speculation, investments, and gambling proceeds (as with the U.S.). The United States and a number of other nations permit their citizens to legally reduce the amount of money they pay in taxes by providing sometimes detailed information on permissible deductions against income. In the majority of cases, tax revenue which comes from income earned becomes payable to both the national and state governments.

Property taxes provide revenue derived from ownership of real property or real estate. These funds are commonly levied and utilized by local governments including provinces, states, counties, and parishes. Such taxes come from possession of land and houses. They typically become due every year. Interestingly, cars and other vehicles also become taxed on an annual basis in most jurisdictions. This tax is levied through the purchase of license plates and vehicle registration which has to be updated annually. These taxes which local governments collect they commonly spend on maintaining state, country, or provincial schools, roads, and other types of public facilities (such as parks). Sometimes these monies are deployed to build up members of the community, as with needy families' support programs.

Sales tax is another way that governments collect a tax revenue every single day of the year. They levy these sales or VAT taxes on practically all purchases. Sometimes exceptions will be made for medicines and some necessary foodstuffs. The rate of taxes which they collect occasionally depends on the kind of item which a person or business purchases. Luxury items often quality for steeper tax rates. There are always higher revenues generated by so-called sin taxes. These are activities which governments attempt to discourage participation in and consumption of for their citizens. On gasoline, this is called carbon tax, while on alcohol and tobacco it is excise taxes.

In many countries of the world (the United States being a notable exception), governments collect a considerable national tax revenue from Value Added Tax. The difference between sales tax and VAT is simple. Sales tax is levied on the final point of sale only. VAT is collected on every stage of production where any value is added to the goods (or service). This is why VAT generates far more income for governments.

For example, in a VAT collecting regime a sweater is a good item to consider. Farmers are VAT taxed on the sales of their wool to factories. Factories which produce a yarn from the wool are also taxed when they go to sell their yarn to producers. Other production facilities that knit the yarn into sweaters also pay VAT when they sell the sweater to the outlet store or shop. Finally, the store which sells the sweater itself will eventually collect a VAT tax from the customer who ultimately purchases the item. VAT taxes are generally included in the sticker price of the item, while sales taxes are not usually included in shelf pricing.

Governments cannot function without tax revenues as the are the most critical types of income for modern age governing. Without such tax revenues, the overwhelming majority of governments would not be able to provide the necessary level of support which businesses and individuals require to live decently and to succeed. This is why in the majority of nations of the world today, when businesses or individuals do not pay their taxes, they are severely penalized. Such penalties start with fines and can occasionally lead to jail time, in extreme cases of tax avoidance.

Tax Sheltered Annuities 403(b)

Tax sheltered annuities are retirement savings programs and vehicles that the Internal Revenue Service allows for under the 403(b) section of their tax code. They were created for the benefit of employees who work for churches, educational institutions, and specific not for profit agencies.

They offer the advantage of permitting employees who are eligible to participate to contribute nearly all of their annual income towards retirement savings and investments in the plan. As an example of the generous limits with these particular plans, employers who choose to contribute can put in as much as $53,000 as of 2016 for any single tax year.

This supplemental program for retirement savings gives participating individuals a variety of ways in which they can choose to contribute funds. They may invest on an after tax basis, as with a Roth plan. They may also choose to contribute using funds that are pre-taxed. They can also opt to use a combination of the two methods. These plans and their participating contributions are entirely voluntary. Employees generally make the majority of these contributions as there is not always an employer match involved with them.

A variety of employees of eligible organizations may participate in these tax sheltered annuity plans. Employees of public schools, universities, and state colleges are allowed to participate. Many employees of churches are also allowed to become involved. Those who work for the school systems run by Indian tribes and their governments may participate. Not for profit 501(c)(3) churches' and organizations' ministers are included in them, as are ministers who are self employed who serve as part of a tax exempt organization. Chaplains are also usually qualified to participate.

There are several good reasons to become involved with these tax sheltered annuity plans. With automatic payroll deductions, it is a simple and relatively painless means of building up extra savings which individuals will require to increase their after retirement income.

They can get involved in a low cost program that is flexible enough to offer a good selection of investment choices. People can make contributions on a Roth after tax basis, a pre tax basis, or a combination of the two. Finally these plans are portable, meaning the owners can take their retirement vehicles with them when they move to a different job or another not for profit organization.

Thanks to these plans and vehicles, account holders are able to invest tax money that would otherwise go to the IRS. They can move money between the various funds in the plans without suffering from capital gains taxes or additional fees. This gives these TSA pre tax accounts a greater return than a taxable account would enjoy if it earned similar returns. For any individuals who use these account vehicles as Roth after tax accounts, all qualified distributions at retirement will be enjoyed completely tax free.

Money from these accounts can not be taken out without penalties until the individual reaches the government mandated minimum retirement age of 59 ½. They must begin taking distributions by the time they turn 70. An exception to the minimum retirement age is for individuals who stop working for their not for profit company before they reach retirement age. In this case, they are allowed to go ahead and begin receiving distributions without having to pay the extra 10% early withdrawal penalty tax. Only any taxes that were due for monies which had been contributed as pre tax dollars would apply in this particular case.

Tax-Deferred

Tax deferred money and status pertains to earnings on investments. This includes dividends, interest, and capital gains which are allowed to accumulate without taxes paid until the owner withdraws the earnings and gains. The two most popular kinds of these deferred investments are found in IRAs and tax deferred annuities. Growth that is tax deferred permits gains to be compounded instead of having taxes paid on them.

Investors gain in two different ways from having taxes deferred on their investment returns. The first method is through growth on investments which is tax free. Instead of having to pay taxes on the present returns of the investment, the taxes are not paid until a later time. This allows the investment to increase without setbacks.

The second method from tax deferral pertains to investments which are entered in pre-retirement accumulation phases. At this point, the earnings and taxes on them are generally significantly higher than earnings will be when the owners retire. This means that withdrawals drawn out of deferred accounts typically happen after individuals are bringing in less taxable income. The end result is that their tax rate is at a lower level than the one the IRS applies with they are still working.

There are a number of qualified and approved tax deferred vehicles available today. Probably the most common and popular is the 401(k). Employers provide these plans as a company benefit to help their employees to increase their retirement savings.

Third party administrators act to deduct contributions from employee payrolls and help manage the plans. The employees then get to choose from several options in which to invest their tax deferred savings. These include company stock, mutual funds, or some fixed rate choices. All gains made in these accounts do no add to the taxable earnings of the employees participating. These contributions they make to the 401(k) and other qualified accounts like most IRAs come from pre-taxed dollars. This means that the employee's taxable income amount becomes reduced.

When the employees surpass the minimum 59.5 retirement age, they are able to take distributions from these plans. The taxes they pay are only those which apply on their earnings as they are received. So investors who may earn enough to pay 33% tax bracket while employed will likely pay as little as 10% to 15% taxes on distributions they take from their 401(k) plans at retirement that they have along with their any other income from interest, social security, or pensions.

401(k)s typically involved employer dollar matching programs that inspire employees to set aside a greater amount of their earnings in order to increase the size of their retirement nest egg. In putting the money off to the future, they will pay fewer taxes in the end.

It is important to understand the difference between tax deferred and non tax deferred retirement vehicles. Some retirement investment accounts are not tax deferred. The owners pay the taxes on the earnings before they contribute them to the accounts. The advantage to this is that all interest, dividends, and capital gains grow without any other taxes being owed on them when they are taken out as distributions at retirement age. One beloved insurance product that works this way is an annuity.

Retirement plans like traditional IRAs have annual contribution limits of $5,500 per year as of 2016. Annuities do not come with such annual restriction levels. Employees can contribute even millions of dollars per year to them if they wish.

The earnings made in these insurance backed products grow without having taxes taken out of them even at retirement. This means that any and all earnings in these account compound fully from the second year of the annuity contract. So long as the gains earned are taken out after the employee reaches 59.5, there will not be any taxes or early withdrawal penalties of 10% levied against the earnings in these pre-taxed contribution accounts.

Term Life Insurance

Term life insurance is a form of life insurance. It offers coverage for a preset and limited amount of time that is called the relevant term. The coverage provided is a fixed rate of payment coverage. Once the term expires, the individual's coverage at the rate of the premiums that were charged before are not assured any more.

The client will be forced to drop their term life insurance coverage or to get a different coverage with varying payments and terms. Should the person who is insured die within the term, the death benefit amounts are paid out to the insured person's beneficiary. This term life insurance proves to be the most affordable means of buying a major dollar value of death benefit coverage based on the premium cost charged.

Term life insurance turns out to be the first type of life insurance created, and it stands in contrast to permanent forms of life insurance like universal life, whole life, and variable universal life. These coverage types promise an individual pre set premiums that can not go up for the person's entire life. People do not usually employ term insurance for strategies involving charitable giving or their needs for estate planning. Instead, they are thinking about a need to replace an income if a person passes away on his or her family unexpectedly.

A great number of the permanent life insurance policies also offer the advantage of increasing in value during the person's contract. This cash value can then be withdrawn when certain conditions are met by the policy holder. Generally, withdrawing these cash amounts closes out the policy. Beneficiaries of permanent life insurance products get the insurance policy face value but not the cash value upon the holder's death. Because of this, financial advisers will suggest that people purchase term life insurance for their insurance needs and then invest the money saved over permanent products in retirement accounts that provide tax deferred contributions and investment gains, like 401k's and IRA's.

Like with the majority of insurance policies, term life insurance pays out claims for the insured, assuming that the contract is current and the premiums are paid as due. Assuming that a claim is not filed, the premium is not given back to the policy holder. This makes term life insurance like home owners' insurance policies that pay claims if a home becomes destroyed or damaged as a result of fire, or like car insurance policies that pay drivers if they have a car accident. Premiums are not refunded when the product is no longer required. Because of this, term life insurance like these other products only provides risk protection.

Underlying Assets

Underlying assets refer to any asset or valuable commodity which determines the value of a derivative based upon the asset. This term is frequently and importantly utilized to discuss derivatives trading. Options are a good example of this. Derivatives themselves prove to be financial instruments that investors trade. Their price is derived from the asset that underlies them. This underlying asset will be the investible instrument like an individual stock, a stock market index, a currency or currency pair, a commodity, or futures. The price of the derivatives will be based upon these.

Options for a given stock provides the holder of the option with the right (but not the obligation) to purchase or sell the stock at a certain strike price (a given price point) on a particular date at some expiration point (a future date that is predetermined). In the case of an option, the underlying assets will always amount to the stock of the company in question.

This underlying asset helps to identify the financial instrument in the agreement that gives the contract its value. Investors in such a contract will always have the right, or option, to purchase the underlying assets for a pre-arranged price on the expiration date. The asset that underlies the contract provides the security of the agreement itself. The two trading parties consent to exchange the underlying asset if necessary as a contract clause in the derivative agreement.

Famed and legendary investor Warren Buffet has notoriously and correctly declared such derivatives to be "financial weapons of mass destruction." This proved to be the case in the Global Financial Crisis of 2008-2009. A wide range of derivatives based on shaky underlying assets literally blew up the world economy and banking system in financial carnage that is still reverberating throughout the economies of the world nearly ten years later.

Take some real world examples that will help to clarify the complex ideas. Berkshire Hathaway sells stock market index put options on worldwide stock market indices that range from the FTSE 100 in London to the American-based S&P 500. These options are unusual because the do not have an expiration date until the years ranging from January of 2018 to

January of 2026. On those particular dates of the varying contracts, it will be the underlying assets of the relevant stock market indices which will decide the amount of money that Berkshire pays out to the option holders.

In theory, the indices could approach zero, though this is highly unlikely. Yet Berkshire Hathaway would be forced to come out of pocket to the amount of up to $27.6 billion to these put holders if they did. When Berkshire sold these puts, they received $4.2 billion as premiums for their risk when they sold these during the years from 2004 to 2008. Guarantor of the options and Berkshire Hathaway founder Warren Buffet has cheerfully invested these billions in premiums and made considerable returns on them since those years in which they sold them.

Another classic example surrounds PepsiCo. The California-based company always reports its earnings in U.S. dollars. Yet it has operations all over the world because of its diversified soft drinks, bottled water, chips and snacks, alternative energy drinks like PowerAde, and juices divisions. This means that it must borrow, invest, and earn money in a range of currencies on every continent. The company has utilized currency swap agreements to help reduce the volatility of changing currency exchange rates on its costs to borrow and earn money in other currencies. The underlying assets would be Euros, British pounds sterling, Canadian dollars, Australian dollars, Japanese yen, Swiss francs, and other major world currencies.

In the end, there are literally trillions worth of derivatives which derive their actual value from an underlying asset of one type or another. This might be interest rates determined in London (the now-infamous LIBOR), stock market index values, or oil and gold hard commodities. Such derivatives make it possible for investors to engage with another party in a zero sum game where the stakes depend on the rises and fails of most any asset or market in the world. Neither party has to be directly involved in the underlying market or asset, thanks to these financial weapons of mass destruction called derivatives.

Underwriting

Underwriting refers to a means of determining if a consumer is eligible or not for a particular kind of financial product. These products vary depending on the person's or business' requirements. They might include home mortgages, insurance coverage needs, business mortgages, lines of credit, or financing for venture start up projects. The bank or other financial institution undergoing the underwriting evaluation procedure will look into the odds of the business transaction successfully providing them with a profit in exchange for their offer of financial help.

As banks and insurance firms go through the underwriting process, two different things will occur. The first of these is showing an interest in the project that the borrower is proposing for finance. They demonstrate this by offering the financial aid that the customer is requesting. Next, with a bank or institution underwriting an insurance policy, residential or commercial mortgage, or venture, they are looking to make money on their investment one day in the future. They might either gather these profits at one time in the form of a lump sum at a future date or little by little in monthly payments. In these underwriting activities, compensation is expected, which is commonly paid via finance charges or other fees.

Underwriters contemplate more than simply the amount of risk that an applicant demonstrates. They also consider the potential risk that working with the new customer might bring to other customers of their company. In order to ensure that the bank or firm does not suffer too much harm to keep up with commitments made to already existing clients, they have developed underwriting standards.

Insurance companies heavily rely on underwriting in performing their business. Health insurance is one example of this. Health insurance providers seriously look into the past and present health of a person applying. Sometimes their underwriting will show that they need to exclude various pre-existing conditions for a certain amount of time when they insure the person. Other times, underwriting will reveal a medical history that demonstrates too much risk for the company. In this case, a health insurance company will refuse to provide the requested health insurance coverage. Their goal is to not insure individuals who they believe will need significant medical treatment over time, so that they can provide a solid financial backing for their existing clientele.

In business, underwriting is commonly employed to determine if new ventures should be given financing. An example of this might be a company that has created a new technology that it wishes to sell. These underwriters will consider how marketable the product appears, the applicant's marketing plan, the expense of creating and selling the new items, and also the odds of the company realizing profits on every piece that they sell. Sometimes, underwriters of these business ventures will express an interest in having shares of stock in the start up company as a portion of their payment for services. Other times, they will only require a set interest rate for the dollar amount invested.

Variable Interest Rate

Variable Interest Rate refers to the applicable interest rate which comes with a security or loan. When such rates are variable, it means that they will fluctuate up or down in time. The reason for this is that a specific index or interest rate benchmark underlies them. This rate or index will change from time to time in the natural course of events. There is a potential great benefit to having such a variable interest rate when this index or interest rate goes down. This is because the interest payments of the borrowers will similarly decline. On the other hand though, when such underlying benchmarks go up, the interest payments will also rise, sometimes painfully.

Not every loan, mortgage, or security will utilize the same benchmark index or interest rate as its underlying comparison point with these Variable Interest Rates. In fact it actually comes down to the kind of security or loan in question. With credit cards, car loans, or mortgages, the Variable Interest Rates are often based on the prime rate for the nation in which the loan is based. Naturally the financial institutions, lenders, and banks will assess a spread between their rate and the true benchmark rate. The amount of this spread form of fee depends on many factors. Some of these are the credit rating of the individual getting the loan and the kind of asset to which the loan is attached.

Where credit cards are concerned, most of them work on a Variable Interest Rate arrangement. Their APR annual percentage rate happens to be fixed to a specific interest index. In most cases, this is the prime rate. With the prime rate, it generally moves up or down in lockstep alongside the federal funds rate that the United States Federal Reserve sets as part of their fiscal and monetary policy tools. A move up or down in this rate eventually leads to a net change in the underlying interest rate of credit cards across America. Such rates for these credit cards working off of variable interest rates are able to shift up or down at will. The credit card companies are not even required to provide written or verbal advance notice to their cardholding customers before adjusting the rates when the benchmark moves.

In the accompanying terms and conditions of such credit card accounts, the applicable interest rates will generally be described as the underlying prime rate added to a certain percentage rate. This specified additional percentage is always heavily based upon how credit worthy the card holding individual proves to be. As a real world example, many cards will assess an interest rate addition of 10.9 percent on top of the prime rate to come up with their credit card customer interest rates.

With other forms of loans that have Variable Interest Rates, the payment schedule proves to be different. The majority of non-credit card forms of loans are actually installment loans. These payments to repay them are fixed and pre-arranged. This leads to the loan reaching pay off on a pre-set specified day. All that changes as interest rates rise or fall is the amount of the payment. This will similarly increase or decrease per the amount of the interest rate change as well as the numbers of payments that remain to fully pay off the loan.

Mortgages have their own specific features. When they carry Variable Interest Rates, such loans are known as ARM adjustable rate mortgages. A great number of such ARMs actually begin their repayment life with a fixed lower interest rate during the initial years of the loan life. Once this pre-determined time frame expires, they will adjust up, sometimes steeply. The most typical periods of fixed interest rates on these adjustable rate mortgages turn out to be either three or five years. Loan officers refer to this as 5/1 or 3/1 ARMs.

Wire Transfer

A wire transfer is the quickest, safest, most reliable means of sending money within the United States, in other countries, or around the world. They are often essential in the more critical financial activities of life such as purchasing a house. The reason larger transactions occur in this form of payment is because the recipient can receive and verify the funds transfer the same day it is done, or as near to immediately as possible (besides Western Union and Money Gram, which cost substantially more to utilize).

A wire transfer actually represents a means to electronically transfer money from one party to another via a bank as intermediary. A traditional and typical wire transfer starts at a credit union or bank and electronically processes through either Fedwire or SWIFT networks. Another common name for such a wire transfer is a bank wire, which also encompasses the standard bank to bank transfers.

Ultimately the wire transfers have become so successful and utilized throughout the United States and rest of world simply because they are capable of moving even enormous sums of money to any destination bank in the world in only a day or two. If they are affected within the same country such as the United States then same day wires can be done. For an international transfer via wire transfer, it often requires another day or even two to complete.

Since the funds move rapidly through the financial system, recipients are not required to wait a material amount of time for the funds to become cleared. This means they can access and utilize the money without significant delays. No holds are typically placed on wire transfer monies. The safety issue means that merchants prefer the wire mechanism. This is because checks can bounce because of insufficient funds, while wires never do so. In other words, these are guaranteed funds.

There are some particular requirements that wire transfers need in order to be possible to transact. At least in the United States, both parties would require a functioning bank account in order for a bank to act as intermediary. Since thieves can not open a bank account too easily, nor bank anonymously in the United States, it is difficult for them to carry out scams using bank wires. This is because it leaves a paper trail which is easy for law enforcement officials to follow.

This does not mean that wire transfer scams are unknown entirely. It is possible for a person to be tricked into wiring money to a fraudster for a purchase or service they never receive. Examples of this are fake insurance policies or false retirement or investment products. Once the wire has cleared the recipients account, they can either withdraw the funds in person or wire it to an offshore overseas account.

By the time the victims realize that they have been scammed, the funds sent by wire will be long gone. They would no longer be recoverable by traditional U.S. law enforcement or even court order methods once they have been transferred offshore. Pulling money back after it has been dispatched via bank wire is extremely difficult in any case. This is true even if the funds remain in the recipient's bank account.

Wire transfer fees can be significant. In many parts of the United States, they run as high as $40 to dispatch a bank wire. Many banks charge upwards of $10 in order for a bank wire to be received into an account. The costs to send one are higher if the wire is funded by utilizing a credit card cash advance. Cash advance fees would then apply, as well as typically large interest rates, plus the wire transfer fee. This is why it is typically most financially sound to effect a bank wire directly from the sender's bank account.

Other Financial Books by Thomas Herold

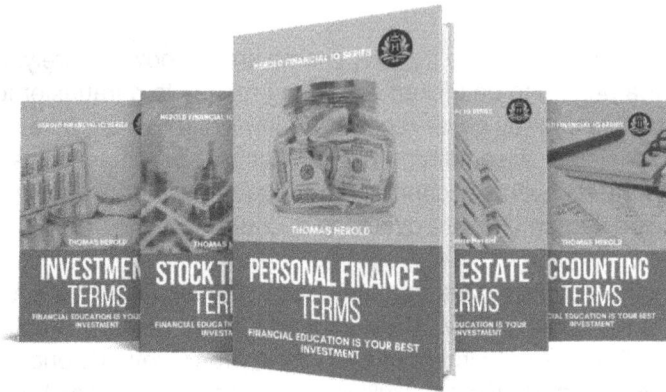

Herold Financial IQ Series
Financial Education Is Your Best Investment

Get Smart with the Financial IQ Series
The Herold Financial IQ series covers all major areas and aspects of the financial world. Starting with Personal Finance, Real Estate and Banking term. Covering Corporate Finance, Investment as well as Economics.

It also includes Retirement, Trading, and Accounting terms. In addition, you'll find Debt, Bankruptcy, Mortgage, Small Business, and Wall Street terminology explained. Not to forget Laws & Regulations as well as important acronyms and abbreviations.

Available on Amazon as Kindle, Paperback and Audio Edition
Go to Amazon.com and search for 'Herold Financial IQ' or copy and paste this link below.

http://bit.ly/herold-financial-iq

High Credit Score Secrets - The Smart Raise And Repair Guide to Excellent Credit

Poor Credit Score Could Cost You Hundreds of Thousands of Dollars
A recent financial statistic revealed that increasing your score from 'fair' to 'good' saves you an average of $86,200* over a lifetime. Imagine what you could do with that extra money?

Improve Your Credit Score in 45-60 Days or Even Less
This practical credit compendium starts off by demonstrating over 50 guaranteed methods of how you can almost immediately boost your credit score. Follow these simple, effective and proven strategies to improve your credit score from as low as 450 points to over 810.

Don't let bad credit hold you back from achieving financial freedom. Your credit score not only influences all your future choices, but it also can save you thousands of dollars.

Available on Amazon as Kindle, Paperback and Audio Edition
Go to Amazon.com and search for 'High Credit Score Secrets' or copy and paste this link below.

http://bit.ly/high-credit

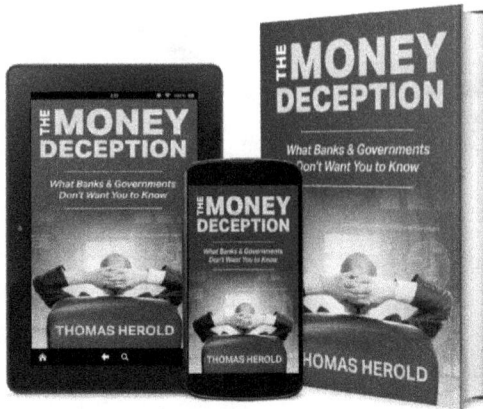

The Money Deception
What Banks & Governments Don't Want You to Know

„It is well enough that people of the nation do not understand our banking and monetary system, for if they did, I believe there would be a revolution before tomorrow morning." - Henry Ford

The Catastrophic Results of Money Manipulation
This money has been souped up by the 1% that now controls 50% of the world's wealth. The fastest and biggest wealth transfer in history is underway. Money evaporates from the middle class, leaving them struggling and without hope for retirement.

What's Happening to Your Money?
Going all the way down into the rabbit hole, it shows you the root of the problem and also lays the foundation for the future. It describes the most likely transition into a new worldwide crypto-based currency, which will become the new basis of our financial system.

Available on Amazon as Kindle, Paperback and Audio Edition
Go to Amazon.com and search for 'Money Deception' or copy and paste this link below.

http://bit.ly/money-deception

Other Books in the Herold Financial IQ Series

99 Financial Terms Every Beginner, Entrepreneur & Business Should Know

Personal Finance Terms

Real Estate Terms

Bank & Banking Terms

Corporate Finance Terms

Investment Terms

Economics Terms

Retirement Terms

Stock Trading Terms

Accounting Terms

Debt & Bankruptcy Terms

Mortgage Terms

Small Business Terms

Wall Street Terms

Laws & Regulations

Financial Acronyms

www.ingramcontent.com/pod-product-compliance
Lightning Source LLC
Chambersburg PA
CBHW071546210326
41597CB00019B/3140